Ernst L. Freud, Architect:
the Case of the Modern Bourgeois Home

Ernst L. Freud, Architect: the Case of the Modern Bourgeois Home

❖

Volker M. Welter

Berghahn Books
New York • Oxford

Published in 2012 by

Berghahn Books

www.berghahnbooks.com

©2012 Volker M. Welter

All rights reserved. Except for the quotation of short passages
for the purposes of criticism and review, no part of this book
may be reproduced in any form or by any means, electronic or
mechanical, including photocopying, recording, or any information
storage and retrieval system now known or to be invented,
without written permission of the publisher.

Library of Congress Cataloging-in-Publication Data

Welter, Volker.

Ernst L. Freud, architect : the case of the modern bourgeois home / Volker M. Welter. -- 1st ed.

p. cm. -- (Space and place; v. 5)

Includes bibliographical references and index.

ISBN 978-0-85745-233-7 (pbk. : alk. paper) -- ISBN 978-0-85745-234-4 (ebook)

1. Freud, Ernst L., 1892-1970--Criticism and interpretation. 2. Architecture, Domestic--Europe--History--20th century. I. Freud, Ernst L., 1892-1970. II. Title. III. Title: Case of the modern bourgeois home.

NA997.F74W45 2012

720.92--dc23

[B]

2011029401

British Library Cataloguing in Publication Data

A catalogue record for this book is available from the British Library

Thanks to the Paul Mellon Centre for Studies in British Art
for a generous publication grant which helped make this book possible.

ISBN 978-0-85745-233-7 (paperback)
ISBN 978-085745-234-4 (ebook)

To the memory of

Paul Levi
(1919, Leipzig – 2008, Reading)

and

Harry Weinberger
(1924, Berlin – 2009, Leamington Spa)

The trace of my days on earth cannot perish in eons.

J. W. von Goethe, *Faust, Part II*

CONTENTS

List of Illustrations	xi
List of Tables	xv
Acknowledgments	xvi
Introduction	1

CHAPTER 1
Modern Bourgeois Domestic Architecture of the Weimar Republic — 7
   Modern Bourgeois Domestic Architecture *10*
   The Limits of Community, the Chances of Society *13*
   The Bourgeois Home, the 'Unknown Territory' of Modern Architecture? *16*

CHAPTER 2
The Making of an Architect — 24
   Vienna, Austrian Capital of Art and Culture *25*
   Berggasse 19, Vienna *26*
   Studying Architecture in Vienna and Munich *31*

CHAPTER 3
Going Modern with Rainer Maria Rilke and Adolf Loos — 38
   'Learning to See' with Rainer Maria Rilke *38*
   Adolf Loos and Bourgeois *Wohnkultur* *41*

CHAPTER 4
Society Architect in Berlin — 49
   Weimar Germany *49*
   Weimar Republic Architecture *50*
   Setting up Home and Office in Berlin *50*
   'To live in Berlin and to build in the Holy Land' *54*
   Society Architect in Berlin *60*

CHAPTER 5
Houses in and around Berlin — 69
   First Houses in Berlin *70*
   Relationships with Clients *72*

The First Modern House 73
The Frank Country House near Berlin 78
More Houses in and near Berlin 88

CHAPTER 6
Couches, Consulting Rooms, and Clinics 96
Historiography of Psychoanalytic Consulting Rooms 97
The Primeval Consulting Room at Berggasse 19 98
Consulting Rooms and Couches in Berlin 102
Sanatorium Schloß Tegel 105
Psychoanalytic Spaces in London 112

CHAPTER 7
At Home in England 118
Going into Exile 118
Setting up Office in London 122
Houses in and around London 123
The Second World War and its Aftermath 132

CHAPTER 8
Family Architect 139
Berggasse in London 139
Family Homes in Berlin 141
A New Family Home in London 143
From Hiddensee to Hidden House 147
A Home for his Parents 150
Towards a Life without Architecture 154

CHAPTER 9
Architecture without Quality?—Some Concluding Remarks 161

Selected List of Works 173

Selected Bibliography 206

Index 210

LIST OF ILLUSTRATONS

Unless noted otherwise, all architectural designs and interior schemes are by Ernst L. Freud.

1.1. Living room in the barn of a country house in Northease, England, refurbished by J. C. Pocock — 8
1.2. Upper-level living room of the Stein villa, Garches, by Le Corbusier, 1926–27 — 8
1.3. Fireplace in the studio of Ernst L. Freud's second Berlin apartment, 1924–25 — 9
1.4. Townhouses in Berlin by Alexander Klein, 1922–25 — 16
1.5. Floor plans of the townhouses in Berlin by Alexander Klein — 17
1.6. Lower-level living room of the Tugendhat villa, Brno, by Ludwig Mies van der Rohe, 1928–30 — 18

2.1. The Freud family in c. 1898 — 24
2.2. Plan of the apartments number 5 and number 6, Berggasse 19, Vienna — 27
2.3. Collection of antiques in Sigmund Freud's consulting room and study in Berggasse 19, Vienna — 28
2.4. Collection of antiques on Sigmund Freud's desk in his study — 29
2.5. Living room with Aunt Minna's room in background at Berggasse 19, Vienna — 30
2.6. Ernst Freud, c. 1915 — 33

3.1. Adolf and Lina Loos in front of the fireplace of their apartment in Vienna, 1903 — 41
3.2. Reception hall of the Goldmann apartment, Vienna, 1911, by Adolf Loos — 44
3.3. Living room and adjacent stair hall in the Müller house, Prague, 1928–30, by Adolf Loos — 45

4.1. Ernst and Lucie Freud on the island of Hiddensee, Germany, 1920s — 51
4.2. Wedding announcement in *Der Jüdische Student*, June–July 1920 — 52
4.3. Tombstone for Sophie Freud, Hamburg, possibly designed by Ernst L. Freud, 1920 — 53
4.4. Sigmund Freud's tombstone, Golders Green, London, 1939 — 53
4.5. Clement Raphael, Stephan Gabriel, and Lucian Michael (from left to right), the three sons of Ernst L. and Lucie Freud — 55
4.6. Bust of Lucie Freud by Joachim Karsch — 57
4.7. Weizmann house, Rehovot, Israel, by Erich Mendelsohn, 1934–36 — 58
4.8. Letter from Ernst L. Freud to Chaim Weizmann, 1927 — 59
4.9. Brigitte Fischer and her three daughters their nursery, Berlin, 1929–30 — 63

4.10. Unidentified nursery in Germany, possibly in Hamburg, not dated — 64

4.11. Corner in the waiting room of Professor Hamburger children's clinic, after being moved from Berlin to London sometime after 1933 — 64

5.1. Garden façade of the Schimek house, Berlin, 1922 — 71

5.2. Garden façade of the Lampl house, Berlin, 1925–26 — 74

5.3. Sommerfeld housing scheme, Berlin-Zehlendorf, 1923, by Erich Mendelsohn and Richard Neutra — 75

5.4. Lower- and upper-level plans of the Lampl house, Berlin, 1925–26 — 76

5.5. Desk and chair in the study in the Lampl house, Berlin, 1925–26 — 77

5.6. Built-in wardrobe, dressing table, and chair in a bedroom in the Lampl house, Berlin, 1925–26 — 77

5.7. Dr. Theodor Frank in front of his country house — 78

5.8. Margot Frank (centre) among guests at a Deutsche Bank event in 1930 — 78

5.9. Lakeside terraces of the Frank country house, Geltow, 1928–30 — 79

5.10. Lakeside façade of the Frank country house, Geltow, 1928–30 — 80

5.11. Entrance façade of the Frank country house, Geltow, 1928–30 — 80

5.12. Lower- and upper-level plans of the Frank country house, Geltow, 1928–30 — 81

5.13. Lower-level hall of the Frank country house, Geltow, 1928–30 — 83

5.14. Panorama window in lower level hall of the Frank country house, Geltow, 1928–30 — 83

5.15. Stair hall of the Frank country house, Geltow, 1928–30 — 84

5.16. Dining room with lowered glass window to the winter garden, Frank country house, Geltow, 1928–30 — 85

5.17. Living room in Erich Mendelsohn's own house, Berlin, 1929–30 — 86

5.18. Upper-level hall, sofas designed by Ernst L. Freud, tubular steel chairs by Ludwig Mies van der Rohe and Lilly Reich, Frank country house, Geltow, 1928–30 — 87

5.19. Buchthal house, Berlin, 1922–23, by Hans and Wassili Luckhardt with Franz Hoffmann — 88

5.20. Buchthal house after the refurbishment by Ernst L. Freud — 89

5.21. Lower- and upper-level plans of the Scherk house, Berlin, 1930–31 — 90

5.22. Garage and chauffeur building of the never completed Mosse country house, Krampnitz, begun in 1932 — 91

6.1. Sigmund Freud's consulting room, Vienna — 99

6.2. Anna Freud's consulting room, Vienna, with a shelf designed by Felix Augenfeld — 102

6.3. Consulting room, Berlin policlinic, 1928 — 103

6.4. Doctors' room, Berlin policlinic, 1928 — 104

6.5. Meeting room, Berlin policlinic, 1928 — 105

6.6. Kurhaus Schloß Tegel, Berlin, built in 1906, later demolished — 106

6.7.	Single bedroom, Sanatorium Tegel, Berlin, 1927	107
6.8.	Double bedroom, Sanatorium Tegel, Berlin, 1927	108
6.9.	Consulting room, Sanatorium Tegel, Berlin, 1927	109
6.10.	Design for Rosemary (Molly) Pritchard's consulting room, London, by Christopher Nicholson, 1938	109
6.11.	Interior of Rosemary (Molly) Pritchard's consulting room, London, 1938	110
6.12.	Sketch of the consulting couch, Sanatorium Tegel, Berlin, 1927	111
6.13.	Sketch of a consulting couch	112
6.14.	Sketch of a bed couch	113
6.15.	Melanie Klein's consulting cum living room, London, 1933	114
7.1.	Willow house, Cambridge, by George Checkley, 1932	121
7.2.	Garden facade of the Scherk house, Berlin, 1930–31	121
7.3.	Paintings and furniture brought over from Berlin and installed in the Marx house, London, 1935–36	124
7.4.	Garden façade of the Marx house, London, 1935–36	124
7.5.	Garden façade of the Charlton house, Berlin, by Otto Salvisberg, 1928–29	125
7.6.	Exterior of the music room, Pine House, Churt, Surrey, 1936	126
7.7.	Fireplace in the music room, Pine House, Churt, Surrey, 1936	127
7.8.	Interior design of 8 Alexander Place, London, 1937–38	128
7.9.	Living room, with murals by Hans Feibusch, of the Matthew House, London, 1937–38	129
7.10.	Street corner of Frognal Lane townhouses, London, 1937–38	130
7.11.	Street corner of Sommerfeld housing, Berlin-Zehlendorf, by E. Mendelsohn and R. Neutra	131
7.12.	Exterior of Belvedere housing block, London, 1937–38	131
7.13.	Exterior of 'The Weald', Betchworth, Surrey, 1937–39	132
8.1.	Desk and chair in the study of Ernst L. Freud's second Berlin apartment, 1924–25	141
8.2.	Journal cupboard in the study of Ernst L. Freud's second Berlin apartment, 1924–25	142
8.3.	Upper-level living room in Ernst L. Freud's London home, 1935	144
8.4.	Bedroom furniture from the second Berlin apartment in Ernst L. Freud's London home, 1935	144
8.5.	Ernst L. Freud at his desk in the study of his London home, 1935	145
8.6.	Living room with fireplace at 8 Alexander Place, London	146
8.7.	Ernst L. Freud's cottage on the island of Hiddensee, Germany, 1924 or later	148
8.8.	'Hidden House' at Walberswick, England, with the addition of a glass bow window, 1937	149

8.9. Design for the setting of a consulting couch between bookshelves, possibly for 20 Maresfield Gardens, London — 152
8.10. Bookshelves in S. Freud's consulting room cum study, London — 152
8.11. Sigmund Freud's desk and chair, London — 153
8.12. Corner in the living room with paintings and furniture brought over from Berlin, Marx house, London, 1935–36 — 154
8.13. Interior of the British Synagogue, London Jewish Hospital, 1958, since demolished — 156
8.14. Ernst L. and Lucie Freud in front of their London home, 1968 — 157

9.1. Facade of the tobacco warehouse 'Problem', Berlin, 1927–28 — 164
9.2. Living room of the Goldschmidt house, Berlin — 166
9.3. Unidentified living room with antique wood sculpture — 167
9.4. Unidentified living room with a series of Holbein prints — 168
9.5. Bank office of Richard Ginsberg, Berlin, 1930 — 168
9.6. Unidentified office (possibly for Melanie Klein in London) — 170
9.7. Two writing desks in the library (front) and living room of the Matthew House, London, 1937–38 — 170
9.8. Sigmund Freud at his desk in Vienna, etching by Max Pollak, 1914 — 171

TABLES

4.1. Jewish/non-Jewish background of Freud's Berlin clients	60
4.2. Professional background of Freud's Berlin clients	61
4.3. Age structure of Freud's Berlin clients	61
5.1. Private houses designed, built, or refurbished by Freud between 1920 and 1933	70
7.1. Houses designed, built, or refurbished by Freud between 1933 and c. 1965	135

❧ ACKNOWLEDGMENTS ❧

I would like to express my gratitude to the following individuals and institutions for their kind support of this project: Stephen and Ann Freud, Esther Freud, Jane McAdam Freud, and the Freud Museum London; the RIBA Library Drawings & Archives Collections and Photographs Collection; the Paul Mellon Centre for Studies in British Art for a senior fellowship during the fall quarter of the academic year 2007–8; the Centre Canadien d'Architecture / Canadian Centre for Architecture, Montréal, for generous help with images from its collection while I was a visiting scholar during summer 2009; and Rodopi, Amsterdam, for granting permission to reuse in chapters 4, 5, and 7 material from my essay 'Ernst L Freud—Domestic Architect', published in *The Yearbook of the Research Centre for German and Austrian Exile Studies,* vol. 6, 2005.

In addition, I wish to thank all individuals and institutions mentioned in the Selected List of Works, the illustration credits, and the endnotes for granting permission to quote from unpublished and printed materials in their possessions and to reproduce images from drawings and photographs in their collections or for which they administer copyrights.

Introduction

Anybody who sought psychoanalysis in Berlin during the 1920s had the choice between private practitioners and psychoanalytic clinics. A search could have started with a visit to Karl Abraham, who practiced in Berlin-Grunewald until his death in 1925 and continued in a wide, circular sweep through the western parts of the city, meeting along the way Hans and Jeanne Lampl in Berlin-Dahlem, Sandor Radó in Berlin-Schmargendorf, Max Eitingon in Berlin-Tiergarten, and, back in Berlin-Grunewald, René A. Spitz. If these consultations would not have yielded success, there was still the Poliklinik für Psychoanalytische Behandlung nervöser Krankheiten in Potsdamer Straße and, after 1928, in new premises in Wichmannstraße, both in the Tiergarten district. Or, for a longer stay, Ernst Simmel had opened the psychoanalytical clinic Sanatorium Schloß Tegel in Berlin-Tegel in 1927. Possibly unbeknown to our fictive patient, the search for a psychoanalyst would have taken him through a sequence of modern psychoanalytic interiors designed by Ernst L. Freud (1892–1970), the youngest son of Sigmund Freud and a successful domestic architect in Weimar Republic Berlin and in London after 1933.

From the late nineteenth century onwards, the name Freud had become synonymous with psychoanalysis, but in the 1920s, at least in Berlin, the name was also synonymous with the creation of the earliest documented architect-designed psychoanalytical consulting rooms in architectural history. Intellectually, Sigmund Freud's conception of psychoanalysis has long been recognized as a major contribution to Western modernity. Architecturally, his Vienna consulting room and adjacent study, however, seem to illustrate all that contemporaries thought to be wrong with late nineteenth-century domestic interiors. Cramped with furniture and filled with antiques, statues, books, oriental rugs, art works, and aromatic cigar smoke, the rooms were sensuously rich and offered plenty of opportunities for a writer's thoughts and gaze to sojourn, but also for unhygienic dust to settle. These rooms recall the sumptuous period interiors that evoked Walter Benjamin's wrath when reflecting, for example, on the kind of later nineteenth-century domestic setting his Berlin grandmother lived in or of Jugendstil apartments in the early twentieth century. The aspirations, but also errors and faults of bourgeois life and thought, Benjamin argued, could be gleaned from the bodily impressions left in the abundant velvety surfaces covering and housing many objects in these rooms which functioned like a shell for the inhabitant and his possessions.[1]

Compared to his father's quarters, psychoanalytical spaces designed by Ernst L. Freud were free from ornamental lines and decorative figurines. Instead, their interiors were a combination of the essential couch and chair with, perhaps, a print or two of the founder of psychoanalysis, a writing desk with a second chair, a net curtain, and a potted plant. Judging from the very few surviving black-and-white photographs, Ernst L. Freud's psychoanalytical rooms come across as almost inconspicuous modern designs, delineating an interior that obviously aimed to impress itself as little as possible on the patient's mind. While the latter tried to reclaim aspects of his life, his body left an impression, at least momentarily, in the soft upholstery of the couch. Thus, Freud's designs refute a modern architecture of the type Benjamin referred to when he described architectural modernism as the exchange of soft impressionable surfaces for hard, reflective, unwelcoming ones.[2]

Perhaps Benjamin thought of the *Maison de Verre* (1927–32) in his beloved Paris, designed by Pierre Charreau for a Parisian gynaecologist, when he made this observation. That building, with a gynaecological consulting room at its heart, is inscribed in the memory of modern architectural history not least because it was constructed from exposed steel beams and translucent glass bricks—external modernist characteristics which Freud's architecture generally neither relied upon nor would have exposed in a such an overly visible manner.

Architectural modernism experimented with radical political utopias, housing for the masses, and with space, form, and technology. For example, Berlin during the 1920s and early 1930s evokes images of radiant white cubes and regularly paced *Zeilenbau*, both of *Neues Bauen* perfection, proclaiming the will to build a new society within a most-likely socialist order for the masses of *Neue Menschen*. Such a picture at least emerges from many period accounts and those architectural histories that, accordingly, tell of *The Victory of the New Building Style*.[3]

Freud, however, stayed away from most issues that nowadays are considered to represent the architectural, social, and cultural goals of the 1920s and 1930s and, consequently, his architecture has not received much attention beyond the small circles of historians of psychoanalysis and the Freud family. The spatial settings of his consulting rooms illustrate one likely cause for this relative anonymity, viz. the emphasis psychoanalysis placed on the individual versus the one many contemporary modernist architects and later many historians placed on the masses. Another possible cause is the emphasis of Freud's architectural practice on domestic architecture for middle-class and bourgeois clients. Villas, country houses, and interiors for homes and rental apartments were the staple diet of his offices in Berlin and London. Freud also designed some business premises and offices for bankers, members of liberal professions, and others of comparable social standing, but with few exemptions his designs were usually for clients he personally knew.

Following closely his clients' wishes rather than pursuing a set of a priori artistic ideas, Freud created a heterogeneous œuvre that sought neither the expression of a Zeitgeist, such as, for example, the pursuit of the radically new, a fundamental break with the past, nor aligned itself with the opponents of modernism who favoured traditional architecture over any renewal, radical or not, of architectural practice. Looked at today, Freud's architectural works oscillate between the familiar and unfamiliar, the modern and traditional, and the homely und unhomely. Yet this does not point to architecture without qualities but rather at difficulties architectural history experiences when trying to place such œuvre.

The obstacles in handling heterogeneous modern designs, especially ones by a single architect, contrast sharply with the favourable reception Freud received by his contemporaries as both the sheer number of his clients and their illustrious names suggest. The 1936 *Philo-Lexikon: Handbuch des jüdischen Wissens* even included Freud in the section on contemporary architects, which concluded with the entry 'Architects, Jewish',[4] which placed his name right beside those of such famous colleagues as Adolf Messel, Erich Mendelsohn, and Josef Frank. Moreover, looking through period architectural magazines and contemporary books unveils quickly that bourgeois and middle-class architecture like Freud's was representative of a very large section of modern architecture in Germany and elsewhere during the 1920s, 1930s, and beyond.

To concern oneself with bourgeois modern architecture requires redirecting one's gaze towards the social, economic, and cultural background of middle-class clients including the occasionally plain ordinariness of their modern homes. The latter contrasts sharply with the more radical formal language of architectural modernism, but at least contemporaries were aware of the fact that the modernist style created only superficial similarities between buildings that catered to clients of highly disparate social and economic circumstances. For example, Albert Sigrist distinguished in *Das Buch vom Bauen*[5] between bourgeois and proletarian versions of modernist architecture.

The middle classes were also the focus of contemporary sociological writings such as Siegfried Kracauer's study of *The Salaried Masses.* In the first chapter, 'Unknown Territory', Kracauer pointed out that the 'commonplace existence' of salaried clerks and office workers had hidden this rapidly growing section of the middle classes from the eyes of 'radical intellectuals' regardless of the widely visible fact that cities like Berlin were 'no longer industrial cities, but cities of salaried employees and civil servants'.[6] Kracauer emphasized the hopes of the new middle classes to achieve a 'bourgeois way of life', even though he indicated a certain critical distance by calling the latter 'vanished' and citing studies that observed an alleged process of proletarisation of the new middle classes.[7]

Other contemporaries took a much more positive stance towards bourgeois aspirations and culture. The philosopher and sociologist Helmuth Plessner argued in *The Limits of Community: A Critique of Social Radicalism* for a positive perception of society (*Gesellschaft*) as an alternative to the contemporary fascination with radical leftwing and rightwing ideas of community (*Gemeinschaft*). Published in 1924, the book was a refutation of Ferdinand Tönnies's study on *Community and Society* (1887)—an important inspiration for all sorts of visions of overcoming mass society with communitarian schemes, including architectural designs[8]—and a contribution to the heated argument about Germany's social and political future. Plessner charged the middle classes with both the defence of society and the increase of its appeal to all citizens. Moreover, he analysed in spatial terms the ritualized social behaviour that took place in the public and private spaces of society. Plessner's appreciation of both the bourgeoisie and society as a social order and his spatialized discussion of social behaviour provide, by analogy, a useful framework from within to look afresh at bourgeois domestic architecture. In short, then, modern domestic bourgeois architecture is the larger background against which this study presents and analyses Ernst L. Freud's architectural career and œuvre.

Bourgeois modernism has recently become the subject of revisionist architectural historical accounts. For example, John V. Maciuika's *Before the Bauhaus* offers a close and highly political reading of the manifold intersections between early modern architects like, for example, Hermann Muthesius and the cultural politics of the different governmental levels of the German nation state with regards to training and educating architects and craftsmen. His analysis also looks at how the interests of the Deutsche Werkbund, a bourgeois pressure group of designers, industrialists, and mainly liberal politicians, may have overlapped with the imperial longings of the Deutsche Reich.[9] Or Maiken Umbach's excellent study on *German Cities and Bourgeois Modernism, 1890–1924*, which theorises on the urban spatial politics of the bourgeoisie.[10] Using mostly Hamburg as a case study, the author analyses how that class configured the urban environment with regard to nature, sense of time, and place.

The present book employs a different methodology, which, in Kracauer's words, may not offer 'examples of any theory, but … exemplary instances of reality'.[11] Thus in order to add a few tesserae to the mosaic of reality, to paraphrase Kracauer,[12] I pursue Ernst L. Freud's architectural career as a case study; a methodological tool that was, incidentally, perfected by Sigmund Freud in his writings on individual cases of psychoanalysis and their meaning for the development of the discipline at large. Moreover, the emphasis on individuals as acting agents in the cityscapes of twentieth-century architectural history in Berlin and London dovetails nicely with the self-perception of good bourgeois citizens.

The study takes a basic chronological approach to Freud's career and life, a path it deviates from if and when required by the larger argument. The contemporary discussion about bourgeois modern architecture in Weimar Germany, especially its domestic variety, is the topic of chapter 1, 'Modern Bourgeois Domestic Architecture of the Weimar Republic', and of chapter 9, 'Architecture without Quality?' In both chapters, questions concerning the middle classes and bourgeoisie as noted above are discussed. In order to delineate the appropriate bourgeois context in which architects like Freud were operating, great emphasis has been placed on identifying contemporary writers, for example Helmuth Plessner, who did not automatically assume that the middle classes were a disappearing part of modern society.

Sandwiched in between the opening and concluding chapters is the chronological account of Freud's career and architecture both in Germany and the United Kingdom; particular emphasis has been placed on his time in the former country. Chapter 2, 'The Making of an Architect', portraits Ernst L. Freud's youth in Vienna and his studies of architecture there and in Munich. Chapter 3, 'Going Modern with Rainer Maria Rilke and Adolf Loos', looks at two canonical figures of bourgeois modernity who were biographically linked to Ernst L. Freud; connections that turn out to have greatly influenced his evolving sense of bourgeois domesticity. Chapters 4 to 6 take the reader to Weimar Berlin. Chapter 4, 'Society Architect in Berlin', offers an overview of Freud's German works, including a look at the economic and social circumstances of Freud's own career and life, but also at the profession and his clients. Chapter 5, 'Houses in and around Berlin', analyses individual houses in the city and its vicinity while also discussing the expectations and desires of the bourgeois clients.

The following chapter 6, 'Couches, Consulting Rooms, and Clinics', enlarges the scope of the study by presenting the first ever architecturally historical analysis of all of Freud's psychoanalytic spaces known to us. These designs are included in this study as they were often conceived as extensions, conceptually and architecturally, of private homes. This chapter also takes the narrative to the United Kingdom, where Freud's first clients were psychoanalysts aiming to ease the exile experience of Sigmund Freud's son.

Chapter 7, 'At Home in England', moves the story to England where Freud lived in London from late 1933 onwards. The emphasis rests on analysing how Freud negotiated the loss of his home and client base with the need to restore both while also integrating his version of modern domestic architecture into the context of the British hesitation to fully embrace Continental European modernism. In England, I argue, Freud found his true architectural home as suddenly his modern domestic designs blended in almost seamlessly with the pragmatic approach to modern architecture that many English colleagues had adopted in their attempts to modernize the architecture of the United Kingdom. Chapter 8, 'Family Architect', is likewise set in England and looks at Freud's projects for his own and his extended family. Leaving the chronological approach, this chapter presents exemplary analyses of Freud's Berlin and London homes as well as that of his parents in the British capital, including the recreation of the Vienna consulting room.

In order to portray Ernst L. Freud and his works as an example of bourgeois modern architecture, it was necessary to also research the lives of his clients, many, but not all, of them of Jewish background. Inevitably, this research has added to my architectural historical interest the aspect of exile studies. While I cannot claim expertise in this area, I have included many biographical details in the Selected List of Works, though space did not allow turning the latter into a series of miniature case studies. However, to the careful reader, and hopefully also to future historians, the biographical details offer further details about the bourgeois life and aspirations of many of Freud's clients. That these annotations are unequally distributed with regards to individual clients is a consequence of German National-Socialist politics and the Holocaust. Comparable to their architect, many clients of Freud were forced into exile, if they had been so lucky to realize early enough that they were no longer welcome in their home country. Thus, it is hoped that the annotations will contribute not only to the architectural history of the period but also to the remembrances of these émigrés.

Throughout the study, I mostly use the terms *bourgeois* and *bourgeoisie* instead of *middle class*. Regardless of the Marxist overtones, they convey rather well the cultural aspirations of those *bürgerliche* citizens that commissioned architectural works from Ernst L. Freud.

Notes

1. W. Benjamin. 2002. 'Berlin Childhood around 1900' [1938], in H. Eiland and M. W. Jennings (eds.), *Walter Benjamin: Selected Writings, vol. 3 1935–1938*, trans. by E. Jephcott et al. Cambridge, MA: Belknap Press, 344–413 (369). See also H. Heynen. 1999. *Architecture and Modernity. A Critique*. Cambridge, MA: MIT Press, 107–117.
2. W. Benjamin. 2001. 'The Return of the *Flâneur*' [1929] and 'Experience and Poverty' [1933], in M. W. Jennings (ed.), *Walter Benjamin: Selected Writings, vol. 2 1927–1934*, trans. by R. Livingstone et al. Cambridge, MA: Belknap Press, 262–267 (264), 731–736 (734).
3. W. C. Behrendt. 2000. *The Victory of the New Building Style* [1927], trans. by H. F. Mallgrave. Los Angeles, CA: Getty Research Institute.
4. E. bin Gorion, et al. (eds.). 1992. *Philo-Lexikon. Handbuch des jüdischen Wissens* [1936]. Frankfurt: Jüdischer Verlag im Suhrkamp Verlag, 38–39.
5. A. Sigrist (i.e. A. Schwab). 1973. '*Das Buch vom Bauen*.' *Wohnungsnot Neue Technik Neue Baukunst Städtebau aus sozialistischer Sicht* [1930]. Düsseldorf: Bertelsmann, 67, my translation.
6. S. Kracauer. 1998. *The Salaried Masses: Duty and Distraction in Weimar Germany*, trans. by Q. Hoare. London: Verso, 29, 32
7. Kracauer, *Salaried Masses*, 82.
8. See V. M. Welter. 2010. 'The Limits of Community—The Possibilities of Society: On Modern Architecture in Weimar German', *Oxford Art Journal* 33 (1): 63–80.

9. J. V. Maciuika. 2005. *Before the Bauhaus: Architecture, Politics, and the German State, 1890–1920.* Cambridge: Cambridge University Press
10. M. Umbach. 2009. *German Cities and Bourgeois Modernism, 1890–1924.* Oxford: Oxford University Press.
11. Kracauer, *Salaried Masses,* 25
12. Kracauer, *Salaried Masses,* 32.

Chapter 1

Modern Bourgeois Domestic Architecture of the Weimar Republic

In August 1928, the German architectural monthly *Die Pyramide* published three distinctly different architectural projects: an English country house, a villa by Le Corbusier, and a domestic interior by Ernst L. Freud. The English country house Northease in Rodmell, Sussex, had been owned by consecutive generations of one family since the time of Henry VIII.[1] The photographer and writer E. O. Hoppé presented a recent refurbishment and extension of the house by the architect J. C. Pocock. The owners are described as 'assiduous, practicing farmers—she is in charge of the cows, while her brother-in-law takes care of the fields and sheep', but this was not a homestead of hard working farm folk; instead, 'the impression of the mansion is rather poetic, and Romanticism constitutes without doubt the background to the daily life.'[2] Built in parts from local flint stone, the renovated house was furnished with an eclectic collection of historic and traditional furniture and objects. The interior fostered the romantic ambitions of the farming occupants but did not recreate a particular historic period (fig. 1.1). Even more, the sparsely decorated rooms, some of them underneath the visible rafters of an old barn, could almost be called an attempt at reinventing traditional interiors in light of the contemporary debates about modern architecture.

The contrast between Northease and the building presented in the next article could not have been greater. 'A Villa by Le Corbusier and Pierre Jeanneret' is the rather dull title of a tedious and stilted, but luckily short essay about the Stein villa in Garches, France.[3] With words as devoid of meaning as the interior of the villa's drawing room (fig. 1.2) was empty of furniture, the author tried to capture—in vain—the effects of the free plan and the free façade on the inhabitants: 'One can see, when light, air, and space penetrate the building in all directions, how the drawing room—the centre of the domestic life—pulls together and lets shine through all dimensions, *viz.* lengths, widths, and heights of both the interior space and the entire grounds. Thus a feeling of a new and free monumentality is conveyed to the inhabitant.'[4]

No such shortage of meaningful words characterizes the third essay that is entitled 'Zu Hause' [At Home]. 'What a world of imaginations is contained in these words: *Zu Hause*!' the text begins. It continues asserting that the *Zu Hause* has to keep at bay the 'questionable, wicked, threatening, and alien outside world.'[5] Ultimately, both the home and its architect have more constructive roles than a mere defence against the uncanny:[6]

> The *Zu Hause* begins with the earliest childhood. ... Here, within the security, the child begins to grasp thankfully and with fresh senses the environment. How constructive

Figure 1.1. Living room in the barn of a country house in Northease, England, refurbished by J. C. Pocock. Photograph from *Die Pyramide*, August 1928, used with permission of the Collection Centre Canadien d'Architecture / Canadian Centre for Architecture, Montréal.

Figure 1.2. Upper-level living room of the Stein villa, Garches, by Le Corbusier, 1926–27. Photograph from *Die Pyramide*, August 1928, used with permission of the Collection Centre Canadien d'Architecture / Canadian Centre for Architecture, Montréal; ©Artists Rights Society (ARS), New York / ADAGP, Paris/F.L.C.

childhood impressions are! The pattern of wallpaper, the form of a table is transformed into unheard of experiences. Such memories remain at work in the realm of the unconscious, and even with thirty years of age we experience their undiminished influence each time we are about to make a choice.[7]

The Freudian overtones of the essay are not accidental because the accompanying photographs, while not referred to directly in the text, are of interior designs by Freud (fig. 1.3).[8] All but one show the architect's own home in Berlin's elegant Tiergarten quarter where the Freuds and their three sons, Stephan Gabriel, Lucian Michael, and Clemens Raphael, lived in an apartment in Regentenstraße 23 from c. 1924 to 1931.

At first sight, the publication of the three designs combines an example inspired by traditions with a modernist one that rejected links with the past, and a third one that was stylistically somewhat undecided but tended towards modern architecture as is suggested, for example, by the lack of ornament. In short, the juxtaposition illustrates the Zeitgeist that, in the form of Le Corbusier's modernist design, pointed toward the future from among numerous traditionalist and other architectural schemes. While this approach ties together traditionalist and modernist architecture it leaves little to no room for designs like Freud's, works that are stylistically neither clearly modernist nor traditionalist.

However, the magazine made no explicit argument for or against any of the three designs. Instead, by publishing them it endorsed apparently all three as noteworthy exam-

Figure 1.3. Fireplace in the studio of Ernst L. Freud's second Berlin apartment, 1924–25. Photograph from *Die Pyramide*, August 1928, used with permission of the Collection Centre Canadien d'Architecture / Canadian Centre for Architecture, Montréal.

ples of contemporary architecture. Thus a different interpretative framework is needed, other than the earlier one that suggests a linear development from traditional styles to modernist architectural principles. Beyond possible aesthetic-stylistic considerations, the three examples share that they were designed for bourgeois clients. The three homes were not competing against each other in order to decide which of them was the most modern. Rather, all three together constitute a call to recognize bourgeois models of dwelling as adequate for life in modern society. They argued with other contemporary models of modern living that aimed at overcoming bourgeois domestic ideals such as, for example, social housing for the masses, experiments with apartment blocks with centrally provided services, bachelor housing, and other forms of communal or even collectivist living.

This chapter concentrates on the contemporary debate about bourgeois domestic architecture as it was conducted in many architectural publications of the Weimar Republic. It will also look briefly at a parallel debate about the future of the bourgeoisie as a social class, especially at the arguments made by the philosopher and sociologist Helmuth Plessner in his 1924 book *The Limits of Community: A Critique of Social Radicalism*. Plessner's book provides a framework that, by analogy, helps to shed light from a different angle on the architectural history of the Weimar Republic. For a long time, the discipline has favoured aesthetic-stylistic approaches that primarily focused on the opposition between modernist-designed architecture and more-traditionally dressed buildings, possibly best exemplified in the tug of words that was waged primarily in the pages of professional journals during 1925 and 1926 over the appropriateness of modernist flat roofs versus traditionally pitched roofs.[9] Over time, such stylistic criteria have been elevated to a methodological approach to Weimar Republic architecture with much less attention being paid to types of modern architecture, for example domestic buildings of the bourgeoisie for whose analysis similarities in the social and spatial programs are perhaps more important than differences in style.

Modern Bourgeois Domestic Architecture

The August 1928 issue of *Die Pyramide* was not an isolated publication of recent bourgeois domestic architecture and interior design as a number of contemporary publications prove. Books like, for example, Gustav Adolf Platz's *Die Baukunst der neuesten Zeit* and *Die Wohnräume der Gegenwart*,[10] Grete and Walter Dexel's *Das Wohnhaus von heute*,[11] Walter Müller-Wulckow's *Wohnbauten und Siedlungen*,[12] and Leo Adler's *Neuzeitliche Miethäuser und Siedlungen*[13] assembled a vast number of social housing projects in modernist and traditionalist architectural styles that illustrate the contemporary concern with improving the living conditions of the masses. However, the authors did not restrict themselves to such buildings. They also presented at least as many, if not more, examples of bourgeois domestic architecture. For example, Platz discussed in his book on modern interiors many recently built country houses including the luxurious residence on the outskirts of greater Berlin for Dr. Theodor Frank, a manager of the Deutsche Bank that Freud began in 1928; this project will be analyzed in chapter 5.[14]

These books illustrate that the architectural debate during the Weimar Republic was conducted across both aesthetic-stylistic fault lines with modernist and traditionalist architecture on the opposing sides and socio-political ones that separated mass social housing for the working classes and lower middle classes from domestic bourgeois architecture. The architect Albert Sigrist (1887–1943) summarized in his *Das Buch vom Bauen* the distinction between bourgeois and proletarian modernist architecture when he wrote 'the new architecture has two faces. Indeed, it is bourgeois and proletarian, highly capitalistic and socialist. One can even say it is autocratic and democratic. However, one thing it is not, it is no longer individualistic.'[15] True to his socialist conviction, Sigrist claimed exclusive ownership in modernist architecture for socialist politics.

Other writers argued that in the long run modernist domestic architecture was a means to overcome social differences. For example, Grete and Walter Dexel published in 1928 *Das Wohnhaus von heute*, a sequel to Adolf Behne's *Neues Wohnen—Neues Bauen* from 1927.[16] The couple stated specifically that the 'detached single house on a reasonably large plot of land' is 'for the time being still the most ideal form of dwelling.'[17] They also remarked that 'it may appear as odd that we do not discuss separately plans of minimum dwellings and those of so-called bourgeois apartments, but speak alternately now about the one and then about the other.' Their answer was that those differences that used to determine the plans of both types of housing had given way to the recognition 'that the basic demands are nowadays of a general character. There is no longer any reason to classify the plans into groups that are rooted in financial and social differences.'[18] Significantly, there also was no reason to dismiss the assumption that the bourgeoisie and the middle classes required different types of dwelling than other classes. Accordingly, the Dexels discussed with equal fervour both bourgeois and working-class domestic architecture. Their overview ranged from modernist single-family dwellings to modernist multi-apartment buildings for both social groups.

A third possible position, viz. a strongly worded defence of bourgeois domestic architecture, was formulated by Gustav Adolf Platz (1881–1947), the author of *Die Baukunst der neuesten Zeit*, one of the earliest contemporary accounts of modern architecture.[19] To this comprehensive overview both of the history and the developments of modern architecture, Platz added in 1933, with *Wohnräume der Gegenwart*, a volume on interior designs.[20] Platz neither dismissed bourgeois architecture as a historical phenomenon nor argued that diminishing social differences rendered it superfluous. Instead, confrontation characterized the period: 'For the radicals, the housing [*Wohnung*] of the masses is the only valuable subject. For the moderates, the issue of bourgeois living [*Wohnung*] still exists.' Even more, the latter was 'more pressing than ever before, because a self-conscious bourgeoisie is rising once again.' Setting bourgeois aspirations as the norm, Platz put housing for the minimum existence into its place when he referred to it as the 'lowest levels of bourgeois living ... nothing else than an apartment ... for the poor.'[21]

Wohnräume der Gegenwart is not so much a history of bourgeois living than a manual, as exemplified by two large sections of the introductory essay. The first one, 'Basic Questions of Building a House,'[22] deals with the contemporary conditions of living in rental apartments within city blocks and with various forms of detached houses in the suburbs and the countryside. The second part, 'Individual Rooms and their Relationships,'[23] sets out the spatial and functional requirements of, for example, a living room, hall, gentleman's room or home office, reception room, lady's room, dining room, bedroom, child's room, rooms for bodily hygiene and sport, and, finally, economy rooms to run a household. In short, the ideal type of home that Platz's essay dissects is a bourgeois house.

It is instructive to compare Platz's book with another such manual, which was published earlier. In 1919, in the immediate post-war period, the third edition of Hermann Muthesius's book *Wie baue ich mein Haus?* was released.[24] The main part of the volume is dedicated to a room-by-room analysis of a hypothetical bourgeois house. It begins with the gentleman's room, followed by the music room, lady's room or reception room, dining room, living room, bedrooms and dressing rooms, bathrooms, children's rooms, sport rooms and sunrooms.[25] Rooms dedicated to specific activities like games of billiards, amassing collections, conducting business, and producing art complement this evocation of a basic version of bourgeois living.

The two books illustrate different approaches to an architecture that was conducive to a bourgeois way of life while at the same responsive to the dire economic circumstances of the times. Muthesius propagated the traditional stand-alone urban or suburban villa and country house thus showing his continuous familiarity with English models of dwelling. In 1903, he had initiated almost single-handedly the early twentieth-century efforts to reform German bourgeois domestic architecture with his book *Das Englische Haus*. That book was the result of an official assignment to the embassy in London from 1896 to 1903 where Muthesius gathered information about the British industry and crafts in a government-driven attempt to modernize Germany's production of commodities.[26] This official function and Muthesius's privately executed, later architectural works illustrate well the ongoing transformation of Berlin—and by implication Germany—into a bourgeois city and society.[27] The 1919 edition of *Wie baue ich mein Haus?* was aimed at matching the bourgeois ideal with the circumstances of the time, most notably by recommending shrinking the house, its volume, and number and sizes of rooms.[28]

Platz argued differently. He emphasized the advantages of modern architecture with regard to the efficient accommodation of the paraphernalia of bourgeois life. When considering the necessity to economize, Platz recommended the modernist open plan as the appropriate environment of the new man:

> The singular living room replaces for him the abundance of rooms that he either does not use or cannot heat. This living room will be a combination of dining area, office area, or music area. The room will be dissected into suitable compartments through built-in features, furniture, partial walls, and sliding doors. The room will be flexible, elastic, separable, it can be increased or reduced—it is an instrument of life even in modest circumstances.[29]

By economic necessity, the bourgeois home of the future was to be much smaller than envisioned, but there was no need to give up on such signifiers of bourgeois life like, for example, house music: A corner in the living room was sufficient if a dedicated music salon was out of reach.

Platz's quote also circumscribes the range of commissions an architect like Freud could receive from clients whose social and cultural aspirations led them to ask a professional to satisfy their domestic needs. These could range from entire houses to interiors of villas, large and small rental apartments, individual pieces of furniture—representative and space-saving devices—to, finally, '*Heimberatung*', advice on how to furnish and decorate a home, as Platz called it.[30] Regardless of the size of a project, each commission fulfilled both societal needs and individual ones. According to Platz, 'in the moulding of our apartments and our houses the individualistic designs of the individual existence' will continuously be expressed because society's 'contemporary division into estates [*Stände*] leaves open a wide field for different attitudes towards life.'[31] Platz concluded that his readers should not decide whether an individual had a right to live in luxury. Rather, they should be inspired by the generous and spacious bourgeois domestic designs that some architects were privileged to realize during the Weimar Republic.

Many more books and journal articles could be cited to buttress the argument that bourgeois domestic buildings were a well-established part of the architectural culture of the Weimar Republic, but this selective account must suffice. The debate about this type of architecture continued an earlier one from the turn of the nineteenth century to the twentieth. According to Peter Gay, the Great War was the watershed that had separated bourgeois politics from bourgeois high culture. With regard to the former the war constituted a clear break between the past and the future, 'but what held true in the domain of political action ... did not hold true in the regions of high culture.'[32] Domestic architecture had always been a part of the latter and it remained so throughout the Weimar Republic. At the beginning of the period, Muthesius's book signalled the hopes that bourgeois architecture, even if in much reduced form, would survive the many great changes that were anticipated in the aftermath of the war. At the end of the period, in 1933, the examples assembled in Platz's book illustrated that bourgeois architecture not only had survived but thrived even if in reduced, though much modernized architectural form.

The Limits of Community, the Chances of Society

The debate about bourgeois domestic architecture (as much as the one about mass social housing) paralleled and even mirrored a larger societal argument about the future of the social groups of German society. Leaving aside in this book those opinions that dismissed, for example from a Marxist point of view, any contemporary or future relevance of the middle classes, especially of the bourgeoisie, these social classes were analysed from a variety of angles ranging from critically sympathetic over scientifically sociological to appreciative.

Several years before he wrote *The Salaried Masses* in 1930, Kracauer had observed the life and habits of urban, educated citizens like 'scholars, businessmen, doctors, lawyers, students, and intellectuals of all sorts'.[33] The 1922 essay 'Those Who Wait' presents a highly critical picture of a social group whose members' lives were emptied of meaning by a historic process of secularization. The resulting void had neither been filled by bourgeois education and aspiration nor abolished as access to the 'religious sphere' was the key to either action.[34] Kracauer describes various attempts—among them anthroposophy, messianic communism, life philosophy, and the neo-classicism of the Stefan-George circle—to regain both the lost sense of religiosity and a feeling of belonging to a community. He distinguishes three types of personalities depending on their handling of the meaninglessness of bourgeois life. The apparently enlightened sceptical type who as a matter of principle lived without any will to belief is juxtaposed with the so-called short-circuit person who subscribed on impulse to whatever religious and communitarian ideology came his way.[35] Yet Kracauer's respect belongs to the third group who did not fall for activism but patiently waited to enter, however tentatively, the 'world of *reality* and the domains it encompasses'.³⁶ In those spheres they would be taught that the lawfulness of social life could not be grasped by either theoretical reasoning or arbitrary subjective acts.

The middle classes were also the subject of detailed scientific-sociological inquiries. One of the most comprehensive analyses was part of the study *Die Soziale Schichtung des Deutschen Volkes* published in 1932. Its author, the sociologist Theodor Geiger (1891– 1952), drew on many contemporary investigations of social classes and their relationships with each other in Germany. Geiger aimed at replacing a Marxist-inspired model of capitalists, middle classes, and proletariat with a multi-layered social stratification model. With the latter the author hoped to capture in addition to the 'old middle classes'—as described by Kracauer in 'Those Who Wait'—what contemporaries called the 'new middle classes', the salaried masses of clerks and office employees. The goal was to account better for the increased social flexibility up and down the social ladder. Moreover, by correlating the middle classes' increased number with a more adequate statistical weighting Geiger argued that his expanded model would represent more accurately the growing social and political importance of these central social layers of the Weimar Republic.³⁷

The future of the middle classes, especially the bourgeoisie, and an appreciation of its historic achievements stand at the centre of *The Limits of Community: A Critique of Social Radicalism* by the philosopher and sociologist Helmuth Plessner.³⁸ Today, Plessner is known as one of the founders of philosophical anthropology and this early book was already influenced by his developing interest in that field of philosophy. More immediately, *The Limits of Community* was a polemic contribution to the post–Great War debate about the future social order of Germany. Plessner adopted a historical perspective that placed his own contribution within the debate about community or society as appropriate social order, which, in turn, went back to the book *Gemeinschaft und Gesellschaft*, which the sociologist Ferdinand Tönnies (1855–1936) had published in 1887.³⁹ This study was reprinted in 1912, but soared to popularity in the 1920s when it saw five more editions.⁴⁰ Tönnies's inquiry was academically balanced, even though it did argue that the emergence of capitalism had run in parallel with a general development towards society as the most adequate social order. The book's success, however, was grounded in the contemporary popularity of all sorts of notions of community that promised salvation from the harsh reality of post-war society.

Already Kracauer had pointed in his 1922 article to the contemporary fascination with community, which became also the starting point for Plessner's book. Plessner did not merely juxtapose community and society. Rather, after acknowledging Tönnies's 'well-known antithesis'⁴¹ he moved immediately towards a tri-partite matrix. He argued that two basic types of community existed, a community of blood (*Blutgemeinschaft*), and an ideal-based community (*Sachgemeinschaft*) that were both nurtured by social radicalism. Society (*Gesellschaft*), a possible third, non-radical social order complemented them. As a philosophical anthropologist, Plessner considered the three concepts not as alternatives but as parallel existing spheres that also encompassed aspects of individual human existence. Accordingly, the community of blood was related to the body, the community of the ideal to the human spirit (*Geist*), while society was the realm of the human soul. As a sociologist and a citizen of the Weimar Republic, Plessner preferred on the larger societal level the concept of society over the other two. Moreover, he charged the bourgeoisie and those members of other classes with bourgeois ambitions with the responsibility to defend their society and to increase its appeal.

Regardless of all differences between the two types of community, Plessner stressed their common origin in social radicalism. Social radicalism was also the source of the contemporary popularity of notions of community as people in war-torn Germany pinned eschatological hopes on either socialist and communist modern utopias or on retrograde and reactionary returns to pre-industrial forms of communal life. Four main points characterized the social radicalism that underpinned such visions.[42]

First, social radicalism could only think in fundamental categories. Second, it searched for first principles with which to envision the world in radically new form. Third, the socially radical insisted on the destruction of the existing in anticipatory preparation for the new and perfect. And, fourth, social radicalism was either based on more irrational ideas or more rational ones. Resorting to art and architecture, Plessner argued that the former became visible, for example, in 'roughly impressionism-expressionism'.[43] The latter he found illustrated in exemplary manner in the 'cry for physical cleanliness—satisfied easily with overhead windows and tiled walls',[44] hints at a modern functionalism that anticipated 'the exaggerated radicalism of the radical-functionalist period' of modernist architecture whose emergence coincided with Plessner's book.[45]

Beside the two types of community, Plessner set the concept of society, the realm of 'the conditioned and limited, small things and steps, restraint, discretion, and the unconsciousness'[46] where 'such things run their own course as they will.'[47] While social radicalism dragged ultimate truths into the limelight, society operated by veiling what stood at the centre of attention, not in order to deceive but to make possible forms of social interaction that would protect the individual soul. Recalling Georg Simmel's notion of modern metropolitan life, society was 'the unity of interactions among an indeterminate number of persons unknown to each other, who because of limited opportunities, time, and reciprocal interests can at most establish acquaintances.'[48] In this world of chance encounters the 'forced distance between persons becomes ennobled into reserve. The offensive indifference, coldness, and rudeness of living past each other is made ineffective through the forms of politeness, respectfulness, and attentiveness. Reserve counteracts a too great intimacy.'[49] Those public social interactions that took such forms as, for example, prestige, ceremony, diplomacy, and tactfulness were a consequence of the 'ontological ambiguity'[50] of the human soul. With this term Plessner referred to the soul being torn between the opposing forces of 'the impetus to disclosure—the need for validity; and the impetus to restraint—the need for modesty.'[51] In order to safeguard it, society and its individual members required form and limits, social masks and roles, restraint and compromise; in short, formalized social interaction.[52]

Finally, Plessner argued that formal social encounter created spatial relations, both real and metaphorical ones, between human beings. For example, prestige and ceremony especially relied on, and also generated, bodily distance, whereas 'diplomatic and tactful conduct ... describe the way of conduct of persons in the public domain.'[53] Thus spaces of society like, for example, the general public domain and public rooms in private dwellings—drawing rooms and music rooms, for example—were more than places to conduct business encounters and to hold polite conversations. They were spaces to stage and choreograph human encounters so that they could cater to the two sides of the human soul by accommodating, for example, a 'dance-like spirit', an 'ethos of grace', 'forms of play where persons come close to each other without meeting', and the 'establishment of distance without damaging each other through indifference'.[54]

The Bourgeois Home, the 'Unknown Territory' of Modern Architecture?

Sigfried Kracauer titled the first chapter of his study on the middle classes 'Unknown Territory' because the public visibility of the life and the culture of this segment of society meant that barely anybody cared to take a closer look.[55] A comparable common visibility characterizes bourgeois architecture like modern domestic designs. Because this architecture was such a common part of the built environment it is often, for example by architectural history, considered not to be worth much attention unless it is of modernist design. For example, the Berlin architect Alexander Klein (1879–1961) is today perhaps best known for his studies of rationalized floor plans for standardized minimum housing during the 1920s. At the same time, he also built sumptuous townhouses in a neo-classical mode (fig. 1.4).[56] The latter's spatial arrangement of a central open stair hall and flanking dining room and living room on the ground floor was ideally suited

Figure 1.4. Townhouses in Berlin by Alexander Klein, 1922–25. Photograph from E. M. Hajos and L. Zahn (eds.). 1928. *Berliner Architektur der Nachkriegszeit.* Berlin: Albertus, used with permission of the Collection Centre Canadien d'Architecture / Canadian Centre for Architecture, Montréal.

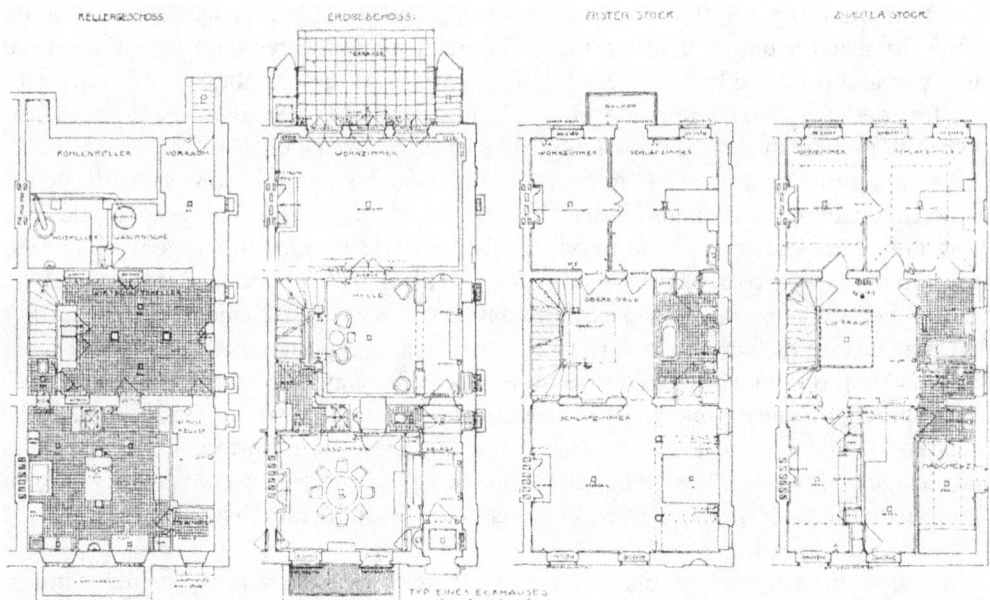

Figure 1.5. Floor plans of the townhouses in Berlin by Alexander Klein. Photograph from E. M. Hajos and L. Zahn (eds.). 1928. *Berliner Architektur der Nachkriegszeit*. Berlin: Albertus, used with permission of the Collection Centre Canadien d'Architecture / Canadian Centre for Architecture, Montréal.

for formal dinner parties and is therefore understood to have mirrored 'the functional sequence of Wilhelminian society' (fig. 1.5).[57] Thus, the houses were not only out of sync with modern Weimar Germany but Klein himself contradicted with them his otherwise impeccable modernity: 'Even an architect who was quite open to contemporaneous ideas about typology and standardization was nevertheless capable of building a very traditional house—not only on the exterior with its classicistic decoration of columns but also in the interior.'[58]

Only a comparison with, for example, Ludwig Mies van der Rohe's modernist Tugendhat villa (1928–30) in Brno, Czech Republic, can integrate Klein's architecture into the discourse about modern period architecture: 'Inside the Tugendhat villa a new world is conjured up, whereas inside the Kleinian houses the old one is preserved obstinately.'[59] This comparison equates differences in style with ones in social behaviour, for example, when the interiors are described as 'closed spaces versus a flowing continuum of space divided only by guiding, freely placed walls; the static principle of social ritual versus the principle of movement and openness.'[60] While modernist designs are often analyzed as allowing freedom of movement and, accordingly, are interpreted as freeing from societal conventions, Grete Tugendhat stressed that her home liberated by imposing formalized social interaction. She recalled the house as 'large and austerely simple—however, not in a dwarfing but in a liberating sense'. This experience rested on the spacious open plan enforcing a distinct formal behaviour: 'This austerity makes it impossible to spend your time just relaxing and letting yourself go, and it is precisely this being forced to do something else which people, exhausted and left empty by their working lives, need and find liberating today' (fig. 1.6).⁶¹ Similarly, the lower-level plan of the villa, while open, catered to the ritualized habits of bourgeois life. The living spaces were comprised of a formal dining area, supper and breakfast zone, sitting area, music area, a library cum study with a writing desk, and, on the upper level, a waiting area adjacent to the main entrance complete with tubular steel chairs and a table on which to leave calling cards.⁶²

Plessner himself suggested an interpretive line from his two-fold concern with society as the adequate framework for modern life and formalized social behaviour to Mies van der Rohe's domestic designs and to bourgeois domestic architecture in general. On the occasion of the twenty-fifth anniversary of the Deutsche Werkbund in October 1932 the philosopher spoke on the 'Wiedergeburt der Form im technischen Zeitalter'.⁶³ Earlier that year he had delivered a lecture to the Bauhaus, accepting an invitation that most likely had come from Mies van der Rohe who was familiar with some of his writings.⁶⁴ In his speech, Plessner identified with modernism in architecture, for example, when he remarked favourably on recent modernist housing projects in Rotterdam, Amsterdam, and Dessau.⁶⁵ However, Plessner qualified this siding by insisting on a renaissance of form as a precondition for a new, playful relationship between human beings and the objects of the man-made world.

The speech castigated as tight corsets of 'closed forms'⁶⁶ mid-nineteenth century historicism, late nineteenth-century *Jugendstil*,⁶⁷ and the recent rational-functionalist architecture. The latter especially shed all aesthetic concerns in favour of subordinat-

Figure 1.6. Lower-level living room of the Tugendhat villa, Brno, by Ludwig Mies van der Rohe, 1928–30. Photograph from G. A. Platz. 1933. *Wohnräume der Gegenwart*. Berlin: Propyläen, used with permission of the Collection Centre Canadien d'Architecture / Canadian Centre for Architecture, Montréal; © Artists Rights Society (ARS), New York / VG Bild-Kunst, Bonn.

ing 'all space-creating considerations to the purposes of technology'[68] while often aligning itself socio-politically with socialism and Marxism.[69] Continuing his criticism of a rational-functionalist architecture, which his 1924 book had already begun as cited above, Plessner developed now the idea of an 'open form'[70] that would accept the continuous changes enforced by technology because it would match the technological world's 'essentially non-enclosed and open character'[71] with regard to space, time, and objects or commodities.

In *The Limits of Community* the two radical types of communities were balanced by society; Plessner's Werkbund talk was structured comparably. The two extreme positions were facing modern technology with either the rigidity of historic and new styles or a dogmatic functionalism. Both required as a check the renaissance of a form characterized by, for example 'bond, ... moderation, ... equilibrium';[72] qualities that echoed those Plessner had earlier already ascribed to society. This open form would allow man to reach a new, playful relationship with human-designed objects and architecture.[73] This relationship extended beyond the mere practical use of objects towards acknowledging that the latter had 'a membrane, a physiognomy, an appearance, a face!', and therefore required a focus on the often overlooked 'value of the sight [*Anblickswert*]'.[74] Accordingly, the playful engagement centred on an aesthetic experience that was quite comparable to the aesthetic character of play as a type of formalized social behaviour to which Plessner had referred in his 1924 book. By regaining playful relationships with his own creations man would achieve true sovereignty; a condition that, like the open form, had thus far been achieved only by a few of 'the great masters of the "new Style"'.[75] Plessner did not mention a particular architect, but his acquaintance with Mies van der Rohe allows one to tie back in exemplary manner the philosopher's thoughts to the Tugendhat villa and to bourgeois architecture in general.

Seen from this perspective, a modernist villa like the Tugendhat's is much closer to the neo-classical townhouses of Klein than, for example, to modernist housing estates. With the latter it may share superficially some modernist architectural detailing, on the strength of which modernist buildings are often considered as the endpoint of a linear historical development of modernism in architecture similar to my initial reading of the three bourgeois homes in *Die Pyramide* from August 1928. With the former the Tugendhat home shares the aspirations and ideologies of the bourgeois middle classes, for example those ideas about spatially formalized social rituals of society and the playful relationship of man with his own artistic and architectural creations that would help, Plessner hoped, establish the adequate social order of modern life and modern architecture as its material form.

Plessner's analysis of social radicalism helps to understand the contemporary arguments between architectural modernists and traditionalists as a squabble between siblings rather than strangers. Modernists imagined a tabula rasa on which to erect model housing without roots in either the known world or history. Equally radical was the dialectical opposite idea that architecture should strictly follow historical precedence and thus deny all changes that had taken place in modern times. While social and architectural radicals were thus metaphorically fighting with each other, other architects stayed away from expressing in their work radical positions of any such kind.[76]

To the latter belonged Ernst L. Freud, whose subtle domestic architecture seems to have almost gone lost among the excitements of avant-garde architectural and artistic experiments in the Berlin of the 1920s and early 1930s. Equally, his British work was no shining beacon that cut through the mist of traditional vernacular and neo-classical architecture hovering over the British architectural scene well into the 1950s when it began to lift slowly. The heterogeneous character of Freud's architecture recalls Plessner's remark that the 'everyday life' which is lived in the realm of society is the 'epitome of *pure individual cases,* even when general ideas and duties—with regard to which it is not possible to appeal to a higher authority … —runs [sic] through it'.[77] This seems to be an appropriate guideline to study the modern domestic architecture of an individual architect like Freud whose career began with his studies in Vienna and Munich, the topic of the next chapter.

NOTES

1. The house was owned by the Marquess of Abergavenny when it was put up for auction in 1919 (letter from Philip Bye, Senior Archivist, East Sussex County Council, to the author, 3 September 2002).
2. E. O. Hoppé. 1928. 'Ein englisches Landhaus', *Die Pyramide* 15 (August): 231–240 (231), my translation.
3. G. Vedres. 1928. 'Eine Villa von Le Corbusier und Pierre Jeanneret', *Die Pyramide* 15 (August): 241-245 (242), my translation.
4. Vedres, ' Le Corbusier und Pierre Jeanneret', 242, my translation.
5. A. H. 1928. 'Zu Hause', *Die Pyramide* 15 (August): 248–257 (248). Nothing is known about the author, A. H. He may have been the conservative cultural critic Adolf Halfeld (1898–1955), possibly best known for his anti-American *Amerika und der Amerikanismus. Kritische Betrachtungen eines Deutschen und Europäers.* 1927. Jena: Eugen Diederichs and his 'Amerika und die neue Sachlichkeit'. 1928. *Der Diederichs-Löwe* 2 (4): 244–248.
6. A. Vidler. 1992. *The Architectural Uncanny: Essays in the Modern Unhomely.* Cambridge, MA: MIT Press.
7. A. H., 'Zu Hause', 255.
8. The essay is also illustrated with images of a new museum in Cologne by Adolf Abel.
9. B. Miller Lane. 1968. *Architecture and Politics in Germany 1918–1945.* Cambridge, MA: Harvard University Press, 133–135.
10. G. A. Platz. 1927. *Die Baukunst der neuesten Zeit.* Berlin: Propyläen; G. A. Platz. 1933. *Wohnräume der Gegenwart.* Berlin: Propyläen.
11. G. Dexel and Walter Dexel. 1928. *Das Wohnhaus von heute.* Leipzig: Hesse & Becker.
12. W. Müller-Wulckow. 1928. *Wohnbauten und Siedlungen.* Königstein i. Taunus: Karl Robert Langewiesche.
13. L. Adler. 1931. *Neuzeitliche Miethäuser und Siedlungen.* Berlin: Ernst Pollak.
14. Platz, *Wohnräume,* 74–75, 237, 252, 352.
15. A. Sigrist (i.e. A. Schwab). 1973. *'Das Buch vom Bauen.' Wohnungsnot Neue Technik Neue Baukunst Städtebau aus sozialistischer Sicht* [1930]. Düsseldorf: Bertelsmann, 67, my translation.
16. A. Behne. 1927. *Neues Wohnen—Neues Bauen.* Leipzig: Hesse & Becker.
17. Dexel and Dexel, *Wohnhaus von heute,* 56, my translation.
18. Dexel and Dexel, *Wohnhaus von heute,* 137, 138, my translation.
19. Platz, *Die Baukunst.*
20. The volume was commissioned in January 1931 with a submission date of December 1931. Platz completed the manuscript in March 1933 and the volume was published in May 1933. The publication during early Nazi government resulted apparently in a rather subdued recep-

tion of the book (R. Jaeger. 2000. *Gustav Adolf Platz und sein Beitrag zur Architekturhistoriographie der Moderne.* Berlin: Gebr. Mann, 85, 97–98).
21. Platz, *Wohnräume*, 13, my translation.
22. Platz, *Wohnräume*, 90–102.
23. Platz, *Wohnräume*, 103–129.
24. H. Muthesius. 1919. *Wie baue ich mein Haus?* Munich: F. Bruckmann. The second edition had appeared in 1917.
25. Muthesius, *Wie baue ich mein Haus?*, table of contents.
26. On this aspect of German cultural politics see, for example, J. V. Maciuika. 2005. *Before the Bauhaus: Architecture, Politics, and the German State, 1890–1920.* Cambridge: Cambridge University Press.
27. The extent of the actual influence of this one social class on the larger society is argued over. See for example P. Gay. 2002. *Schnitzler's Century: The Making of Middle-Class Culture 1815–1914.* New York: W. W. Norton, especially chapter 1. See also R. König. 1949. *Soziologie heute.* Zurich: Regio-Verlag, especially the section on 'Strukturwandel des kapitalistischen Systems', 49–87; and R. König. 1961. 'Zur Soziologie der zwanziger Jahre oder Ein Epilog zu zwei Revolutionen, die niemals stattgefunden haben, und was daraus für unsere Gegenwart resultiert', in L. Reinsch (ed.), *Die Zeit ohne Eigenschaften. Eine Bilanz der zwanziger Jahre.* Stuttgart: Kohlhammer, 82–118
28. Muthesius, *Wie baue ich mein Haus?*, 6.
29. Platz, *Wohnräume*, 65, my translation.
30. Platz, *Wohnräume*, 66.
31. Platz, *Wohnräume*, 67, my translation.
32. P. Gay, *Schnitzler's Century*, xx.
33. S. Kracauer. 1995. 'Those Who Wait', in T. Y. Levin (trans.), *The Mass Ornament: Weimar Essays.* Cambridge, MA: Harvard University Press, 129–140 (129).
34. Kracauer, 'Those Who Wait', 130.
35. Kracauer, 'Those Who Wait', 135–136.
36. Kracauer, 'Those Who Wait', 139, italics in original.
37. T. Geiger. 1932. *Die soziale Schichtung des deutschen Volkes. Soziographischer Versuch auf statistischer Grundlage.* Stuttgart: F. Enke. For other contemporary contributions to the debate about the changes of the social composition of Weimar Germany see, for example, H. Quigley and R. T. Clark. 1928. *Republican Germany. A Political and Economical Study.* London: Methuen; A. Vierkandt. 1931. *Handwörterbuch der Soziologie.* Stuttgart: F. Enke; and P. Kosok. 1933. *Modern Germany. A Study of Conflicting Loyalties.* Chicago, IL: University of Chicago Press.
38. H. Plessner. 1924. *Die Grenzen der Gemeinschaft. Eine Kritik des sozialen Radikalismus.* Bonn: Friedrich Cohen. In the following I refer to the English edition: H. Plessner. 1999. *The Limits of Community: A Critique of Social Radicalism*, trans. by A. Wallace. Amherst, NY: Humanity Books.
39. F. Tönnies. 1887. *Gemeinschaft und Gesellschaft: Abhandlung des Communismus und Socialismus als empirischer Kulturformen.* Leipzig: Fues.
40. F. Tönnies. 1912. *Gemeinschaft und Gesellschaft: Grundbegriffe der reinen Soziologie.;* Berlin: Karl Curtius. The third edition was published in 1920, followed by two combined editions, the fourth and fifth edition in 1922, and the sixth and seventh in 1926. All these editions were published by Karl Curtius in Berlin. An eighth edition appeared in 1935, published by H. Baske in Leipzig.
41. Plessner, *Limits*, 41.
42. Plessner, *Limits*, 48–53.
43. Plessner, *Limits*, 52.

44. Plessner, *Limits*, 167, I substituted 'overhead window' for 'small, high window' as the term for *Oberlicht*.
45. H.-J. Dahms. 2002. 'Mies van der Rohe und die Philosophie um 1930', *Arch+* issue 161 (June). www.archplus.net/archiv_artikel.php?show=1998, accessed 10 July 2007, column 10.
46. Plessner, *Limits*, 48.
47. Plessner, *Limits*, 49.
48. Plessner, *Limits*, 131.
49. Plessner, *Limits*, 131.
50. Plessner, *Limits*, 109.
51. Plessner, *Limits*, 109.
52. See also H. Plessner. 1960. 'Soziale Rolle und menschliche Natur', in H. Plessner [1966], *Diesseits der Utopie. Ausgewählte Beiträge zur Kultursoziologie*. Düsseldorf: Eugen Diederichs, 23–35.
53. Plessner, *Limits*, 169, my italics. On the differences between Plessner's public domain or public sphere and that of Habermas, see Plessner, *Limits*, 101, endnote 3.
54. Plessner, *Limits*, 131.
55. S. Kracauer. 1998. *The Salaried Masses: Duty and Distraction in Weimar Germany*, trans. by Q. Hoare. London: Verso, chapter 1, 'Unknown Territory', 28–32.
56. Terraced villas in Ballenstedter Straße, Berlin-Wilmersdorf, 1922–25, *Architekten im Exil*. http://www.ikg.uni-karlsruhe.de/projekte/exilarchitekten/architekten/klein.htm, accessed 14 August 2007.
57. G. Kähler. 1996. 'Nicht nur Neues Bauen! Stadtbau, Wohnung, Architektur', in G. Kähler (ed.). *1918–1945 Reform, Reaktion, Zerstörung*. Stuttgart: DVA, 303–452 (349), my translation.
58. Kähler, 'Nicht nur Neues Bauen!', 349, my translation.
59. Kähler, 'Nicht nur Neues Bauen!', 350, my translation.
60. Kähler, 'Nicht nur Neues Bauen!', 349, my translation.
61. G. and Fritz Tugendhat. 2000. 'The Inhabitants of the Tugendhat House give their Opinion', in D. Hammer-Tugendhat and W. Tegethoff (eds.). *Ludwig Mies van der Rohe: The Tugendhat House*. Vienna: Springer, 35–37 (35).
62. W. Tegethoff. 2000. 'A Modern Residence in Turbulent Times', in Hammer-Tugendhat and Tegethoff, *The Tugendhat House*, 43–97 (78).
63. H. Plessner. 2001. 'Wiedergeburt der Form im Technischen Zeitalter', in S. Giammusso and Hans-Ulrich Lessing (eds.). *Helmuth Plessner, Politik—Anthropologie—Philosophie: Aufsätze und Vorträge*. Munich: Wilhelm Fink Verlag, 71–86.
64. The Dessau lecture 'Mensch und Umwelt' from February 1932 has been lost, but see the reference to it in 'Die letzten zwei Jahre des Bauhauses. Auszüge aus Briefen des Bauhäuslers Hans Keßler', in P. Hahn (ed.). 1985. *Bauhaus Berlin: Auflösung Dessau 1932, Schließung Berlin 1933, Bauhäusler und Drittes Reich*. Weingarten: Kunstverlag Weingarten, 157–182 (163–164). Mies van der Rohe owned copies of *Die Einheit der Sinne* (1923) and *Die Stufen des Organischen und der Mensch: Einleitung in the philosophische Anthropologie* (1928), see F. Neumeyer. 1991. *Mies van der Rohe: The Artless Word. Mies van der Rohe on the Building Art*, trans. by Mark Jarzombek. Cambridge, MA: MIT Press, 358, notes 27 and 39.
65. Plessner, 'Wiedergeburt', 85.
66. Plessner, 'Wiedergeburt', 76, my translation.
67. Plessner, 'Wiedergeburt', 71–73.
68. Plessner, 'Wiedergeburt', 81.
69. Plessner, 'Wiedergeburt', 77, 78–80.
70. See P. Bernhard. 2007. 'Plessners Konzept der *offenen Form* im Kontext der Avantgarde der 1920er Jahre', *ARHE Časopis za filozofiju* 4 (7): 237–252.
71. Plessner, Wiedergeburt', 77.

72. Plessner, 'Wiedergeburt', 71, my translation.
73. Plessner, 'Wiedergeburt', 82.
74. Plessner, 'Wiedergeburt', 82, my translation.
75. Plessner, 'Wiedergeburt', 82, my translation.
76. See V. M. Welter. 2010. '*The Limits of Community*—The Possibilities of Society: On Modern Architecture in Weimar German', *Oxford Art Journal* 33 (1): 63–80.
77. Plessner, *Limits*, 130, italics in original.

❦ Chapter 2 ❧

The Making of an Architect

Born on 6 April 1892, Ernst Freud was the fourth of the six children of Sigmund and Martha Freud. One sister, Mathilde (1887–1978), and two brothers, Jean Martin (1889–1967) and Oliver (1891–1969), were born earlier, two more sisters, Sophie (1893–1920) and Anna (1895–1982), later (fig. 2.1). In Ernst Freud's own words his early education took an orderly course: 'I attended in Vienna the Volksschule for five years and afterwards the Oberrealschule for seven years.'[1] Freud completed his secondary-school education in July 1911. In the following autumn he enrolled for architecture at the *Kaiserliche und Königliche Technische Hochschule Wien* (TH Vienna). Whatever the ultimate reason for this decision, Freud had already made up his mind to study architecture before he finished at the Oberrealschule, so at least reported his father in a letter from mid June 1911.[2] This chapter will outline some influences from his childhood and youth that may have

Figure 2.1. The Freud family in c. 1898, back row (from left): Martin and Sigmund Freud; middle row (from left): Oliver and Martha Freud, Minna Bernays, Ernst Freud; front row (from left): Sophie and Anna Freud. Used with permission of the Freud Museum London.

contributed to Freud's decision to study architecture. Moreover, the chapter will briefly discuss Freud's studies in Vienna and Munich where he completed his formal education.

If any of the six siblings were destined to become an architect, one would have suspected it to be Oliver or Anna. Both signed a contract on the 17 August 1908 in which Oliver called himself a builder and committed to erect for his sister a two-storey house in the countryside. Anna, in turn, was to pay him one Mark and one piece of chocolate upon completion of the commission, a fee she promised to hold until 1 September of that year. Oliver was successful and the country house—presumably a doll house or a model—was completed on time on 31 August 1908.[3]

However, Oliver eventually chose civil engineering as his profession and Anna became a child psychoanalyst, though she never lost her interest in building. When in 1931 her recently acquired country cottage Hochrotherd near Vienna was rebuilt according to a design that she had developed in co-operation with Ernst, Anna reported proudly in a letter to him that she had erected some parts of a brick wall and also tried roofing work both in an attempt to be prepared for future maintenance.[4] The thoughts of the site architects, Felix Augenfeld (1893–1984) and Karl Hofmann (born 1890), about their client's self-help ambitions have not been recorded.

No comparable interest in architecture is recorded from Ernst Freud's childhood and early youth. Notwithstanding, it is conceivable that both siblings' interest in architecture was influenced by the friendship their brother struck during his final years at school with Richard J. Neutra (1892–1970) whose early interest in architecture has been documented.[5] Even though Neutra attended Vienna's humanistic Sophiengymnasium, a different school than Freud, the latter's inclination towards architecture may have been triggered by his friendship with Neutra. But growing up in Vienna during the decades flanking 1900 offered in any case many opportunities to watch building sites and to observe buildings going up.

Vienna, Austrian Capital of Art and Culture

Turn-of-the-century Vienna was a major European centre for art and architecture. Since the mid-nineteenth century, Gottfried Semper (1803–1879) and others had erected palatial neo-Renaissance and historicist buildings along Vienna's Ringstraße, the broad boulevard built in lieu of the historic city walls. Towards the end of the century it was, however, Otto Wagner (1841–1918) who dominated the architectural scene of the imperial capital. The *Stadtbahn*, the urban light railway with its many stations and above-ground rail tracks (1894 onwards), the postal savings bank (1904–12), the Steinhof church (1903–7), the Majolica house (1898–9), and almost everywhere in Vienna Wagner's restrained classicism was visible. Wagner strove to achieve a monumental metropolitan architecture that reconciled modern construction technologies and cladding materials with timeless aesthetic principles. Since 1894, Wagner held a chair for architecture at the Kunstakademie. His students began likewise to transform the urban fabric of Vienna, most notably Joseph Maria Olbrich (1867–1908). The latter designed in 1898 the new exhibition building for the Vienna Secession founded only a year earlier. Under its gold-leafed dome, architects and artists such as Gustav Klimt (1862–1918), Josef Hoffmann (1870–1956), Olbrich, Wagner and other members of the Secession battled against the prevailing imperial historicism. Together with Koloman Moser (1868–1918), Hoffmann was one of the driving forces behind the establishment of the Wiener Werkstätten in 1903. Inspired by the British Arts and Crafts movement, the Wiener Werkstätten worked for exemplary reforms of interior design, furniture design, and applied arts. Due to the increasingly difficult economic situation of its mainly bourgeois clients, the enterprise went out of business in 1932. And there was of course Adolf Loos (1870–1933), beside Wagner perhaps the most important Austrian modern architect, and a known, but little-documented influence on Freud to which chapter 3 will return.

Vienna was also a European centre for other art forms like, for example, literature with writers like Arthur Schnitzler (1862–1931) and Hugo von Hofmannsthal (1874–1929) and music with composers like Gustav Mahler (1860–1911) and Arnold Schoenberg (1874–1951); each representing the respective avant-garde of their time and discipline. Most of these attempts to modernize art and architecture strongly relied on the perception of the artist and architect as a lonesome, Nietzschean genius, whose task was to guide the ignorant masses. This idea underpinned, for example, the contemporary Beethoven cult that held in its sway alike artists, architects, and their audiences. When Freud was ten years old, the cult was famously celebrated at the annual Vienna Secession exhibition in 1902 when a Beethoven sculpture by Max Klinger (1857–1920) was exhibited in a room decorated with Klimt's Beethoven fries.

Finally, the capital of the Austro-Hungarian Empire was also a centre for political ideas. Theodor Herzl (1860–1904) published in Vienna in 1896 *Der Judenstaat*,[6] the pamphlet that became the manifesto of the Zionist movement that was formally established at the first Zionist congress in Basel the following year. Until his death in 1904, Herzl was an editor for *Die Welt* in Vienna, the official newspaper of the movement, and published other important Zionist writings. Among the latter was the novel *Altneuland* that tells about the transformation of Palestine into a modern-day utopia.[7] Architects and engineers occupy a central role in the endeavour. Perhaps the twelve-year-old Freud read the slim volume when it was first printed in 1904, but in 1920 he pinned his hopes on Zionism when he began to establish himself as an independent architect.

Berggasse 19, Vienna

Even though Sigmund Freud did not entertain close contacts in Vienna's artistic circles,[8] a broad interest in architecture was nevertheless present in the Freud household. Ernst Freud's elder brother Martin recalled that a regular visitor to Berggasse 19, both as a family friend and a patient, was Marie Ferstel.[9] She was related to Freiherr Heinrich von Ferstel, architect of the Votivkirche (1855–79) in Vienna. The church stood near one end of Berggasse where the Freud family lived in number 19. A different church, the Romanesque cathedral in Trento, gave Sigmund Freud opportunity to prove his knowledge of architecture. On the occasion of a holiday to northern Italy he apparently explained the cathedral's 'architecture and stylistic development which could be read on the magnificent building'.[10] Possibly, the elder Freud had acquired this respectable knowledge of architectural history through his interest in archaeology. Ever since Sigmund and Martha Freud had moved into Berggasse 19 in 1891, Sigmund had begun to build up collections of antique statuettes, sculptures, engravings, and prints.[11] Among the latter were many images of ancient cities and buildings that may have stirred the youngest son's fascination with architecture.

Ernst Freud was the first child to be born in Berggasse 19. Initially, the Freuds rented apartment number 5 on the first floor of the new building, right above the shops on the ground floor.[12] On the same stair landing, Rosa Graf, a sister of Sigmund Freud, lived in the adjacent apartment number 6 since her marriage in 1897. His parents had settled nearby in 1892. Sigmund Freud's first consulting room was inside the family apartment, but towards the end of 1896 it was moved to apartment number 4 one floor below. When Ernst Freud was in his mid teens, his father's consulting rooms were relocated into apartment number 6, in 1907 or 1908,[13] after Sigmund Freud's sister had moved out. From then onwards, the Freuds occupied the entire first floor of Berggasse 19 (fig. 2.2). Inter-

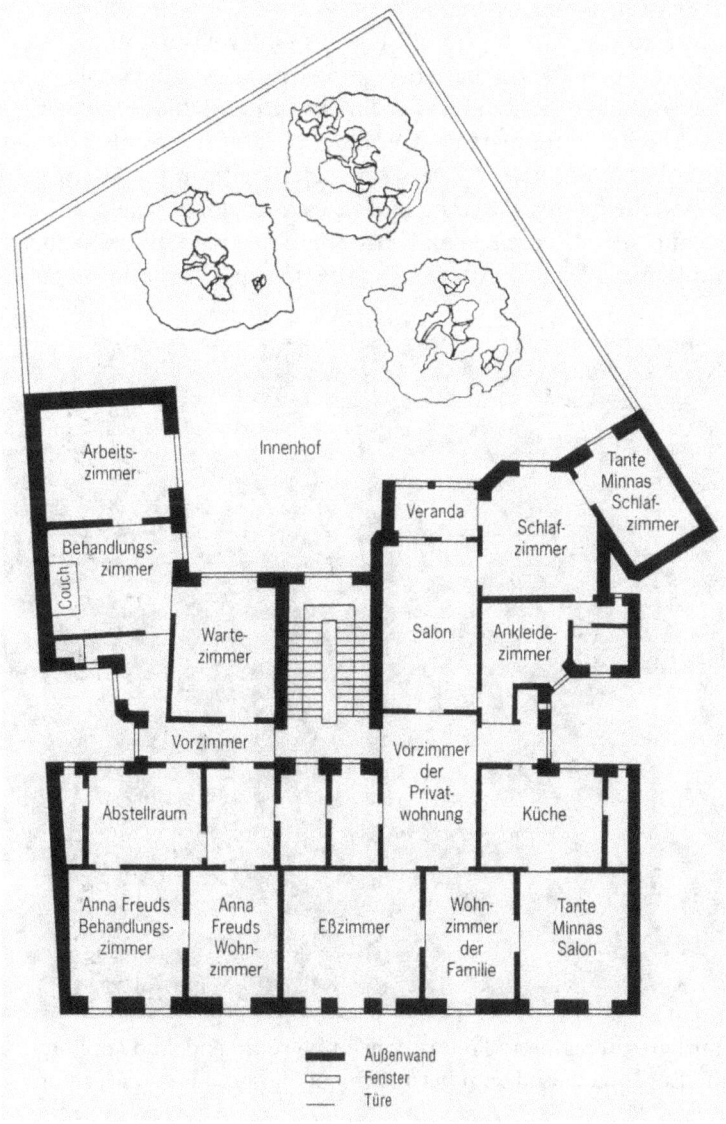

Figure 2.2. Plan of the apartments number 5 and number 6, Berggasse 19, Vienna. Used with permission of the Sigmund Freud Museum, Vienna.

nally, the two apartments were linked by removing some walls; externally the two entrance doors remained functional. Through the door on the right of the stair landing one accessed the working quarters of Sigmund Freud, and later also of Anna Freud, whereas the left door gave access to the private apartment. While thus both spheres of his life were spatially united, Sigmund Freud strove to keep work life and family life as separated as the two entrance doors suggested.

The daily schedule was determined by a strict routine of dedicated work hours that Freud spent in his office quarters. At fixed times during the day, for example after a consultation or at mealtimes, Freud would appear in the family quarters.[14] On very special occasions, he would allow his children into his study. Martin Freud remembered how his father, for example, took him there in order to talk to him about an argument that took place at the local ice-skating ring that left him feeling that he had unjustly been punished for something his brother Ernst had done wrong.[15]

Perhaps Ernst Freud was also taken to the study when his father wished to talk seriously to his youngest son. In that case, he will have had glimpses of the father's collection of antique statues, stone carvings, and engravings (fig. 2.3). Eventually, this art collection filled the consulting room and study in apartment number 4; later it was also moved upstairs into apartment number 6. But it was always kept separate from Freud's private apartment.[16] What impression the figures, carvings, and vases from, for example, ancient Egypt, Italy, Greece, and China may have made on Ernst Freud can perhaps be deduced from the diary of his friend Richard Neutra. After seeing the treasures the latter wrote: 'I

Figure 2.3. Collection of antiques in Sigmund Freud's consulting room and study in Berggasse 19, Vienna. © Edmund Engelman, used with permission of Sigmund Freud Museum, Vienna.

was able to look at the collection and the books while the professor was at the desk. Pompeian frescoes ... mummy fragments, many Egyptian bronzes, ceramics, antique vase paintings, sculptures ... Greek gold ornaments and these books ... the erotic work. Terrific."[17] On this or similar occasions, Sigmund Freud may have even explained to the two budding architects that among the figures that gazed at him from the edge of his writing desk was that of Imhotep, the builder of the stepped pyramid of Saqqara, and one of the world's earliest known architects (fig. 2.4).[18]

While Freud's working quarters opened a window on the world of art and, of course, the human soul and mind, the family quarters constituted a much more closed world. The family apartment had eight rooms plus a kitchen, bathroom, and storage spaces, which at times were shared by Sigmund and Martha Freud, Minna Bernays, a sister of Martha, and the six children plus household employees. At least while the children were still living at home the apartment was certainly not spacious. After the Freuds had taken over apartment number 6, the children, for example, slept all together in the two rooms facing Berggasse.[19] Before that, a bedroom for the children may have been either in the rear of apartment number 5 next to the parental bedroom, or towards the street in the room that later became the salon of Minna Bernays, but it is not known which.[20] Paula Fichtl, the housekeeper since 1929, never had her own room. This cramped living situation in the two apartments changed gradually only after the children, with the exception of Anna Freud, began to leave home.

Figure 2.4. Collection of antiques on Sigmund Freud's desk in his study. © Edmund Engelman, used with permission of Sigmund Freud Museum, Vienna.

Today the Freud home is best known from the photographs with which the photographer Edmund Engelman recorded the apartment in 1938 just before the Freud family left for exile to London. At that time it had been the latter's home for almost forty-seven years. Engelman's images show the home of a bourgeois family that was well-off but not overly rich. The apartment was filled—today one would even say overcrowded—with carved furniture, decorative coverings, table cloths, memorabilia, and plenty of other objects (fig. 2.5). The latter will have had meaning to the inhabitants, but remain silent to a current student of the images. The apartment did not obey 'some decorator's program',[21] but it lived up to Sigmund Freud's homely evocation of the future family abode. In a letter from 1882, when he was courting his future wife Martha Bernays, Freud envisioned having two or three rooms. Calling them the diminutive '*Zimmerchen*', little rooms, he wrote:

Figure 2.5. Living room with Aunt Minna's room in background at Berggasse 19, Vienna. © Edmund Engelman, used with permission of the Sigmund Freud Museum, Vienna.

And just think of all the things that have got to go into the rooms! Tables and chairs, beds, mirrors, a clock to remind the happy couple of the passage of time, an armchair for an hour's pleasant day-dreaming, carpets to help the housewife keep the floors clean, linen tied with pretty ribbons in the cupboard … pictures on the wall, glasses for everyday and others for wine and festive occasions, … a small larder, … and an enormous bunch of keys—which must make rattling noise. And there will be so much to enjoy, the books and the sewing table and the cosy lamp.

In short, Freud dreamt of 'a small world of happiness'[22] whose foundation he and Martha were about to establish. After their marriage in 1886, the Freuds embarked successfully on the creation of this small cosmos that, in turn, became the home in which Ernst Freud and his siblings grew up. This was not a household that was interested in pursuing aesthetic and artistic ideas for its private home. Instead, Berggasse 19 embodied 'solid Victorian comfort' reflecting 'an accumulation of objects that … speaks of the uncomplicated pursuit of domestic enjoyment'.[23]

Besides enjoying these pleasures, an equal part of educated bourgeois family life was sharing knowledge about the local buildings of one's hometown, parental explanations of cathedrals in Italy, and even having a collection of engravings of historic monuments. Somewhat exceptional was perhaps the collection of antique statues. Still, there was no surprise in Sigmund Freud's attitude towards the arts which has been summarized as 'simply and unambiguously conventional'.[24] In Ernst Freud's case, contemporary knowledge about the most modern architecture was more likely contributed by Neutra. The latter was fascinated from early on by Wagner's architecture,[25] and it is reasonable to assume that his enthusiasm may have infected his school friend. The explorations of architecture by the two friends took likewise bourgeois forms. For example, in 1912 when both young men were already architecture students, they went together on two miniature grand tours. The first was a trip along the east coast of the Adriatic Sea. Later in the year, the Freud family stayed for a holiday in Italy. Neutra met up with Ernst Freud in order to travel to Venice, Florence, Genoa, and Milan, where they 'savored the classics of ancient and Renaissance Italy'.[26]

Studying Architecture in Vienna and Munich

Freud spent the first two years of his studies at the TH Vienna where he was exposed to a traditional academic architectural education. This comprised during his first academic year from autumn 1911 to summer 1912 tuition in the subjects of higher mathematics, mechanics, elements of structural engineering, architectural forms and drawings, sketching after nature, and proportions of architecture and the human body. His second year ran from autumn 1912 to summer 1913 and consisted of much the same classes with architectural history and architectural and art history of Italy as well as of Austria-Hungary as additional subjects.[27] Among his fellow students were his friend Neutra, already enrolled since 1910. Another fellow student was Augenfeld, with whom Freud was to cooperate occasionally during the 1930s, for example in the design for Anna Freud's country house Hochrotherd.[28] On 12 July 1913, Freud passed the *1. Staatsexamen*, the first major university examination halfway through a typical course of studies. Subsequently, Freud decided to continue his studies in Munich. Thus, he adhered to the tradition of changing one's alma mater after the intermediate examination, then and now a common step for students at universities in German-speaking countries.

Comparable to Vienna, the Bavarian capital was an important European centre of contemporary art. Ever since the two journals *Pan* and *Die Jugend* were founded in 1895 and 1896 respectively, Munich had been a major centre of German *Jugendstil*. Even though the latter no longer represented the avant-garde of architecture and art during the years immediately preceding the Great War, Munich continued to hold a fascination for artists and architects, not least because the Deutsche Werkbund had been founded there in 1907. Prominent Werkbund members such as Theodor Fischer (1862–1938) and Richard Riemerschmid (1868–1957) worked and taught in Munich. The former held a chair for *Baukunst*, the art of building, at the *Technische Hochschule München* (TH Munich) from 1909 onwards, the latter became the director of the local *Kunstgewerbeschule* (school for applied arts) in 1912.

Architecturally, Munich was, however, dominated by the buildings of the neo-classical architect Leopold von Klenze (1784–1864), court architect to the Bavarian King Ludwig I. Among von Klenze's buildings were such influential masterpieces as the Glyptothek and the Pinakothek. The former accommodated a collection of ancient sculptures; the latter housed the courtly painting collections. *Jugendstil* was most prominently represented in Munich by a single building, the photographic studio *Elvira* that August Endell (1871–1925) had erected in 1897–98. Endell's architecture relied on floral motives and curling lines, whereas a severe neo-classically inspired style dominated the design by the symbolist painter Franz von Stuck (1863–1928), a co-founder of *Pan*, for his own villa. The main building was erected in 1897–98 under the supervision of the architects Jakob Heilmann and Max Littmann (1862–1931). When Freud lived in Munich, the complex was about to be completed with a large studio wing with accommodation for the servants and personnel working in the home. Even though it was a private home, the lavish interior was widely noticed and discussed among those interested in architecture and interior design. With his luxurious villa, von Stuck continued the tradition of successful artists celebrating their achievements by establishing homes. Another well-known example in Munich was the Italianate villa for Franz von Lenbach (1836–1904) that had been designed by the historicist architect Gabriel von Seidl (1848–1913). From the mid 1900s onwards, Seidl was also occupied with the design of the Deutsches Museum in Munich, a task that after his death was continued by his brother Emanuel von Seidl. Littmann was also the architect of the Germanic neo-Renaissance *Hofbräuhaus* (1896–97). Students would have visited this beer cellar for more reasons than only an interest in the design. Many architecture students will also have attended Munich's chamber theatre (1902) that Littmann had designed together with Riemerschmid. Finally, the Bavarian capital offered plenty of study opportunities for budding architects because of the various urban design and planning interventions in the city's urban fabric that had been drawn up by Fischer. From 1893 to 1901 Fischer had been the director of the municipal office in charge of the extension of the city.

When Freud arrived in Munich in 1913, the city still held its position as the major centre for the arts in Germany, a distinction that would pass over to Berlin only with the end of the coming war. For students of architecture Munich remained attractive even then because Theodor Fischer taught at the TH Munich until 1928.[29] Fischer's importance as a teacher rested on his rejection of historicist styles as the basis for contemporary architectural design. Instead, the importance to develop each design from the unique demands of the individual commission was emphasized. This resulted in compositions that while occasionally picturesque were always carefully integrated into their urban settings. Among Fischer's students were many who during the 1920s became well-known figures of German and European modernist architecture, for example Erich Mendelsohn (1887–1953), Hugo Häring (1882–1958), Ernst May (1886–1970), Dominikus Böhm (1880–1955), and Lois Welzenbacher (1889–1955).

Freud studied in Munich during the winter semester 1913–14 and the summer semester 1914 before the Great War interrupted his academic career.[30] During this prewar period, Freud enrolled for two design courses that together made up the bulk of the *Hauptstudium*, the major phase of the two-partite architectural studies. Each course was comprised of lectures, tutorials, and an actual design project. One course was dedicated to a design in a medieval architectural style which was taught by Heinrich Freiherr von Schmidt. Freud also enrolled in a course that focused on Renaissance architecture as the inspiration for contemporary design tasks. This class was offered by Friedrich von Thiersch (1852–1921), a well-known specialist for high-Renaissance architecture who taught at the TH Munich from 1879 up to his death in 1921.

Thiersch preferred a historicizing architectural language. At the same time, his buildings, for example the new stock market building (1889–1901) and the new justice building (1902–5), both in Munich, were characterized by a thoughtful integration of advanced technical systems like central heating, sanitary equipment, and elevators.

Among Thiersch's students had been, for example, Theodor Fischer, his later colleague at the university, Fritz Schumacher (1869–1947), who held the speech at the founding of the Werkbund, Heinrich Tessenow (1876–1950), who became a proponent of a stripped down neo-traditional domestic architecture, Walter Gropius (1883–1969), in 1919 the founder of the Bauhaus, and Otto Rudolf Salvisberg (1882–1940), a Swiss-born architect who was Freud's colleague in Berlin in the 1920s. Besides technical subjects, Freud also completed classes in the typology of buildings that were taught by Professor Karl Hocheder who favoured a neo-Baroque architecture as the appropriate vernacular building style.[31] In 1914, military service interrupted Freud's time in Munich; he only returned to the city for the winter semester 1918–19.

After his initial rejection for health reasons, Freud eventually volunteered for the Austrian-Hungarian army on 9 October 1914 (fig. 2.6). After military training in early 1915,

Figure 2.6. Ernst Freud, c. 1915. Used with permission of the Historisches Archiv, Technische Universität München.

he was stationed with a heavy gun unit at the Doberdoplateau near Montefalcone. The position came under attack during the third Isonzo battle in late October. On 22 October, a direct hit wiped out the small unit; Freud was the sole survivor only because he had left the dugout shortly before the attack. This shocking event led to Freud's first award of a medal; by the end of the war he would have earned three.[32] It also resulted in Freud's first architectural commission as he was asked to design a memorial for his five killed comrades.[33] A lack of archival evidence prevents us from knowing if the memorial was indeed built, or even conceived.

With his first known architectural commission having been a memorial, Freud's architectural career began almost exactly the way the German-Jewish architect Alexander Baerwald (1877–1930) had mocked in an article in a Jewish newspaper in 1912. Baerwald traced the deplorable condition of contemporary Jewish funeral architecture to the fact that 'the majority of Jewish families nowadays show forth a member that studies architecture'. He continued: 'These young people wish to earn their first laurel with a monument for their deceased aunt and usually draw for this first commission on the treasure trove of forms that they have learned at the technical universities. Most unfortunately, not everybody of the young, Jewish architecture students is artistically talented.'[34] Apparently, Freud was an exception to this final conclusion because Baerwald was one of his first employers after the young architect had relocated to Berlin at the end of 1919.

During the war, Freud remained a student at the university in Munich. With the end of the hostilities he returned to Munich in late 1918 for the winter semester 1918–19. He passed the final diploma examinations in April 1919[35] amidst revolutionary unrests in the Bavarian capital.[36] Subsequently, Freud worked in an unsalaried position with the Munich architect Fritz Landauer (1883-1968), but toward the end of the year he decided to move to Berlin.[37] The immediate cause for this move was Freud's engagement with Lucie (Lux) Brasch, the daughter of a wealthy Berlin grain merchant family who had studied classical philology in Munich. The couple married on 18 May 1920, on which occasion Ernst added in honour of his wife the letter 'L' as a middle initial to his name.[38]

Freud's architectural studies in Vienna and Munich were a standard architectural education that equated architectural design with the adaptation of historical styles to various, often entirely new types of buildings. Moreover, Freud was obliged to enrol into a broad range of technical subjects, among them classes on reinforced concrete construction, a subject that had only gradually been integrated into the syllabus of technical universities since the late nineteenth century. This was probably one of the most modern aspects of architecture that Freud encountered during his time as a student.

If Freud ever had the wish to study with Wagner at Vienna's Academy of Fine Arts, this would not have been possible as Wagner retired by the end of 1912 from his professorial chair.[39] Also noteworthy is that Freud did not study with Fischer while being a student at the TH Munich. Apparently he tried in his last semester to enrol in Fischer's architectural design class; at least Fischer's name is noted on the official list of Freud's courses. Yet either a change of mind occurred or Freud was not accepted, because he crossed out Fischer's name and replaced it with von Thiersch's.[40]

While Freud thus missed out on two teachers that influenced generations of modern architects, two other names stand out from the spare archival sources that cover his time as a student in Vienna and Munich: that of the poet Rainer Maria Rilke (1875–1926) and that of architect Adolf Loos. Sigmund Freud occasionally called his youngest son a

'Rilke enthusiast.'[41] In 1915, Lou Andreas-Salomé (1861–1937), a recent convert to psychoanalysis and a new confidant of Sigmund Freud, even detected a 'resemblance to R. M. Rilke'[42] in Ernst Freud when the latter was twenty-four years old in 1916. Contacts between a Viennese architecture student and Loos are almost to be expected, especially during the 1910s when Loos started his private *Bauschule*. The next chapter will consider the influence both men may have had on Freud's developing sense of architecture.

NOTES

1. *Student file Ernst Freud*, p. 33. Historisches Archiv Technische Universität München (HATUM), my translation.
2. Letter from Sigmund Freud to Oskar Pfister, 15 June 1911 (E. L. Freud and H. Meng [eds.]. 1963. *Sigmund Freud/Oskar Pfister: Briefe 1909–1939*. Frankfurt: Fischer, 50–51).
3. Contract between Anna and Oliver Freud, 17 August 1908 (Anna Freud papers, box 30, Freud Museum, London).
4. Letter from Anna Freud to Ernst Freud (Berlin), 22 October 1931 (Lucie Freud papers, box A–K, Freud Museum, London).
5. T. S. Hines. 1982. *Richard Neutra and the Search for Modern Architecture: A Biography and History*. New York: Oxford University Press, 18.
6. T. Herzl. 1967. *The Jewish State: An Attempt at a Modern Solution of the Jewish Question*. London: Pordes.
7. T. Herzl. 1997. *Old New Land*, trans. by Lotta Levensohn. Princeton, NJ: M. Wiener.
8. P. Gay. 1998. *Freud: A Life for Our Time*. New York: W.W. Norton, 130.
9. M. Freud. 1958. *Sigmund Freud: Man and Father*. New York: Vanguard Press, 29, 74–75.
10. M. Freud, *Sigmund Freud*, 126.
11. L. Gamwell and R. Wells (eds.). 1989. *Sigmund Freud and Art: His Personal Collection of Antiquities*. Binghamton, NY: State University of New York.
12. For details about the dates and occupancy of the various apartments, see I. Scholz-Strasser. 1993. 'Berggasse 19', in E. Engelman (ed.). *Sigmund Freud Wien IX: Berggasse 19*. Vienna: Christian Brandstätter, 7–21.
13. The literature notes variously both years as the date for the move.
14. P. Roazen. 1993. *Meeting Freud's Family*. Amherst, MA: University of Massachusetts Press, 152–166.
15. E. Weissweiler. 2006. *Die Freuds: Biographie einer Familie*. Cologne: Kiepenheuer & Witsch, 99–100.
16. L. Gamwell. 1989. 'The Origin of Freud's Antiquities Collection', in Gamwell and Wells, *Sigmund Freud and Art*, 21–32 (27).
17. Richard Neutra, Diary, 1910, cited in Hines, *Neutra*, 12.
18. Gamwell, 'Freud's Antiquities Collection', 44.
19. Later these rooms were Anna Freud's consulting room and her adjacent living room (email from Christian Huber, Freud Museum, Vienna, 14 January 2008).
20. Email from Christian Huber, Freud Museum, Vienna, 15 January 2008.
21. Gay, *Freud*, 165.
22. Letter from Sigmund Freud to Martha Bernays, 18 August 1882 (E. L. Freud [ed.]. 1960. *Letters of Sigmund Freud*, trans. by Tania and James Stern. London: Hogarth Press, 43–46 [44–45]).
23. Gay, *Freud*, 165–166.
24. P. Gay. 1976. 'Introduction: Freud/For the Marble Tablet', in E. Engelman (ed.). *Berggasse 19: Sigmund Freud's Home and Offices, Vienna 1938. The Photographs of Edmund Engelman*. New York: Basic Books, 13–54 (35).

25. M. Boeckl (ed.). 1995. *Visionäre und Vertriebene: Österreichische Spuren in der modernen amerikanischen Architektur*. Berlin: Ernst & Sohn, 1995, 339–340. Hines, *Neutra*, 18.
26. Hines, *Neutra*, 14.
27. Technische Universität Wien Archiv (TUWA), k.k. Technische Hochschule in Vienna, Hauptkatalog 1911/12, Matr.-Nr. 307-1911/12.
28. R. Hanisch, 'Die unsichtbare Raumkunst des Felix Augenfeld', in Boeckl, *Visionäre und Vertriebene*, 227–247, 327–328.
29. See W. Nerdinger. 1988. *Theodor Fischer: Architekt und Städtebauer 1862–1938*. Berlin: Ernst & Sohn.
30. While the Technische Hochschule in Munich accepted the intermediate exam from Freud's studies in Vienna, it was stipulated that he had to pass additional exams in technical subjects. Freud successfully passed these additional exams at the end of the summer semester as testified by a letter dated 23 July 1914 (*Student file Ernst Freud*, pp. 15–17, 34, HATUM). The journal of the corporations of Jewish students printed in its November 1914 issue the July 1914 report of the Jordania corporation of Jewish Students at the University of Munich. This report stated that Freund [sic] had successfully passed the intermediate exam at the Technische Hochschule (*Der jüdische Student* [Neue Folge], XI [1914–15], November 1914, issue 5, 139). In earlier issues Freud's name had been misprinted as Freund (*Der jüdische Student* [Neue Folge], X [1913–14], January 1914, issue 9, p. 326).
31. *Student file Ernst Freud*, pp. 7–11, HATUM. For information on Freud's Munich teachers, see H. K. Marschall. 1982. *Friedrich von Thiersch 1852–1921: Ein Münchner Architekt des Späthistorismus*. Munich: Prestel, 12–14.
32. Subsequently, Freud was awarded the 'Silberne Tapferkeitsmedaille 2. Klasse' for his 'most exemplary display of bravery' facing an enemy attack that had lasted for hours (Belohnungsakten des Weltkrieges 1914–1918, Mannschaftsbelohnungsanträge [MBA] Nr. 324 471 [Kt.166], Kriegsarchiv Wien, my translation). For Freud's second medal from 1917: Belohnungsakten des Weltkrieges 1914–1918, Offiziersbelohnungsanträge (OBA) Nr. 151 980 (Kt. 175), Kriegsarchiv Wien. For his third medal—the K.T.K. (Karl-Truppenkreuz)—no archival documentation has survived. For Freud's general military career, see Grundbuchblatt Ernst L. Freud, geb. 1892 in Wien, Personalevidenzunterlagen ('Grundbuchblätter'), GBBL/Wien/1892 (Kt. 175), Kriegsarchiv Wien.
33. Letter from Sigmund Freud to Lou Andreas-Salomé, 18 November 1915 (E. Pfeiffer. 1972. *Sigmund Freud and Lou Andreas-Salomé Letters*, trans. by W. and E. Robson-Scott. New York: Harcourt Brace Jovanovich, 36). No design has been found in both of Freud's papers at the RIBA and in the Kriegsarchiv Vienna.
34. A. Baerwald. 1912. 'Der Friedhof in Weißensee', *Allgemeine Zeitung des Judentums* 76 (88, 12 July): 333–334 (334).
35. Grundbuchblatt Ernst Freud, geb. 1892 in Wien, Kriegsarchiv Wien, Personalevidenzunterlagen ('Grundbuchblätter'), GBBL/Wien/1892 (Kt. 175). A special dispensation of the university allowed Feud to remain enrolled during active military service. In January 1918 Freud asked the TH Munich to confirm that he needed only one more semester in order to complete his studies. On 5 March 1919 Freud applied to the TH Munich to be accepted for the final diploma examinations due to hardship suffered through lost time because of military service and despite missing an eighth (summer) semester. In a note from 7 March 1919, setting out his educational career, he stated that he took up his studies again in winter semester 1918–19 and that he had also enrolled for winter semester 1919. The latter must be an error, for the winter semester 1919 would have only started by October that year. Presumably, he was referring to his intention to enrol again for the summer semester 1919. However, he was accepted for the final diploma examinations which he passed on 17 April 1919 with the final grade of 'Mit Auszeichnung bestanden', eleven days after his twenty-seventh birthday (*Student file Ernst*

Freud, pp. 22–41, HATUM.) In total, Freud studied four semesters at the TU Vienna (winter semester 1911–12 through to summer semester 1913) and three semesters at the TU Munich (winter semester 1913–14, summer semester 1914, and winter semester 1918–19). However, Freud's student file at the TH Vienna records that he had enrolled there again for summer semester 1918. He himself never referred to this semester in his correspondence with the TH Munich. It is doubtful that he actually attended classes, as the student file does not record any marks for attendance or passing of examinations (TUWA, k.k. Technische Hochschule in Vienna, Hauptkatalog 1917–18, Matr.-Nr. 563, 21 February 1918).

36. E. Falzeder et al. (eds.). 2000. *The Correspondence of Sigmund Freud and Sándor Ferenczi*, 3 vols. Cambridge, MA: Harvard University Press, letter 808, 20 April 1919.
37. R. A. Paskauskas (ed.). 1993. *The Complete Correspondence of Sigmund Freud and Ernest Jones 1908–1939*. Cambridge, MA: Harvard University Press, letter 248. S. Klotz. 2001. *Fritz Landauer (1883–1968): Leben und Werk eines jüdischen Architekten*. Berlin: Dietrich Reimer, 67–68.
38. Occasionally, the 'L' is misread as Ludwig, a mistake I have also made, for example, in my 1992 conservation reports on various Freud buildings.
39. Hines, *Neutra*, 20.
40. *Student file Ernst Freud*, p. 12, HATUM. Worbs claims that Ernst Freud went to Munich to study with Fischer (Dietrich Worbs. 1997. 'Ernst Ludwig Freud in Berlin', *Bauwelt* 88: 2398–2403 [2398]).
41. Letter from Sigmund Freud to Lou Andreas-Salomé, 9 November 1911 (Pfeiffer, *Sigmund Freud and Lou Andreas-Salomé Letters*, 35).
42. Letter from Sigmund Freud to Lou Andreas-Salomé, 27 July 1916 (Pfeiffer, *Sigmund Freud and Lou Andreas-Salomé Letters*, 51).

Chapter 3

Going Modern with Rainer Maria Rilke and Adolf Loos

In the early twentieth century, both Adolf Loos and Rainer Maria Rilke (1875–1926) were dealing with the consequences of modernity on bourgeois life. Loos was fighting unnecessary ornament in order to define simpler standards for the aesthetic and economic refinements of the life of a cultured bourgeoisie. Rilke was 'learning to see',[1] for example in his *New Poems* and *The Notebooks of Malte Laurids Brigge*, that poetry had little to do with expressing inner feelings but much more to do with the things that constituted the world of man. While the two artists displayed anti-bourgeois streaks in their public utterances and their lives, they nevertheless heavily relied on the social class many artists often habitually despised. Loos's writings were highly critical, if not too say acerbic, of the bourgeois ways of life that the architect attempted to improve upon. At the same time, members of the bourgeoisie commissioned some of Loos's most artistic houses. A comparable reliance characterized Rilke's life. The poet wandered endlessly around Germany, France, and many other locations, staying in whatever castle, summer residence, or winter refuge financially potent members of the bourgeoisie and the nobility made available to him.

'Learning to See' with Rainer Maria Rilke

Soon after Ernst Freud had begun his studies in Munich in autumn of 1913, his father wrote to Andreas-Salomé that his 'youngest son ... who is so enthusiastic about R[ainer] M[aria] R[ilke], reported to me that he was very disappointed not to have met you.'[2] Presumably, the older Feud dropped this remark as a reminder of how much it would mean to his son to meet with the former lover of the poet, if not with Rilke himself. Only a little earlier, during the fourth psychoanalytical congress in Munich at the beginning of September 1913, Andreas-Salomé had introduced Sigmund Freud and Rilke to each other.[3] Apparently, Andreas-Salomé told Rilke about the admiration the youngest Freud son held for him because the poet returned the compliment in a postscript to a letter from Andreas-Salomé to the older Freud. With a few words Rilke instructed Sigmund Freud to convey his greetings to Freud's son. Thoughtfully, Rilke added 'if he is at home',[4] thus indicating that he knew about Freud's army service.

These polite gestures of Rilke towards Freud's youngest son continued. After Freud had survived the shell attack in October 1915, Rilke dedicated to him in the following December a book by Regina Ullmann, a writer friend of the poet, appropriately titled *Field*

Sermon.[5] By that time, Rilke had been drafted and was working, due to his weak health, in the archive of the war office in Vienna for the first half of 1916.[6] When Freud was on leave and stayed at home in Vienna between 26 February and 1 March,[7] he and Rilke met in person. 'Ernst ... has at last met his hero Rilke. But not at our house. Rilke was not to be persuaded to visit us a second time, though his first visit before his call-up had been so very cordial', Sigmund Freud wrote to Lou Andreas-Salomé.[8] In her diary, Andreas-Salomé recorded one more meeting between Rilke and Freud on the evening of 23 April 1919,[9] six days after the latter had been awarded the final diploma at the TH Munich.

No records of the conversations between the poet and the future architect seem to exist, nor is it not known which books by Rilke Freud had read.[10] The surviving collection of Rilke books owned by Anna Freud gives, however, an idea about her brother's likely acquaintance with the poet's works. Freud's younger sister owned almost all writings that Rilke had published in the first two decades of the twentieth century.[11] Individual books were given to her by Rilke, her older brother, Lucie Brasch, and colleagues of her father. This collection indicates the serious interest in Rilke by Anna Freud, and possibly also by Ernst. It certainly illustrates the spell Rilke had cast over the youth in German-speaking countries in the years flanking the Great War. Many recognized in Rilke 'a seer and a saint',[12] even though he was both 'the most reluctant of prophets' and 'thoroughly aware of the differences between life and poetry'.[13] The latter distinction allows us to pinpoint a possible influence of Rilkean poetry on Freud's understanding of architecture as it was formed in the 1910s.

During the 1900s, Rilke began to redraw the line along which poetry and life intersected.[14] Up to that junction, his poems had been concerned with the immediate expression of feelings. Objects and scenes of any poem had been mirrors reflecting the subjective confessions of the poet because 'all things solely exist in order to become in some sense images for us'.[15] Now Rilke was interested in a 'more objective dealing with reality',[16] as the protagonist of *The Notebooks of Malte Laurids Brigge* explained: 'Verses are not, as people think, feelings (those one has early enough)—they are experiences. For the sake of a verse one must see many cities, men, and things, one must know the animals, feel how birds fly, and know the gesture with which the little flowers open in the morning.'[17] From a realm of overwhelming and eternal feelings—that could only be grasped by making the self subjective to the essence of the object, nature for example—the world was transformed into an environment of things in their own rights. To ponder them rendered them both comprehensible and into 'sensuous equivalents of inner experiences'.[18] But they would never again become identical with the innermost feelings both of poet and reader.

This shift in the relation between poetry and life in Rilke's writings recalls the distinction, as set out in chapter 1, between the different attitudes towards societal life that, according to the sociologist Plessner, resulted in two principle forms of social organization. Rilke's earlier, romantic thoughts about poetry's function in life can be seen as an analogue to Plessner's socially radical attitude. Both wished to make the world conform to fundamental ideas and authentic feeling. Rilke did not replace this poetic radicalism with a more, or even exclusively, rational concept. That would have been equally radical in so far as it would have denied any attachment of man to the things in his life. Rather, with the so-called 'thing poems' as exemplified in the *New Poems*, Rilke aimed for an equilibrium between the subjectivity both of the writer and the reader and the objectivity of the world. Thus, these poems may be taken as an analogue illustration of Plessner's notion of a non-radical attitude.[19]

The *New Poems* were published in 1907 and 1908; thus, Freud may have read them when he was in his mid teens. The two volumes presented things in the broadest understanding, encompassing material objects, human beings (mythical, historical, and contemporary), landscapes, plants, animals, and the 'occasional presentations of more or less timeless human situations and predicaments'.[20] Chronologically ordered from ancient periods to modern times, the two series of poems constituted a panorama of the world as it was endlessly made and remade by human beings who, in turn, found themselves bound into both the cosmos of nature and the ever-growing collection of human-made objects. In addition, some poems such as 'In the Drawing-Room', 'The Group', and 'Meeting in the Chestnut Avenue'[21] depicted human encounters and social interactions.

'The Meeting in the Chestnut Avenue' describes the passing of two humans that have entered an avenue at opposing ends.[22] Rilke's words evoke the colours and the outlines of the approaching person as they change from a distant whitish blot to a clearly focused, yet passing face. The poem's sole subject matter is the experience of the diminishing distance between two strangers and the social behaviour that lets both figures pass each other while they let pass the sudden flash of a longing for intimacy. The formation of a crowd of spectators surrounding an athlete is the subject matter of 'The Group'. One long sentence recreates over several stanzas the constantly changing spatial constellation of this ad-hoc group as faces in the crowd come closer or grow further apart depending on the distances between them.[23] These poems are vignettes depicting the spatialized social behaviour that, to use once more Plessner's sociological terminology, led to the formation of society.

The *New Poems* do not invite the reader to identify with the poet's inner feelings and thus to blend into the collective of readers who all feel the same. Nor are they an analysis of either logical transactions between human beings or a rational consideration of things as commodities. Instead, while things exist in their own right, they nevertheless come alive only when gazed at by the poet. Rilke's newly discovered fascination of apparently objective things was really a love of 'animate objects'.[24] These things as they were gathered together, for example, in and around a home were the guarantors of 'humanness': 'Even for our grandparents a "House", a "Well", a familiar tower, their very dress, their cloak, was infinitely more, infinitely more intimate: almost everything a receptacle in which they both found and enlarged a store of humanness. ... The animated, experienced things that *share our lives* are running out and cannot be replaced. *We are perhaps the last to have still known such things.*'[25]

Ultimately, Rilke's encounter with the world of things was dominated by the poet's wistfulness for a bygone era. For a young man with an artistic sensibility like Freud, who was about to become an architect, the *New Poems* and *The Notebooks of Malte Laurids Brigge* may have had the opposite effect. The focus on things in the poems may have taught Freud that objects were hardly ever mere commodities but could well be holders of memories. In the novel, Freud may have read that in order to make the experiences that went into writing poetry it was necessary 'to think back to streets in unknown neighborhoods, to unexpected encounters, ... to partings ... , to days of childhood, ... to days in quiet, restrained rooms'. Yet, Rilke emphasized that 'memories themselves are not important. Only when they have changed into our very blood, into glance and gesture, and are nameless, no longer to be distinguished from ourselves—only then it can happen that in some very rare hours the word of a poem arises in their midst and goes forth from them.'[26]

By analogy, to create a home was not primarily about the fulfilment of minimum spatial requirements or about the creation of memorable nooks and corners. Instead, it meant to conceive houses which the occupants and their animate objects could fill so that both together would create the home and thus would come alive. The notion of the home and the architect's role in its creation also stood at the centre of the work and thought of the Viennese architect and cultural critic Adolf Loos. In opposition to Rilke, however, Freud specifically met Loos in connection with his architectural studies when he attended events of the latter's private *Bauschule*.

Adolf Loos and Bourgeois *Wohnkultur*

Loos had been a cultural critic and a commentator on architecture ever since his return from a three-year stay in the US in 1896. At that time he took up writing for various newspapers as one way of making a name for himself among the educated bourgeoisie in the Austrian capital. His presence as public commentator paid off as Loos gradually established a circle of friends from which he received many commissions for interior designs and buildings as well as financial support (fig. 3.1).[27]

Figure 3.1. Adolf and Lina Loos in front of the fireplace of their apartment in Vienna, 1903. Used with permission of Albertina, Vienna.

One attraction of Loos was his often sharp and highly ironic criticism of various cultural phenomena as recalled by Augenfeld, a friend of both Neutra and Freud: 'I was well familiar with the name Loos from the moment onwards that I could read newspapers. Between 1900 and 1914, Loos wrote highly readable *Feuilletons* in the *Neue Freie Presse* that expressed his radical reform intentions with regard to themes critical of art and culture.'[28]

In 1910, when Freud entered his last year at school, Loos became even more widely known because of the fierce public argument that surrounded the Michaelerhaus (1909–1911) in Vienna. Loos's design for an apartment building with the gentlemen's tailor firm of Goldman & Salatsch occupying the two lower floors had received planning permission. Yet when the six storeys rose upwards, a scandal erupted over the façade's unadorned nakedness. Located opposite the Hofburg, the house was erected in the centre of imperial Vienna. The design was also a statement against the historicist architectural high culture of its time. When the municipality tried to revoke the permit, Loos defended the design as inspired by eighteenth-century Viennese inner-city buildings. Typically, these had rental apartments on the upper floors behind little adorned facades and more visibly designed business premises on the lower two floors. In short, crucial to the modernity of Loos's design was an evocation of traditional buildings from around 1800 rather than the reduction of the modern architects' work to either the invention of new artistic and architectural forms, or the copying of historical details. The former was the error Loos found in the efforts of the Wiener Werkstätten and the Wiener Secession, the latter was the fault of historicist architects.

With Otto Wagner retiring in the summer of 1912, Loos became the focal point for many aspiring young architects. This contributed to Loos's decision to start a *Bauschule*, a private school of architecture.[29] By selecting for the name of the school the slightly old-fashioned sounding word *Bau*, rather than *Architektur*, Loos again emphasized that traditions in building were of importance to his understanding of modernity. The school offered a three-year program with classes in art and architectural history, interior design and outfitting, and technology of materials. Excursions to foreign countries were to complement the annual course of studies. Ordinary enrolled students were also admitted to Loos's private office where they worked on his commissions, whereas other students just attended public lectures and seminars.

It has been claimed that Freud was a student of Loos,[30] but this statement needs to be qualified. First, it was only during his second academic year in Vienna, from fall 1912 to summer 1913, that Freud could attend events of the newly founded *Bauschule*. During the latter's second year of instruction, Freud was already studying in Munich. Second, the only source known that identifies Freud as a pupil of the *Bauschule* is a memoir by Augenfeld. Augenfeld listed, as members of a 'very small group of students', Neutra, Rudolf Schindler (1887–1953), Giuseppe De Finetti (1892–1952) from Milan, Paul Engelmann (1891–1965), who later worked with Ludwig Wittgenstein (1889–1951) on the Stonborough-Wittgenstein house (1926–28) in Vienna, Helmut von Wagner-Freinsheim, and Freud. This list differs from one by Gustav Schleicher who entered the *Bauschule* in the winter of its first year of instruction.[31] Schleicher did not mention Freud. Accordingly, Augenfeld was most likely correct to describe Freud as 'not a very conscious participant or fanatic disciple' of the *Bauschule* 'but nevertheless strongly influenced by Loos.'[32]

The *Bauschule* wasn't Loos's first venture into teaching. Rather than restricting his cultural criticism and reform efforts to the printed word, Loos invited the public in 1907, for example, to a self-guided walking tour of apartments for which he had designed the interior. During the school year 1911–12, Loos taught art history at the *Schwarzwaldschule* in Vienna, a private school for young female adults. Its director, Dr. Eugenie Schwarzwald, and her husband had been friends with Loos and repeatedly also his clients. For example, in 1905 Loos refurbished an apartment for the couple which was included two years later in the public tour of Loos apartments.[33] Comparable to his walking tour, Loos's teaching at the *Schwarzwaldschule* incorporated many excursions to important buildings from Vienna's history and to site visits of Loos's own projects, for example the Michaelerhaus. Excursions were also favoured at the *Bauschule:* 'The word "school" was hardly applicable to this small working group. ... Rather, it was a kind of seminar ... that did not meet in a lecture hall or a studio, but on improvised walks or at round tables in the city centre, in the Kärntnerbar [with an interior design by Loos], in cabarets and night clubs, in marble yards, and in apartments that had been rebuilt and refurbished by Loos.'[34]

The diary of Richard Neutra confirms this practice-oriented approach to teaching. Neutra noted on 10 November 1912 that he had given up working for Loos, but that he took part in visits to building sites and to villas in Hietzing, a suburb of Vienna. Moreover, he went every Thursday evening to the *Deutsches Haus,* a restaurant where a table was reserved for regulars.[35] Regardless of Augenfeld's recollections, Loos's teaching did incorporate traditional lectures that were delivered in the premises of the *Schwarzwaldschule.* Loos proudly pointed out that his audience filled at times two interconnected classrooms with each seating forty. Moreover, he was extremely pleased that a large number of his audience came from among the students of both the TH Vienna and the Academy.[36] What could a young architecture student like Freud have learned from these lectures and site visits? There are at least three areas in which Loos possibly influenced Freud's developing ideas about architecture.

First, the argument around the Michaelerhaus emphasized the relationship between clients and architect. The former not only commissioned and financed a project, but were expected to stand by their architect should a project run into difficulties. Reversely, the architect should not impose on the clients a design, a style, or his private taste. Loos had criticised such an approach already in his 1900 essay 'The Poor Little Rich Man'[37] and raised a similar charge against the Wiener Werkstätten.

Second, when Freud attended *Bauschule* events in 1912–13, 'The Civilized Home' was the topic for the first year that Loos taught the class on interior design and outfitting. The course dealt with technical installations and standards as well as the requirements for a typical private home that comprised, for example, a 'hall, the reception room, the dining room, the bedroom etc., kitchen and bath room.'[38] This list not only circumscribed the scope of the task to design a home but also indicates that, at least at that time, Loos focused on bourgeois homes. The site visits to private apartments that accompanied the lectures reinforced that last point.[39]

Most of Loos's domestic architecture evolved around the concept that 'architecture arouses sentiments in man', which meant that for the private home 'the room has to be comfortable; the house has to look habitable' (fig. 3.2).[40] Accordingly, Loos's domestic designs shared internal divisions into individual rooms and clearly defined inglenooks that

Figure 3.2. Reception hall of the Goldmann apartment, Vienna, 1911, by Adolf Loos. Used with permission of Albertina, Vienna.

could accommodate the changing needs of the inhabitants during a typical day at home. Moreover, the rooms were filled with a mixture of furniture including pieces designed and selected by the architect, or already owned by the clients. Finally, most interiors demonstrated Loos's ambition to reduce or completely remove ornament as called for in the essay 'Ornament and Crime' from 1908.[41] However, these interiors were not sensuously impoverished. Rather the opposite—attention to colours, surfaces, patterns, and the reflection or absorption of light by materials and furnishings increased the appeal to the senses of a Loosian interior.

Third, and finally, there was the question whether domestic design and architecture in general belonged to the realm of art. Loos's answer was that 'man loves everything that satisfies his comfort'.[42] It followed from this that an ideal home should be conservative as it had to please the public, meet present needs rather than recreating past or anticipating future ones, and generate feelings of being comfortable. On all accounts, art pursued opposite goals as, for example, was demonstrable when one considered the grave and the monument, the only two forms of architecture that qualified as art.[43]

Once again Loos's idea of modernity, especially where domestic architecture and interiors were concerned, ran counter to many of his contemporaries' convictions. For Loos, architecture was a service both to the public and the individual clients. Major public buildings should stand out in their surroundings, but domestic architecture should avoid being overly visible, for example through unusual artistic means, and thereby possibly causing offence. These ideas, however, were severely tested by several of the houses that Loos had designed in such a plain and inconspicuous architectural language that they stood out for exactly that reason.

While thus the exterior belonged to the public and the architect, the interior was a hierarchically ordered sequence of spheres of responsibility of architect, craftsmen, and the client or inhabitant. Beginning from the outside, the architect created the enclosing volumes and spaces including interior walls and built-in furniture.[44] Beyond these latter two, craftsmen were to build all moveable furniture, while the inhabitants were both arranging the latter and filling all spaces with their things and possessions. A house was for Loos like a case for a precious piece of jewellery, it had to be plain so that nothing would distract from the sparkle of the things inside (fig. 3.3).[45]

For both Rilke and Loos, things were more than just objects that clogged up the spaces of the modern house and mind. Loos raised the awareness that an architect should restrict himself to design the mere space that the inhabitant was obliged to fill with his possessions once architect and craftsmen had left. Things were thus turning the house into a home. Rilke went a step further when he taught that, besides spaces in homes, things required places in humans' lives in order to stimulate imaginative thought. This meant that we needed to recognize the animated character of things; one of the important tasks of the time as Rilke explained it: 'On us rests the responsibility of preserving, not merely their memory (that would be little and unreliable), but their human and laral worth ("Laral" in the sense of household-gods).'[46]

Figure 3.3. Living room and adjacent stair hall in the Müller house, Prague, 1928–30, by Adolf Loos. Used with permission of Albertina, Vienna.

Sigmund Freud's relationship with things in his home provides a suitable illustration of what Rilke was hinting at. In a letter from August 1882 to his future wife, Freud noted not only the list of rooms and furniture of their future home as quoted in the last chapter. He also added that these possessions needed to be well looked after because he felt the heart of the housewife was divided into small pieces, each of which was attached to various possessions.[47] But Sigmund Freud himself expressed such a personal emotional attachment to things. For example, every morning upon entering the study, Freud petted a marble baboon and greeted the figure of a Chinese sage.[48] Thus he literally evoked the 'laral worth' of 'household-gods', to apply Rilke's words to the collection of antiquities that had filled Freud's study and consulting room over the years. A comparable indicator of domesticity stood also at the centre of the essay 'At Home' in *Die Pyramide* from August 1928, which was accompanied by images showing Freud's apartment in Berlin. The anonymous author claimed that the imagination of children would be triggered, for example, by the pattern of wallpaper and the form of furniture. Thus the provision of a sensuously rich interior was recognized as an important task of an architect or interior designer.[49]

The illustrated apartment in the German magazine was the second home in Berlin that Freud and his wife inhabited. They had married in early 1920 and shortly thereafter established their own family when they became parents for the first time. Hence, issues of domesticity which Freud had thus far experienced during his childhood and youth in Vienna, reflected upon in response to Rilke's writngs, and thought about when listening to Loos, now moved to the centre of both his private life and his burgeoning professional career.

Notes

1. R. M. Rilke. 1983. *The Notebooks of Laurids Malte Brigge* [1910], trans. by S. Mitchell. New York: Random House, 5.
2. Letter from Sigmund Freud to Lou Andreas-Salomé, 6 November 1913 (E. Pfeiffer. 1972. *Sigmund Freud and Lou Andreas-Salomé Letters*, trans. by W. and E. Robson-Scott. New York: Harcourt Brace Jovanovich, 14).
3. Pfeiffer, *Sigmund Freud and Lou Andreas-Salomé Letters*, 218, note 41. The meeting between Sigmund Freud and Rilke took place on 8 September 1913 (E. Pfeiffer. 1975. *Rainer Maria Rilke Lou Andreas-Salomé Briefwechsel*. Frankfurt: Insel, 298).
4. Letter from Lou Andreas-Salomé to Sigmund Freud, 30 March 1915 (Pfeiffer, *Sigmund Freud and Lou Andreas-Salomé Letters*, 28). This letter resulted in Sigmund Freud instructing Andreas-Salome to let Rilke know that Anna Freud also was a great fan of the poet and had envied that Ernst had received greetings from Rilke (letter from Sigmund Freud to Lou Andreas-Salomé, 1 April 1915 [Pfeiffer, *Sigmund Freud and Lou Andreas-Salomé Letters*, 28]).
5. R. Ullmann. N.d. *Feldpredigt: Dramatische Dichtung in einem Akt*. Leipzig: Insel, inscribed by Rilke with 'Herrn Ernst Freud/mit herzlichsten Weihnachtsgrüßen./Rainer Maria Rilke/22. Dez[ember] 1915' (Freud Museum London). Two days earlier, Rilke had dedicated a copy of *Das Buch der Bilder* to Anna Freud whom he met in person (R. M. Rilke. 1913. *Das Buch der Bilder*. Leipzig: Insel). The dedication reads: 'Fräulein Anna Freud/in ihr Buch dieses Datum der ersten Begegnung herzlich einschreibend: Rainer Maria Rilke 20 Dezember 1915' (Freud Museum London).
6. Rilke served from 4 January to 9 June. His work at the Kriegsarchiv began on 27 January. See 'Zeittafel', in I. Schnack. 1996. *Rainer Maria Rilke: Chronik seines Lebens und seines Werkes 1875–1926*. Frankfurt: Insel, 525–537.

7. Dates from Sigmund Freud's diary kindly provided by Michael Molnar, Freud Museum London, email to author, 28 December 2007.
8. Letter from Sigmund Freud to Lou Andreas-Salomé, 21 March 1916 (Pfeiffer, *Sigmund Freud and Lou Andreas-Salomé Letters*, 39).
9. Andreas-Salomé wrote in her diary, 'Evening at Rilke's. Later Ernst Freud and Hotup [Else Hotop] there' (cited in Schnack, *Rainer Maria Rilke*, 636).
10. After Lucie Freud had passed away in 1989 Freud's books were sold by the book dealers Hans Seeling, Andreas Mytze, and Robert Hornung. Unfortunately, no list of the library was produced (Robert Hornung, email to the author, 27 September, 2002).
11. List 'Rilke books in Anna Freud's library', Freud Museum London, 20 December 2007.
12. P. Gay. 1968. *Weimar Culture: The Outside as Insider.* New York: Harper & Row, 53.
13. Gay, *Weimar Culture*, 55.
14. The following relies on W. Müller. 1971. *Rainer Maria Rilkes 'Neue Gedichte': Vielfältigkeit eines Gedichttypus.* Meisenheim am Glan: Anton Hain.
15. Letter from Rainer Maria Rilke to Frieda von Bülow, 27 May 1899 (cited in Müller, *Rainer Maria Rilkes 'Neue Gedichte'*, 21, my translation).
16. Müller, *Rainer Maria Rilkes 'Neue Gedichte'*, 14, my translation.
17. Rilke, *Malte Laurids Brigge*, 19. I cite here, however, the translation provided by Gay as it comes closer to the original; see Gay, *Weimar Culture*, 56.
18. Müller, *Rainer Maria Rilkes 'Neue Gedichte'*, 24, my translation.
19. H. Plessner. 1999. *The Limits of Community. A Critique of Social Radicalism*, trans. by A. Wallace. Amherst, NY: Humanity Books, 48.
20. J. B. Leishman. 1964. 'Introduction', in R. M. Rilke. *New Poems*, trans. by J. B. Leishman. London: Hogarth Press, 1–41 (5).
21. Rilke, *New Poems*, 111, 221, 261.
22. See Müller's interpretation of this poem in Müller, *Rainer Maria Rilkes 'Neue Gedichte'*, 27–29.
23. Rilke, *New Poems*, 221.
24. Leishman, 'Introduction', in Rilke, *New Poems*, 17.
25. Letter from Rilke to his Polish translator, 13 November 1925 (cited in J. B. Leishman, 'Introduction', in Rilke, *New Poems*, 17–18, italics in original).
26. Rilke, *Malte Laurids Brigge*, 19–20.
27. B. Rukschcio. N.d. [1985]. 'Die Bedeutung der Bauherren für Adolf Loos', in 'Aufbruch zur Jahrhundertwende. Der Künstlerkreis um Adolf Loos', *Parnass* (Sonderheft 2): 6–15.
28. F. Augenfeld. 1981. 'Erinnerungen an Adolf Loos', *Bauwelt* 72 (issue 42): 1907, my translation.
29. In the following, all facts about the *Bauschule* are from B. Rukschcio and R. Schachel. 1982. *Adolf Loos: Leben und Werk.* Vienna: Residenz Verlag, 168–173, 186–190.
30. Especially K. Klemmer. 1998. *Jüdische Baumeister in Deutschland: Architektur vor der Shoah.* Stuttgart: dva, 124. See also D. Worbs. 1997. 'Ernst Ludwig Freud in Berlin', *Bauwelt* 88 (issue 42): 2398–2403 (2398).
31. Rukschcio, Schachel, *Adolf Loos*, 171.
32. Augenfeld, 'Erinnerungen', 1907, my translation
33. Rukschcio, Schachel, *Adolf Loos*, 439–440.
34. Augenfeld, 'Erinnerungen', 1907, my translation
35. R. J. Neutra diary, vol. 2, 1912–17, Box 335, Richard and Dion Neutra Papers, Department of Special Collections, Charles E. Young Research Library, University of California at Los Angeles.
36. A. Loos. 1913. 'Meine Bauschule (1913)', in F. Glück (ed.). 1962. *Adolf Loos Ins Leere gesprochen 1897–1900: Trotzdem 1900–1930.* Vienna: Verlag Herold, 322–325 (324).

37. A. Loos. 1900. 'The Poor Little Rich Man', in A. Loos. 1982. *Spoken into the Void: Collected Essays 1897–1900*, trans. by J. O. Newman and J. H. Smith. Cambridge, MA: MIT Press, 124–127.
38. Quoted from Rukschcio, Schachel, *Adolf Loos*, 169, my translation of '*Die Kultur der Wohnung*'. Loos uses the word *culture* (*Kultur*) here in the sense of the English term *civilisation*.
39. While it is not known which apartments were visited that Loos had designed, the diary (vol. 3) that Neutra began in September 1913 may actually record some of the locations. Neutra drew into his diary thumbnail sketches of the floor plans and notes about the apartments Schwarzwald (Josephstädterstr. 68), Proser (Josephstädterstr.), Schweiger (Alserstr. 22), the villa Steiner in Hietzing, and an apartment [Braun] (Richard J. Neutra diary, vol. 3, 1913–1917, 72, 74–76, 81, Box 335, Richard and Dion Neutra Papers, Department of Special Collections, Charles E. Young Research Library, University of California at Los Angeles).
40. A. Loos. 1910. 'Architecture', in Y. Safran and W. Wang (eds.). 1985. *The Architecture of Adolf Loos*. London: Arts Council of Great Britain, 104–109 (108).
41. Loos, 'Ornament and Crime' (1908), in Safran and Wang, *Adolf Loos*, 100–103.
42. Loos, 'Architecture' (1910), in Safran and Wang, *Adolf Loos*, 104–109 (108).
43. Loos, 'Architecture' (1910), in Safran and Wang, *Adolf Loos*, 104–109 (108).
44. A. Loos. 1924. 'Die Abschaffung der Möbel', in Glück, *Adolf Loos Ins Leere gesprochen 1897–1900: Trotzdem 1900–1930*, 390.
45. Loos, 'Abschaffung der Möbel', in Glück, *Adolf Loos Ins Leere gesprochen*, 389.
46. Letter from Rilke to his Polish translator, 13 November 1925 (cited in Leishman, 'Introduction', in Rilke, *New Poems*, 17–18).
47. Letter from Sigmund Freud to Martha Bernays, 18 August 1882 (E. L. Freud [ed.]. 1960. *Letters of Sigmund Freud*, trans. by T. and J. Stern. New York: Basic Books, 25–28 [27]).
48. L. Gamwell, 'The Origin of Freud's Antiquities Collection', in L. Gamwell and R. Wells (eds). 1989. *Sigmund Freud and Art: His Personal Collection of Antiquities*. Binghamton, NY: State University of New York, 21–32 (23).
49. A. H. 1928., 'Zu Hause', *Die Pyramide* 15 (August): 248–257 (255).

Chapter 4

Society Architect in Berlin

Ernst Freud left Munich for Berlin at the end of 1919. By that time, he had completed his university studies, collected his first experiences of working in his profession, and met and fallen in love with his future wife. He was twenty-seven years old, about the same age at which other contemporary architects likewise began their careers. For example, Mendelsohn and Mies van der Rohe started professional work at the age of twenty-five. Gropius was the same age as Freud when he set up his first office, whereas Bruno Taut (1880–1938) and Salvisberg opened their own firms when they both were thirty years old. The military service had interrupted Freud's studies, but had at most delayed the beginning of his career. Nevertheless, the aftermath of the war was a major influence on Freud's life in Berlin.

Weimar Germany

Politically, the move to Berlin was one to an unsettled city during an unstable time. After the November revolution from 1918, Germany began to transform itself into a federally organized state with a democratically elected government. Officially, this goal was reached in August 1919 when a new constitution was approved, but opposition to the republic continued from the extreme left and right, and from within the state bureaucracy.

Political and economic factors exaggerated the situation. The large number of war victims and returning soldiers, the allegedly unjust vilification of Germany in the Versailles Treaty, political assassinations, and putsch attempts were only some of the events that time and again threw the republic into crisis. The hyperinflation of the early 1920s, the high reparation payments, the French occupation of the Ruhr zone during 1923, and the 1929 Wall Street stock market crash had comparable consequences.

Still, the Weimar Republic was a move toward democracy and a 'free economy'.[1] The latter was favoured alike by capitalists and trade unions, as both abhorred the wartime economy with its state interventions and resulting shortages of goods. The Social Democrats, the Catholic Zentrum party, the German Democratic Party, and the German People's Party—the latter two parties appealed particularly to the bourgeoisie and the middle classes—each worked towards the realization of its ideas for a new Germany without, however, fundamentally opposing the country's transformation into a democracy. They argued fiercely about political issues and formed ever-changing coalitions, but overall 'the Republic ... succeeded in re-establishing a peacetime economy in a relatively trouble-free fashion',[2] despite many attempts by the Communists and the National-Socialists to overthrow the young democracy.

Moreover, continuities across the pre-war and post-war periods had potentially stabilizing effects. The historian Peukert pointed towards administrative continuities, co-operation between employers and employees, and individual citizens like soldiers who 'simply wanted to get home as quickly as possible and, once home, to re-establish their "normal" pre-war way of life'.[3] This goal appeared to be within reach when the economy entered a brief period of relative stability between the currency reform from late 1923 that ended the hyperinflation and the 1929 stock market crash.

Weimar Republic Architecture

Professionally, the move to Berlin was a move into a radicalized architectural environment. During the late 1910s, architecture became more socially focused than aesthetically oriented. Groups like the *Arbeitsrat für Kunst* and the *Novembergruppe* mimicked the workers' soviets that, for example, had ruled Munich in April 1919 when Freud passed his final examinations. These groups either wholeheartedly aligned themselves with the goals of various leftwing movements or argued for a broad, even if often unspecified, cultural renewal.

The latter point is captured well by Expressionist designs for people's houses, cultural institutions, and monuments that were generated between c. 1918 and the early 1920s.[4] The former point, the social and activist turn of modern architecture, moved into the foreground after the economy had begun to stabilize from late 1923 onwards. At that moment numerous social-housing projects and socially oriented buildings like, for example, schools, employment offices, and co-operative stores were initiated by municipalities, state authorities, and building co-operatives.

Together with these increased building activities, modern architecture underwent an aesthetic revolution when architects deliberately designed many of the new buildings in an ahistorical and unadorned manner supposedly symbolizing the new times. Modernist architecture employed a language of cubic forms, flat roofs, horizontally banded windows, open plans, a separation of structural systems and building envelopes, and new urban design principles like *Zeilenbau*. While many of the socially oriented buildings were designed in this new manner, both the building types and the style cannot be equated with each other. Rather, the modernist style was also popular for mainstream capitalist buildings like, for example, department stores and factories, as well as luxurious villas and country houses. In turn, many social housing projects were conceived in traditional styles and building methods.

Thus, to be modern did not require, by definition, being modernist. Architects could respond affirmatively or critically to conditions of modernity, for example by developing a new building type in response to social demands without therefore having to subscribe to principles of radical aesthetic change. Continuities comparable to those in the political and social spheres also existed in the development of modern architecture; see, for example, the issue of bourgeois dwellings and homes as discussed already in chapter 1.

Setting up Home and Office in Berlin

Privately, the move to Berlin was into circumstances—the imminent wedding to Lucie Brasch and the foundation of a family—more likely determined by a wish for stability than a desire for revolutionary change (fig. 4.1). The couple met after the war in Munich

Figure 4.1. Ernst and Lucie Freud on the island of Hiddensee, Germany, 1920s. Used with permission of the Freud Museum London.

where Lucie Brasch had enrolled at the university for the winter semester 1918 to 1919. She had begun her education at Berlin's Friedrich-Wilhelms-Universität where she read German studies from winter semester 1916 onwards. For the next two years, she took classes by such luminaries as, for example, Professor von Wilamowitz-Moellendorf, the great classical philologist.[5] When she was at the university in Munich, her main subject was classical philology, but she also attended classes in art history held by Heinrich Wölfflin.[6] While in the Bavarian capital, Brasch lived in the bohemian quarter of Schwabing, close to her university. Freud's abode was nearby in the borough of Maxvorstadt, on the same street as the TH Munich.[7]

Lucie Brasch came from a bourgeois family of grain merchants in Berlin with connections to Gaglow, near Cottbus, to the southeast of Berlin.[8] Her parents, Josef and Elise Brasch, had four children.[9] Beside Lucie, there was Gerda who married the paediatrician Carl Mosse, a son of Rudolf Mosse, the owner of the Berlin-based publishing house. Later, in the early 1930s, Carl and Gerda Mosse became the last clients of Freud before both families fled Germany. Another sister, Käte Brasch lived with her husband and their three daughters in Hamburg. She passed away in 1932.[10] Lucie's father died around the turn from 1919 to 1920;[11] he has occasionally been described as a 'wise and far-sighted grain merchant who was always open to charitable causes'.[12] Her mother continued to live in Hardenbergstraße 13 in Berlin-Charlottenburg,[13] only one house away from Steinplatz. Around the corner, Freud might have noticed a *Jugendstil* apartment building (1906–7) by Endell whose famous photography studio *Elvira* was very close to where he had lived in Munich.

The wedding took place in Berlin on 18 May 1920. Freud's parents did not travel to the event, but some of Sigmund Freud's colleagues in Berlin and Anna Freud attended.[14]

Afterwards, the event was announced in newspapers like, for example, *Jüdische Rundschau* and *Der Jüdische Student* (fig. 4.2).[15] In June, the couple visited the elder Freuds in Vienna.[16] From mid October to mid November, Ernst and Lucie Freud went on their honeymoon in Anacapri, high up on the island of Capri in the gulf of Naples, though they also visited Rome and, possibly, Venice.[17]

1920 was, however, not just a year of happiness. Early in the year, Freud's sister Sophie had succumbed to the flue. Freud arranged for the gravestone, a stele with chamfered corners surmounted by a shallow vase planted with ivy (fig. 4.3). The dates of Sophie Freud's life were chiselled into the front according to both the Gregorian calendar and the Jewish one. The gravestone anticipates some features of Freud's 1939 design for his father's memorial. Then, Freud chose an ancient urn from Sigmund Freud's collection of antiques that was placed on a stele with chamfered corners (fig. 4.4). A little over a

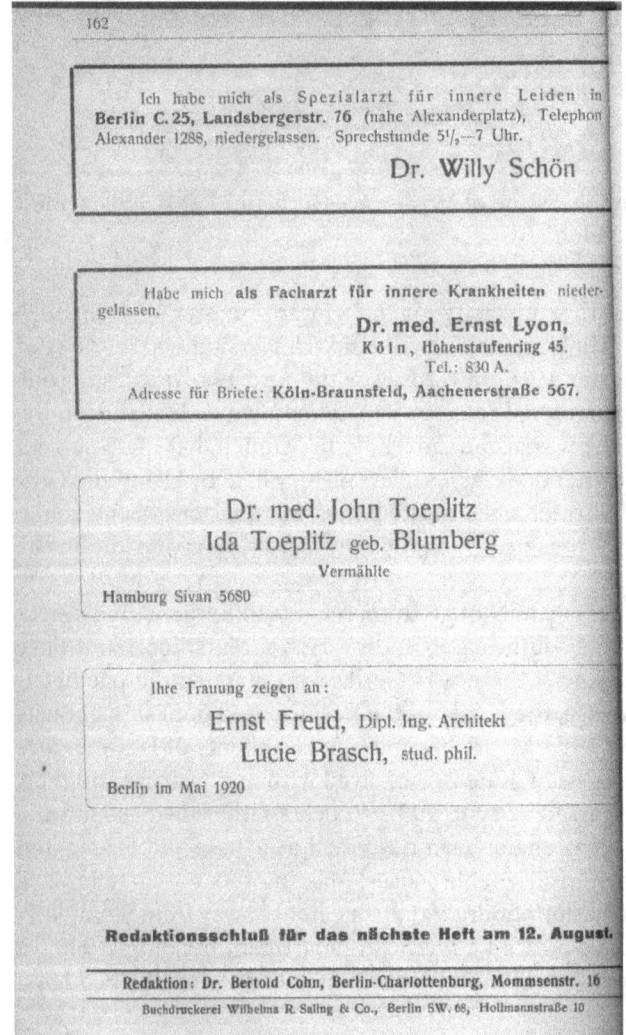

Figure 4.2. Wedding announcement in *Der Jüdische Student*, June–July 1920. Used with permission of the Central Zionist Archives, Jerusalem.

Figure 4.3. Tombstone for Sophie Freud, Hamburg, possibly designed by Ernst L. Freud, 1920. Used with permission of the Freud Museum London.

Figure 4.4. Sigmund Freud's tombstone, Golders Green, London, 1939. Used with permission of the Freud Museum London.

year after the cremation of his daughter, in February 1921, Sigmund Freud thanked his architect son for the beautiful gravestone; by then the photographer Max Halberstadt, Sophie's husband, had send a photograph to Vienna.[18]

Sigmund Freud had to post this letter to Arosa, Switzerland, where Ernst L. was staying for about three months in early 1921 because of a lung condition. This was the second time that the ailment compelled him to seek a cure; the first time had been in February 1920 just before his wedding, when he was advised to seek a change of air and to gain weight.[19] This second occurrence caused Sigmund Freud considerable concern, as he confided to Eitingon, because to visit a Swiss sanatorium 'so short after one has married into a rich family ... I only hope that the Braschs are too refined to suspect anything behind this'.[20] Freud stayed in Switzerland until mid April 1921 when he returned to Berlin, twenty-one pounds stronger, cured, and as Lucie Freud accompanied him back to Berlin, without having caused a fallout over financial issues between the newly related families.[21]

After their wedding, Ernst L. and Lucie Freud set up home in an apartment at Regentenstraße 11 (today Hitzigallee) in Berlin's elegant Tiergarten quarter.[22] This was the first Berlin abode of the new Freud family and which the psychoanalyst Karl Abraham called 'Ernst's charming home' after he and his wife had visited on the occasion of the birth in July 1921 of the young couple's son, Stephan Gabriel Freud (fig. 4.5).[23] Sometime during 1924, the Freuds moved into an apartment in number 23 on the same street; this was the home of which *Die Pyramide* published photograph in 1928. The new family home had become necessary because in April 1924 a third child, Clemens Raphael Freud, was born. Their second son, Lucian Michael Freud, had arrived in December 1922. They gave up the apartment at Regentenstraße 23 in 1932 when they moved to Matthäikirchstraße 4 in the same area of Berlin where they lived until they were forced into exile in 1933.

During the years in Berlin, Freud's office was always part of the family apartment.[24] A lack of archival material concerning the administrative side of the offices in Berlin (as well as later in London) makes it difficult to assess, for example, day-to-day working practices and to establish names of collaborating colleagues. A number of drawings from the Berlin period are stamped 'Architekten Freud—Kurz Dipl[om].-Ing[enieure]' which points towards a co-operation between Freud and the architect Alexander Kurz. Kurz was born in Vienna in 1887, and had worked in Brno, Czechoslovakia, from 1919 until 1928. He most likely began to co-operate with Freud when he settled in Berlin in 1929. In 1933, he went back to his native city of Vienna. Subsequently, he immigrated to England where he lived until the late 1940s when he may have relocated to the US.[25] A few drawings also list an Erna Cohn as a collaborator in Freud and Kurz's office, but no information could be found about her.[26] On other items a professional drafting office—'Hermann Gerson, Zeichenatelier'—is referenced. This suggests a strongly business-minded approach to running an office aimed at keeping down the number of regular employees. Most of Ernst L. Freud's buildings from the Berlin period were published, under his name, if at all, with only two exceptions. One was the two semi-detached houses for G. Levy and Adolf Hofer from 1922, for which an architect named Schäfer was co-listed.[27] The other was a tobacco warehouse for a cigarette company with the fitting name of 'Problem'. The latter was erected in Berlin-Prenzlauer Berg and was credited to Ernst L. Freud with Heinz Jacobsohn (born 1899). Jacobsohn managed to flee Germany; eventually he and his wife Katharina reached Sydney in Australia in December 1937.[28]

'To Live in Berlin and to Build in the Holy Land'

To move to Berlin meant also to settle in a network of friends, colleagues, and students of his father. During the 1920s, Berlin developed, beside Vienna, into a major centre for psychoanalysis. As the son of the founder of this new 'science', Freud benefited from living in this new centre of psychoanalysis because he received commissions for psycho-

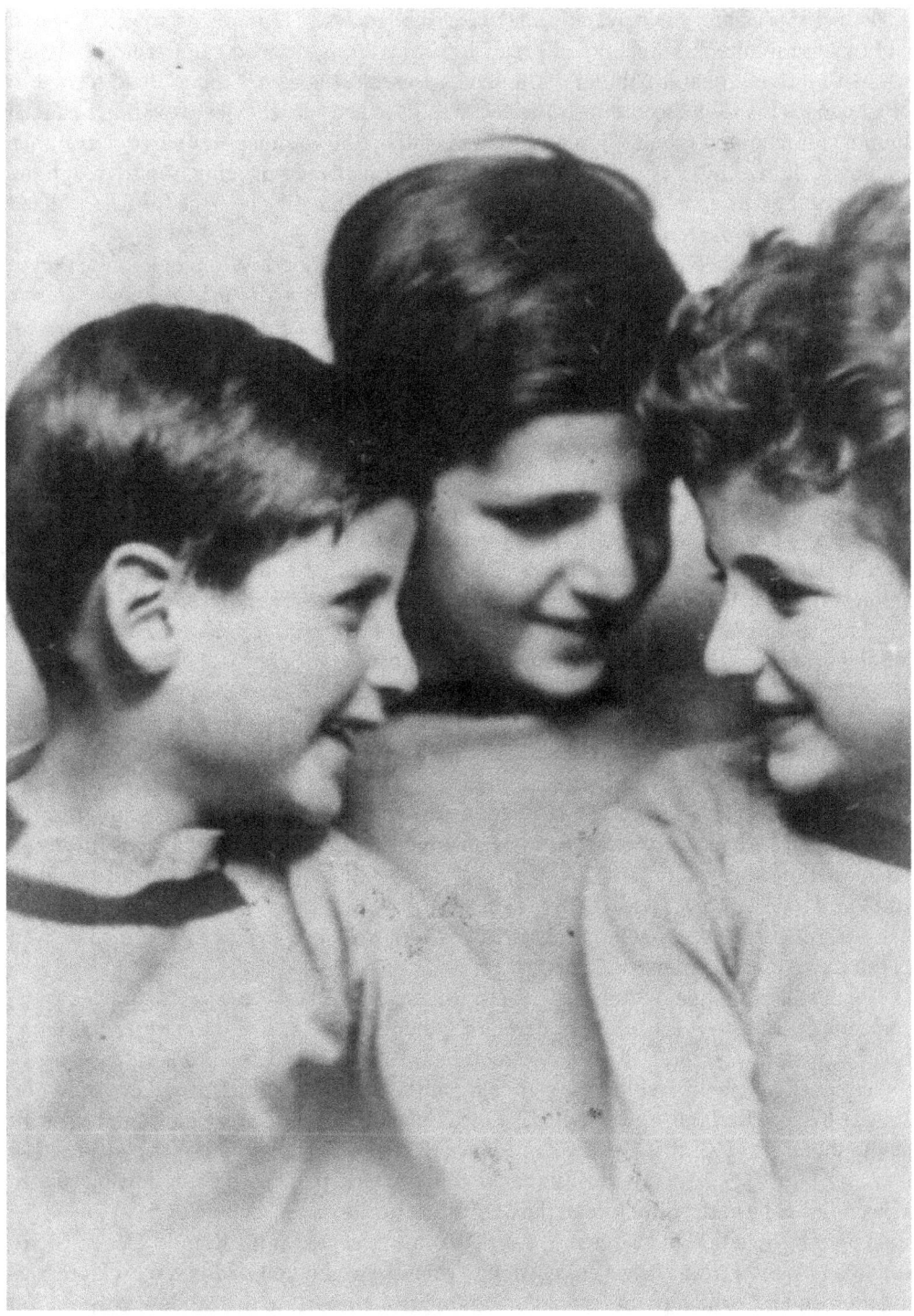

Figure 4.5. Clement Raphael, Stephan Gabriel, and Lucian Michael (from left to right), the three sons of Ernst L. and Lucie Freud. Used with permission of Sigmund Freud Copyrights by arrangements with Paterson Marsh Ltd., London.

analytical spaces and for private homes of psychoanalysts. One of the most dedicated and earliest architectural clients of Freud was Max Eitingon, who came from a Russian family of international fur traders. Trained as a medical doctor, Eitingon had turned to psychoanalysis and dedicated his time and wealth to the cause, even providing financial support for Sigmund Freud.[29] His generosity included the younger Freud by, for example, employing him as interior designer for a new apartment and engaging him to design the interior of the world's first psychoanalytical clinic in Berlin. This became the first realized project in Freud's career.

But even before Freud had settled in Berlin, Eitingon helped. When in anticipation of his move Freud looked for work in Berlin, Eitingon inquired with the well-known Zionist architect Baerwald, whose critical comments on young Jewish architects were quoted in chapter 2. Ever since Baerwald had designed the Hebrew Technical Institute, or *Technion*, in Haifa, Palestine, in 1909–14, he was a prominent figure among both German Zionists, who had financed the institution, and German-Jewish architects.[30] The latter admired the style of the building for its references to local building traditions that were rooted in geography and climate. Baerwald's work illustrated how architects might transform Palestine into a modern country as described by Herzl in the novel *Old-New Land*.

Herzl's vision of a Jewish state had been brought closer to realization by the British Balfour declaration from November 1917, a document that generated much excitement among Zionists. For any Zionist architecture student who faced likely economic hardship in post-war Germany or Austria, the possibility of working in Palestine was doubly attractive because of the noble cause and the financial remuneration. Suddenly, Palestine also seemed to offer business opportunities. Many Zionist entrepreneurs realized that in order to build up the country a capitalist economy was needed. For example, Eitingon was in contact with Baerwald with regard to an oil refinery in Palestine, a project of Eitingon's father, the entrepreneur Chaim Eitingon.[31]

Towards the end of September 1919, Max Eitingon wrote to Freud that 'action regarding the architect Baerwald has already been ushered in.'[32] Mid-October Eitingon informed Freud that the construction of the refinery was to begin shortly and that Freud would be employed on the project with 250 Mark as his monthly salary.[33] Thus at the outset of his new life in Berlin, Freud had not only already found work but he was to become involved in the Zionist resettlement of Palestine.

When still in Vienna, Freud was an active member of Blau-Weiss, a Zionist youth organization.[34] In 1909, his brother Martin had joined *Kadimah*, a Zionist student corporation.[35] Apparently, Freud also became a member of a fraternity while studying in Munich, though only his membership as a senior member (*alter Herr*) of *Hasmonaea* when he already lived in Berlin is documented.[36] Once in Munich, Freud struck a friendship with fellow student and Zionist Gustav Krojanker (1891–1945), a member of the corporation *Jordania*.[37] In 1929, Krojanker would move to Berlin where he rose the following year to a position as one of the directors of the publishing house *Jüdischer Verlag*.[38] On this occasion, Freud would design a large number of furniture pieces for his friend.[39] When corresponding by letter in the intervening years, Krojanker and Freud addressed each other as 'Bundesbruder,'[40] which points towards both men's membership in a student corporation as the root of their friendship. Perhaps the latter began when Freud delivered a lecture on 'Radical Zionism' sometime before the end of 1913 after he had arrived in Munich.[41]

What Zionist position Freud took in this talk remains unknown. However, his acquaintance with Krojanker suggests sympathy with cultural Zionism which goes back to the ideas of the philosopher Achad Ha'am and was propagated, for example, by Martin Buber. Both argued for a cultural renewal of the Jewish people, with Palestine being foremost their spiritual-cultural centre. Incidentally, the images of the second Berlin apartment of the Freuds in *Die Pyramide* provide further proof of an inclination towards cultural Zionism. When one of the photographs is sufficiently enlarged, several volumes of the Zionist magazine *Der Jude* that was published by Martin Buber and for which Krojanker served as one of the editors become visible.[42] Through his involvement with the Zionist student movement Freud apparently met some of his subsequent clients. For example, Richard Ginsberg, later a banker in Berlin, was mentioned in various issues of *Der jüdische Student*.[43] In the 1930s, Freud designed offices including furniture for Ginsberg's bank, the Mitteldeutsche Bodencredit-Anstalt in Berlin Mitte.[44] By that time the banker and the architect moved in the same circles in Berlin, as can be concluded from a series of busts that the sculptor Joachim Karsch (1897–1945) produced of various members of both families. Karsch portrayed Lucie Freud in bronze bust in October 1929 (fig. 4.6). Shortly thereafter he completed a portrait bust of Käthe Ginsberg, the wife of Richard Ginsberg, their daughter Marianne, and, much later, of their son Oliver.[45]

Figure 4.6. Bust of Lucie Freud by Joachim Karsch. Used with permission of the Freud Museum London.

Other than a design for a table, work for Baerwald was not productive and after a few months Freud gave up his first position in Berlin.[46] Like so many of the architectural schemes of early Zionism, the oil refinery never materialized. A similar fate befell a second Palestine project of Freud's, a design for a house for Chaim (1874–1952) and Vera Weizmann (1881–1966) on which he worked in 1926. This house was intended for Mount Scopus in Jerusalem where the Scottish city designer Sir Patrick Geddes (1854–1932) and Sir Frank Mears (1880–1953), his architect son-in-law, had been planning the Hebrew University since Geddes had received that commission from Weizmann, a fellow natural scientist, in 1919.[47] For a long time, Weizmann envisioned settling on Mt. Scopus, but this idea had changed around the mid 1930s when Mendelsohn was asked to design a house for the Weizmanns in Rehovot (fig. 4.7).

Figure 4.7. Weizmann house, Rehovot, Israel, by Erich Mendelsohn, 1934–36. Used with permission of Yad Weizmann, The Weizmann Archives, Rehovot, Israel.

Two designs for a Weizmann house in connection with the Hebrew University are known.[48] One which is dated 1927 is by Baerwald and the other is the design by Freud, plans of which have not been found. Correspondence between Weizmann and Mears allows one to date this project to 1926 with a second design stage handed over by Freud in October of that year.[49] Freud was keen on this prestigious commission; in April 1927 he inquired almost anxiously with Chaim Weizmann if a decision had been reached (fig. 4.8).[50] The connection between Weizmann and Freud had been initiated by Sigmund Freud, who had used his contacts with David Eder (1866–1936), a British Zionist and one of the first psychoanalysts in the United Kingdom.[51] Eder, in turn, was a close friend of Geddes. Weizmann had thought of sending his son for the summer of 1926 to the latter's private university in Montpellier, France.[52]

Freud's design for the Weizmann house is important for three reasons. First, it is one of the very commissions upon which Sigmund Freud commented, even though Martha Freud apparently had to initiate this letter from which the subtitle for this section has been borrowed ('to live in Berlin and to build in the Holy Land').[53] Second, the correspondence about the project implies that Freud was settled in Berlin but not firmly tied to the

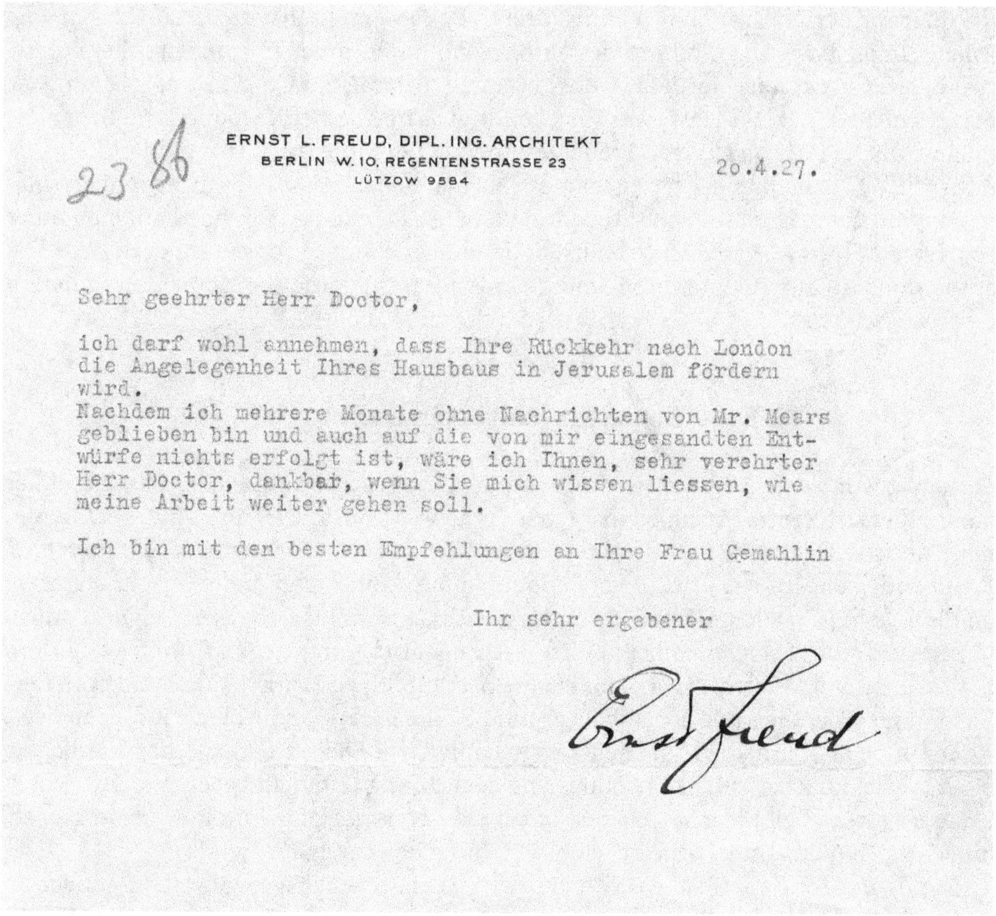

2386

ERNST L. FREUD, DIPL. ING. ARCHITEKT
BERLIN W. 10, REGENTENSTRASSE 23
LÜTZOW 9584

20.4.27.

Sehr geehrter Herr Doctor,

ich darf wohl annehmen, dass Ihre Rückkehr nach London die Angelegenheit Ihres Hausbaus in Jerusalem fördern wird.
Nachdem ich mehrere Monate ohne Nachrichten von Mr. Mears geblieben bin und auch auf die von mir eingesandten Entwürfe nichts erfolgt ist, wäre ich Ihnen, sehr verehrter Herr Doctor, dankbar, wenn Sie mich wissen liessen, wie meine Arbeit weiter gehen soll.

Ich bin mit den besten Empfehlungen an Ihre Frau Gemahlin

Ihr sehr ergebener

Ernst Freud

Figure 4.8. Letter from Ernst L. Freud to Chaim Weizmann, 1927. Used with permission of Yad Weizmann, The Weizmann Archives, Rehovot, Israel.

city. Mears raised, for example, the difficulties Freud would face regarding relocating to Palestine should Geddes and Mears agree with him concerning his involvement in the construction of the university.[54] In the meantime, Freud lived in Berlin and the Weizmann project indicates, third, the direction his practice had taken by 1926. The Eitingon scheme was a contribution to the economic infrastructure of a resettled Palestine; it was idealistic but nevertheless practical. The Weizmann commission was equally idealistic and it was highly symbolic of the entire Zionist project. It was, however, also a design for domestic architecture which had become Freud's main area of work.

Mears understood that domestic architecture was Freud's true specialty. He carefully treaded the fine line between not alienating Weizmann and Eder, who supported the Scotsmen's work on the university, and endorsing Freud's plans for the Weizmann house and thus foreclosing the possibility of he himself designing a home for the Zionist leader. Mears advised Weizmann that he would 'not wish to have a modern German house—quite interesting, but difficult to live up to'. He continued: 'What I mean is, that while the interiors of rooms, as shown in his [Freud's] photographs, have a certain charm, one would almost have to get him to design ones clothes in order to complete the picture. Again, he designs largely for 3-ply wood; I wanted to use it, but Chaikin [a local architect-partner of Geddes and Mears] was very doubtful as to whether it would stand the Palestinian climate.'[55] Mears charged Freud with being more interested in a total piece of art rather than the clients' needs, causing possible maintenance issues by using modern materials, and being ignorant about the local climate as Freud had provided an open inner courtyard.[56] Thus Mears voiced the usual prejudices about European modernism while at the same time misidentifying Freud's less-than-avant-garde position among modern German architects.

Society Architect in Berlin

Socially, the move to Berlin meant to step into the circles of both Lucie Brasch and her family. Richard Neutra explained that Lucie Freud was from a rich family 'but what is even more decisive for the life of this young couple, she has social connections' and therefore, Freud had 'plenty of work and a very good income'.[57] But Freud did not exclusively rely on his wife to gain clients. Some commissions came from his father's colleagues, others he received from fellow members of Zionist student fraternities and from friends from both Vienna and Munich. Most of his clients in the 1920s and early 1930s came from Berlin's bourgeoisie, the same social background as the Brasch family. Except for relatives, it cannot be established which clients were contacts of Lucie Freud and her family. The biographical information, like religious and social background and age structure, which could be researched for many clients, offers exemplary insights into how these aspects influenced and determined the development of Freud's career and work.

The figures for Berlin clients with and without Jewish backgrounds are compiled in table 4.1. While significant gaps in our knowledge continue to exist, it is certain that over half of Freud's clients were of Jewish background with the true number most likely being higher. Considering that Freud was not an avant-garde modernist architect, his clients exemplify that the Jewish bourgeoisie was not unanimously attracted to modernist architecture as one occasionally reads in German architectural histories.[58] Table 4.2 analyses Freud's clients by occupations and professions, indicating that the majority of them stemmed from the bourgeoisie and upper-middle classes. Remarkably, among the named clients of Freud, thirty-five carried the academic title of Dr. or PhD. The distribution of clients according to birth year, ordered by decades, is provided in table 4.3. Most notably, the most prestigious projects, for example the country house for Dr. Theodor Frank, a manager of the Deutsche Bank, and the design for the Weizmann house, were commissioned by some of Freud's oldest clients (born in the 1870s) and came relatively late in his career. In general, the age structure shows that Freud built up his office in parallel to his friends, acquaintances, and clients establishing families, businesses, and careers.

Table 4.1. Jewish/non-Jewish background of Freud's Berlin clients

	Total	Jewish	not Jewish	background unknown
Identified clients	52	31	4	17

Table 4.2. Professional background of Freud's Berlin clients

Profession/occupation	number of designs for each listed profession
Industrialist and businessmen:	11
Psychoanalysts and financiers:	7
Lawyers and bankers:	4
Medical doctors / professions:	3
Publishing and private income:	2
Gymnastics teacher, chemist, politician, writer, academic, architect:	1
Unknown:	18

Table 4.3. Age structure of Freud's Berlin clients

Born in	1870s	1880s	1890s	1900s
	6	9	14	4

Beside his designs for houses that will be looked at in the next chapter, interior designs for apartments and townhouses became the staple diet of Freud's practice in Berlin. This focus recalls Loos's many interior projects for bourgeois clients, some of which Freud will have visited when he attended *Bauschule* lectures. The emphasis also reflects the influences of both the general economic circumstances and those of the architect and individual clients. With the architect and most of his clients at roughly the same age and at comparable stages in their careers, the former could probably not reject requests for designs of single pieces of furniture, whereas the latter most likely could only afford an interior design, if at all, but not necessarily an entire house. Finally, to design interiors for apartments was a standard task for architects in the first half of the twentieth century. Regardless of the popularity of the suburbs at the edges of Berlin from the later nineteenth century onwards, large numbers of citizens continued to live in densely built-up inner-city areas. There five-storey apartment buildings, rather than townhouses or terraced homes for example, were the norm even for the middle classes and the bourgeoisie. The apartments of the latter groups were often large considering the number of rooms and their sizes, and they were usually rented unfurnished. To have such a home fitted out was thus a necessity; yet to have fittings and furniture purpose-designed by an architect fulfilled often cultural and social ambitions of the bourgeois tenants similar to those of clients who commissioned houses or villas from an architect.

Freud did not coherently date all of his drawings or note names of clients and addresses of projects. This made identification often difficult, and in many cases impossible. Usually commissions for interiors consisted of built-in furniture and moveable pieces for apartments and entire houses. Three projects from 1930 are typical with regard to the type of client and the scope of Freud's large-scale interior designs. The project for the home of the research chemist Dr. Fritz Michael and his newly married wife Hannah Schwab was commissioned after the couples' wedding in late 1928 or early 1929. Around

January 1930, Freud worked on forty-four pieces of furniture that were subsequently installed at an apartment at Brückenallee 4, Berlin-Alt Moabit. The large number of pieces indicates the comprehensive character of the commission, yet when the couple fled National-Socialist Germany, the only one they took with them to the United Kingdom was a large Freud-designed desk.[59]

The second interior design was most likely also created in conjunction with a marriage. In September 1930 the surgeon Dr. Albert Salomon (1883–1976) married the singer Paula Lindberg (1897–2000). Charlotte Salomon (1917–1943), the daughter from Albert Salomon's first marriage, recorded in her painted autobiography that around the time of her father's second marriage their apartment on Wielandstraße 15, Berlin-Charlottenburg, was remodelled and refurbished.[60] Albert Salomon had been born in this apartment and he may have wished to set up the place as a new home with Paula Salomon-Lindberg. The refurbishment may also have been an attempt to erase lingering memories of Salomon's first wife who had committed suicide in 1926.

Among Freud's papers exists a set of drawings for thirty-three pieces of furniture; some of the sheets are dated April 1930 and others are inscribed with Salomon, the client's name. Ultimately, it is not known if this refers to Albert and Paula Salomon, but it is likely for a number of reasons. Early on in her musical career Paula Salomon-Lindberg had worked as a nursemaid in the home of Mendelsohn.[61] As a contralto, she had also accompanied the cellist Louise Mendelsohn (1894–1980). Besides this possible link between Salomon-Lindberg and the Freuds, who were acquainted with the Mendelsohns, a second intersection exists via Freud's client Eugen Buchthal.[62] Between 1928 and 1929, Freud remodelled the businessman's house in Berlin-Westend. At that time, Salomon-Lindberg was a lodger in the Buchthal home, where she continued participating in house music after her wedding.[63] Thus Salomon-Lindberg may have met Freud at the Buchthals, even if she had not been familiar with the architect and his wife from the Mendelsohns.

The third and final example is forty-eight pieces of furniture on which Freud worked between August and November 1930 for a client named Stefan Neumann, of whom nothing is known. The commission comprised, among other items, linen cupboards, a shoe cupboard, anteroom cupboards, tables, and dresser tables for verandas. This inventory of furniture characterizes many of Freud's commissions and is representative of the domestic needs of his clients. These larger projects typically consisted of designs to fit out living and sitting rooms, libraries and smoking rooms, often with fireplaces, bedrooms, nurseries, and office quarters. Freud's archives contain many projects of comparable scope which indicates that Freud had a consistent client base with similar ideas about what their homes should offer.

Within the realm of domestic architecture, nurseries and children's furniture emerged as a small area of specialization for Freud. One early example is a nursery for the three daughters of Gottfried and Brigitte Bermann-Fischer. Brigitte Fischer was the daughter of the publisher Samuel Fischer (1859–1934). Her family had lived since 1905 in a villa designed by Hermann Muthesius in Berlin-Grunewald, Erdener Straße 8.[64] After she had married in 1926, the couple moved into a house at Gneiststraße 7 around the corner from her family home. Freud was called upon several times to design interiors—a gentleman's bedroom, a drawing room, a fire place, and another bedroom—but also such items as radiator coverings. From July to August 1930 he was occupied with the nursery that was comprised of a bedroom for the three children, a playroom, a bathroom, and a terrace with an outdoor shower (fig. 4.9). Freud designed some of the furniture, for example the cupboards and the beds with integrated benches at the footends and painted in a light green.[65] The playroom was organized functionally with all furniture lined up against the walls in order to free the centre of the room as a play area. Underneath the windows Freud placed a continuous writing desk with tubular steel chairs marking the individual writing stations. On one wall, a frieze of African animals among palm trees was hand painted by Brigitte Berman-Fischer.

An interior for another, unidentified nursery was again planned for three children.[66] In this case, three school desks were sited individually along the curved glass façade of a large bay window of an older building (fig. 4.10). To the right of the bay window Freud placed a small table of his own design between three chairs made from bent wood. The table is rectangular with four curved metal feet and a colourful linoleum cover for the table top. On the opposite side stood another low table, surrounded by three wooden children's chairs with seats and backrests made from cane. Freud used the same type of chair in the waiting room of a private paediatric clinic for Richard Hamburger (1884–1940), a professor at the Charité in Berlin (fig. 4.11). With their precise geometry softened by the never-quite-so-sharp edges of the wood, these chairs are much more typical of Freud-designed furniture than the metal chairs of the Berman-Fischer nursery. In both cases Freud conceived his children's furniture as diminutive versions of adult furniture, just as other designers did as well.

Figure 4.9. Brigitte Fischer and her three daughters their nursery, Berlin, 1929–30. Used with permission of the RIBA Library Photographs Collection.

Figure 4.10. Unidentified nursery in Germany, possibly in Hamburg, not dated. Used with permission of the RIBA Library Photographs Collection.

Figure 4.11. Corner in the waiting room of Professor Hamburger children's clinic, after being moved from Berlin to London sometime after 1933. Used with permission of the RIBA Library Photographs Collection.

Throughout his career in Berlin, Freud also accepted commissions for individual pieces of furniture. A good example is a single bedstead from November 1930 in green varnish with the headboard and bed end made of cane. In itself, this piece of furniture is insignificant, but it offers another glimpse into Freud's private life in Berlin and later in England. The client for the bedstead was Constanze Marie Matilde Kurella (1904–95), the daughter of a Polish psychiatrist, and a long-standing friend of the Freuds since their days in Berlin. Kurella had lived there since childhood and later trained as a physical therapist with Elsa Gindler (1885–1961).[67] Her future husband, the author and translator James Stern (1904–93), described her lovingly in a letter after the two had met in France in 1934, to where Kurella had fled from the Nazis: 'I'm with one Tania Kurella, a German [sic], … she possesses the somewhat enviable quality of arriving in a strange country, learning its language in a few weeks and then making a quite substantial livelihood by teaching its wealthy folk a weird kind of Kultur-Gymnastik, for the good of their 'ealth.'[68] Later in England, where Kurella and Stern married in 1935, it was Freud who gave her away. The two couples stayed in contact, and even collaborated on a selection of letters by Sigmund Freud that the Sterns translated into English, but Freud never worked again as an architect for his friends.[69] However, this takes the narrative to England too soon; before I will turn to Freud's work in the United Kingdom, the next two chapters will look at his houses in and around Berlin and at his designs for psychoanalytic spaces.

Notes

1. D. J. K. Peukert. 1992. *The Weimar Republic: The Crisis of Classical Modernism*, trans. R. Deveson. New York: Hill and Wang, 47.
2. Peukert, *Weimar Republic*, 48.
3. Peukert, *Weimar Republic*, 47–48.
4. W. Pehnt. 1973. *Die Architektur des Expressionismus*. Stuttgart: Hatje.
5. Matriculation entry Lucie Brasch, 19 October 1916, number 182, 107. Rektorat of the königliche Friedrich Wilhelms-Universität Berlin (today Humboldt-Universität).
6. Studenten-Karte Lucie Brasch, Wintersemester 1918–19, Archiv der Ludwig-Maximilians-Universität München (ALMU). Brasch enrolled for four classes, of which Wölfflin taught two, one on the art of Rome and the other on Dürer and his time. The student card only records Brasch's enrolment for the Wintersemester 1918–19. No other information is given about earlier studies at another university or any indication of Brasch continuing her studies respectively gaining a Magister degree.
7. Lucie Brasch lived at Elisabethstraße 13 (Studenten-Karte Lucie Brasch, Wintersemester 1918–19, ALMU); Ernst Freud lived in Gabelsbergerstraße 3 (*Student file Ernst Freud*, pp. 1, Historisches Archiv Technische Universität München [HATUM]).
8. E. Freud. 1997. *Gaglow*. London: Hamish Hamilton.
9. E. Weissweiler. 2006. *Die Freuds: Biographie einer Familie*. Cologne: Kiepenheuer & Witsch, 350, mentions four daughters. Clement Freud, one of the sons of Ernst and Lucie Freud, refers to three daughters and one son (C. Freud. 1995. *Freud Ego*. London: BBC, 11).
10. Weissweiler, *Freuds*, 350.
11. Weissweiler, *Freuds*, 261.
12. M. Apt. 1927. *25 Jahre im Dienste der Berliner Kaufmannschaft*. Berlin: Sieben Stäbe Verlag, 12, my translation.
13. *Jüdisches Adressbuch für Gross-Berlin: Ausgabe 1931*. Berlin: Arani, 1994, 46; Weissweiler, *Freuds*, 261.

14. Weissweiler, *Freuds*, 263–264.
15. *Jüdische Rundschau* 25 (1 June 1920, issue 35): 277; *Der Jüdische Student* 17 (June–July 1920, issue 3): 162.
16. Letter from Sigmund Freud to Sandor Ferenczi, 17 June 1920 (E. Falzeder et al. [eds.]. 2000. *The Correspondence of Sigmund Freud and Sándor Ferenczi*, 3 vols. Cambridge, MA: Harvard University Press, vol. 3, letter 848).
17. Letters from Sigmund Freud to Ernst Freud, respectively to Ernst and Lucie Freud, 7 October, 17 October, 7 November, 9 November, 15 November, all 1920 (Sigmund Freud papers, Library of Congress [LoC], box 3, folder 2 and folder 10).
18. Letter from Sigmund Freud to Ernst Freud, 21 February 1921 (Sigmund Freud papers, LoC, box 3, folder 2).
19. Letter from Max Eitingon to Sigmund Freud, 29 February 1920 (M. Schröter [ed.]. 2004. *Sigmund Freud Max Eitingon, Briefwechsel 1906–1939*, 2 vols. Tübingen: Edition Diskord, vol. 1, letter 167E, 193).
20. Letter from Sigmund Freud to Max Eitingon, 13 December 1920 (Schröter, *Sigmund Freud Max Eitingon*, vol. 1, letter 191F, 224, my translation).
21. Letter from Max Eitingon to Sigmund Freud, 17 April 1921 (Schröter, *Sigmund Freud Max Eitingon*, vol. 1, letter 207E, 249–250.)
22. Letter from Sigmund Freud to Ernst and Lucie Freud, Regentenstraße 11, Berlin, 7 August 1920 (Sigmund Freud papers, LoC, box 3, folder 10). Up to the move into the first apartment, Ernst Freud apparently stayed with a Dr. Pinner at Detmolder Straße, Wilmersdorf. This address was used by family members for correspondence between 1919 and May 1920. Dr. Pinner may have been an acquaintance of Freud's through the Jewish Student corporation in Munich. *Der Jüdische Student* variously listed members with the name Pinner, including at least one who lived in Berlin. But Pinner may have also been one of the partners of the architecture firm Pinner and Neumann for which Richard Neutra worked after he had moved to Berlin in October 1920. Ernst Freud helped Neutra to obtain that position (R. Neutra. 1962. *Life and Shape*. New York: Appleton-Century-Crofts, 147; T. S. Hines. 1982. *Richard Neutra and the Search for Modern Architecture: A Biography and History*. New York: Oxford University Press, 30).
23. Letter from Karl Abraham to Sigmund Freud, 4 December 1921 (E. Falzeder [ed.]. 2002. *The Complete Correspondence of Sigmund Freud and Karl Abraham 1907–1925*. London: Karnac, letter 404A).
24. For 1923, the Berlin address book lists the following entry: Ernst Freud, Dipl[om].-Ing[enieur], W 35, Steglitzer Straße 69 (today Pohlstraße), which is close to Regentenstraße. See K. Umlauf (ed.). 1983. *Adressbuch für Berlin und seine Vororte 1919–1932*. Munich: Saur. The reason for this address is unknown.
25. Alexander Kurz, biographical file, British Architecture Library, Royal Institute of British Architects, London.
26. See the entries for Margot Joachimsthal 1931 and Schönheimer 1931 in the Selected List of Works at the back of this book.
27. E. M. Hajos and L. Zahn. 1928. *Berliner Architektur der Nachkriegszeit*. Berlin: Albertus, 80, 113; see the entries for G. Levy-Adolf Hofer 1922 and tobacco warehouse 'Problem' 1927–28 in the 'Selected List of Works'.
28. A folder with architectural drawings by Jacobsohn of projects from his German period is today preserved in the Faculty of Architecture, Landscape, and Visual Arts, University of Western Australia, in Perth. Many thanks to Dr. Bronwyn Hanna, University of New South Wales, Sydney, Australia, and Dr. Leonie Matthews, Curtin University of Technology, Perth, Australia, for providing valuable information on Jacobsohn. See also L. Matthews. 1991. 'An Exploratory Study of Women in Western Australian Architecture 1920–1960', BA thesis. Western Australia: Curtin University of Technology, Appendix iv-Biographies, 20–21.

29. Letter from Sigmund Freud to Max Eitingon, 22 December 1919 (E. and L. Freud [eds.]. 1968. *Sigmund Freud Briefe 1873–1939*, 2nd enlarged edition. Frankfurt: S. Fischer, 341–342 [341]).
30. *Alexander Baerwald 1877–1930 Architect and Artist.* N.d [c. 1983]. Exhibition catalogue. Haifa: National Museum of Science, Planning and Technology.
31. Dr. Michael Schröter, Berlin, kindly helped identify the projects by Freud for the Eitingons; see Schröter, *Sigmund Freud Max Eitingon*.
32. Letter from Max Eitingon to Sigmund Freud, 22 September 1919 (Schröter, *Sigmund Freud Max Eitingon*, vol. 1, letter 145E, 162, my translation).
33. Letter from Max Eitingon, Berlin, to Ernst L. Freud, Munich, 12 October 1919 (Freud Museum London, box Lux [i.e. Lucie Brasch] papers, A–K). Eitingon actually financed Freud until the latter was to receive his salary; see letter from Sigmund Freud to Max Eitingon, 22 December 1919 (E. and L. Freud [eds.]. 1968. *Sigmund Freud Briefe 1873–1939*; and Schröter, *Sigmund Freud Max Eitingon*, vol. 1, 193).
34. M. Gresser. 1994. *Dual Allegiance: Freud as a Modern Jew.* Albany, NY: State University of New York Press, 229.
35. P. Gay. 1998. *Freud: A Life for Our Time.* New York: W.W. Norton, 600–601; Gresser, *Freud*, 229.
36. *Adreßbuch des Kartells jüdischer Verbindungen E.V.* 1932. Berlin: Kartell jüdischer Verbindungen, 26.
37. *Adreßbuch des Kartells jüdischer Verbindungen E.V.* 1932, 50.
38. Email from Leorah Kroyanker to the author, 18 November 2005.
39. See the entry for Gustav Krojanker 1929 in the 'Selected List of Works'.
40. Letters from Gustav Krojanker to Ernst Freud, 20 February 1918, 24 September 1919, 15 November 1918 (postcard), Freud Museum London
41. 'Mr. cand. ing. Freund [sic] from Vienna spoke about "radical Zionism"' (*Der Jüdische Student* 10 [January 1914, issue 9]: 326, my translation).
42. *Der Jude* 1 (1916) to 12 (1928). These volumes may of course have been Lucie's.
43. *Der Jüdische Student* 12 (June 1915): 25; *Der Jüdische Student* 12 (Kriegsheft 27 November 1916): 310.
44. See entries for Richard Ginsberg's director's office 1930 and Mitteldeutsche Bodencredit-Anstalt 1930 in the 'Selected List of Works'.
45. F. Karsch. 2005. *Joachim Karsch: Werkverzeichnis der Plastiken.* Weimar: VDG, number 1929-16: portrait of Mrs. Freud, masque, bronze Berlin, October 1929, c. 30 cm tall, whereabouts unknown; 1930-2: Käthe Ginsberg, plaster of Paris, February 1930, c. 35 cm tall, privately owned; 1930-4: portrait Marianne Ginsberg, plaster of Paris, March 1930, c. 25 cm tall; 1932-3: portrait Oliver Ginsberg, February 1932, 22.8 cm tall. In 1929 Karsch also sculpted a likeness of Dr. Rudolf Gleimius, a Berlin banker and industrialist who was, incidentally, also a client of Freud's; see number 1929-5: Dr. Rudolf Gleimius, whereabouts unknown.
46. In a letter from 10 (or 20) March 1920, Richard Neutra admired Ernst Freud's courage to have given up his current position and expressed his hope that Freud would not lose sight of Baerwald and Palestine (Sigmund Freud Museum London).
47. V. M. Welter. 1995. 'The Geddes Vision of the Region as City—Palestine as a Polis', in J. Fiedler (ed.). *Social Utopias of the Twenties: Bauhaus, Kibbutz and the Dream of the New Man.* Wuppertal: Müller + Busmann Press, 72–79.
48. An even earlier design was provided by the German-Jewish architect Fritz Kornberg for a piece of land in Haifa from 1922 (letter from Fritz Kornberg to Chaim Weizmann, 7 July 1928, The Weizmann Archives, Rehovot).
49. Letter from Frank Mears to Chaim Weizmann, 12 October 1926 (L12/39, Central Zionist Archives, Jerusalem); letter from Frank Mears to Chaim Weizmann, 20 October 1926 (file 1099, The Weizmann Archives, Rehovot).

50. Letter from Ernst Freud to Chaim Weizmann, 20 April 1927 (file 1134, The Weizmann Archives, Rehovot).
51. Letter from Sigmund Freud to Ernst L. Freud, 12 October 1926 (Sigmund Freud papers, LoC, box 3, folder 3).
52. Chaim Weizmann to Vera Weizmann, 7 and 10 July 1926 (P. Ofer. N.d. [1978]. *The Letters and Papers of Chaim Weizmann*, 23 vols. New Brunswick, NJ: Transaction Books, v. 13 Series A, letters 43, 44, and 51). The plan fell through when Weizmann learned that Geddes would not personally be in Montpellier that summer.
53. Letter from Sigmund Freud to Ernst L. Freud, 12 October 1926 (M. Schröter [ed.]. 2010. *Sigmund Freud: Unterdess halten wir zusammen. Briefe an die Kinder.* Berlin: Aufbau, 362–364 [363]).
54. Letter from Frank Mears to Chaim Weizmann, 12 October 1926 (L12/39, Central Zionist Archives, Jerusalem).
55. Letter from Frank Mears to Chaim Weizmann, 12 October 1926 (L12/39, Central Zionist Archives, Jerusalem, my inserts in square parentheses).
56. Baerwald's 1927 design for the Weizmann house likewise was arranged as an open courtyard. Within his œuvre this design stands out as the house does not have a dome, which was otherwise typical for Baerwald's designs. The massing, especially of the northeast façade, is much more modern than is usual for Baerwald's houses. The oriel windows with their chamfered corners look like an add-on and are not as well integrated as this trademark of Baerwald's design usually was. Lack of further archival sources do not allow me to consider fully the possibility that Baerwald's 1927 design is an elaboration of Freud's second design stage from October 1926.
57. Letter from Richard Neutra to Dione Niedermann, 15 September 1921 (quoted in Hines, *Neutra*, 35).
58. For example, K. Klemmer. 1998. *Jüdische Baumeister in Deutschland: Architektur vor der Shoah*. Stuttgart: dva, 86.
59. Emails from Ben Schwab to the author, May and November 2004.
60. J. C. E. Belinfante (ed.). 1998. *Charlotte Salomon, life? or theatre?*, trans. L. Vennewitz. Zwolle: Waanders, 98, 131, 283, 708–709.
61. C. Fischer-Defoy (ed). 1986. *Charlotte Salomon—Leben oder Theater?: das 'Lebensbild' einer jüdische Malerin aus Berlin 1917–1943; Bilder und Spuren, Notizen, Gespräche, Dokumente.* Berlin: Das Arsenal, 37.
62. Some members of the Freud family were acquainted with Charlotte Salomon and her grandfather when both lived in exile in southern France. See letter from Martha Wertheim to Henny Freud, 3 February 1945 (Box 3, folder Wertheim, Martha & Ernest 1913–1946, Oliver & Henny Freud Papers, Manuscript Division, Library of Congress, Washington, DC)
63. Email from Christine Fischer-Defoy to author, 13 August 2006.
64. Email from Gisela Braun-Fischer to author, 23 October 2001.
65. Email from Gisela Braun-Fischer to author, 14 January 2002.
66. The photograph may show a nursery that Ernst Freud designed for Käthe Brasch, a sister of Lucie Freud, who had three children and lived in Hamburg. It could also show part of the waiting room of *Gartenhausklinik* of the pediatrician Prof. Richard Hamburger at an unknown location in Berlin.
67. E. Gindler, 'Gymnastik for People Whose Lives are Full of Activity', in D. H. Johnson. 1995. *Bone, Breath, and Gesture: Practices of Embodiment.* Berkeley, CA: North Atlantic Books, 3–14.
68. M. Huddleston. 2000. *James Stern: A Life in Letters 1904–1933.* Norwich: Michael Russell, 57.
69. Huddleston, *James Stern*; N. Jenkins. 1994. 'James Stern 1904–1993', *Auden Society Newsletter* 12 (April); E. L. Freud (ed.) 1960. *Letters of Sigmund Freud*, trans. T. and J. Stern. New York: Basic Books; latter editions were edited by Ernst L and L. Freud.

Chapter 5

Houses in and around Berlin

During his thirteen years in Berlin, Ernst Freud designed eight new houses, with a ninth, the Weizmann house, located outside Germany.[1] In addition, Freud was commissioned to alter, to different degrees, at least another eight houses. A ninth project, the weekend house near Vienna for his sister Anna Freud, was again outside Germany.[2] All of the German houses were located in western parts of Berlin: Grunewald, Dahlem, Nikolassee, Westend, and Lankwitz. The Tiergarten district, where Freud himself lived, was the most central area of Berlin in which he worked on a domestic project; and even that district is to the west of the historic centre of Berlin. What may appear like an undue limitation was, however, a quite precise geographic indication of the clients for whom Freud worked. The western parts of Berlin, especially where the urban fabric turned from densely built-up city blocks into individual, suburban houses, were traditionally among the most popular areas inhabited by the bourgeoisie and the middle-classes.

As table 5.1 shows, Freud's larger domestic projects were distributed unequally during his years in Berlin but the chronological spread reflects the broad movements of the post-war economy in Weimar Germany. The years before the currency reform in 1923 ended the hyperinflation were, relatively speaking, almost a good time for some architects. If private clients had managed to safeguard their monetary wealth throughout the war, they now aimed to protect it from inflation by investing in real estate. Other clients came from abroad, for example the Swiss Dr. jur. Heinz Henneberg,[3] and had access to foreign currency. The fact that between 1924 and 1929 five of Freud's eight Berlin projects, which were completed or begun, were refurbishments possibly reflects the greater difficulties in securing financing for buildings during this period of relative economic stabilization. With the passing of the hyperinflation, the time had also passed during which it was relatively easy to pay back the principle of a mortgage loan. After the stock market crash in 1929, Freud could only acquire two commissions for new houses in addition to the completion of three houses whose construction had begun before 1929. Overall, Freud's was not an overly busy practice as far as new houses were concerned, once the ups and downs of both the larger economy and his own commissions have been accounted for. Regardless, he received a steady, even if smaller, number of commissions for new single-family houses and the remodelling of existing ones. This pattern matched that of the larger demand for this type of housing in Berlin.

The statistical yearbooks of the Weimar Republic record relatively stable numbers of new constructions of single-family houses at least for the years 1923 to 1929, the only ones during which figures for 'new buildings for dwellings with one apartment', the statistical term for single family dwellings, were collected.[4] For Berlin, the figures show that every year between approximately 1300 and 1450 such buildings were completed. Exceptions

Table 5.1. Private houses designed, built, or refurbished by Freud between 1920 and 1933 (excluding houses for his own family)

	1920–23	1924–29	1930–1933
new designs (begun)	4	2 (1)	2
refurbished (begun)	2	5 1	1

were 1924, when in the aftermath of the currency reform the absolute figure dropped to a low of 799 homes, and 1926 and 1927 when between 1929 and 2175 buildings were noted. Percentage-wise, the statistics indicate a steady decline of this building type in comparison with the parallel increase of multi-apartment buildings like, for example, the large social-housing estates of the later 1920s.[5] But for architects who specialized in domestic architecture it mattered more that the absolute figures remained more or less stable, as that indicated a steady demand and, therefore, possible commissions.[6]

First Houses in Berlin

Freud's first three houses of 1921 and 1922 were all located in Dahlem and Westend, suburbs at the western edge of the city in which the bourgeoisie lived in leafy comfort with easy access to Berlin's central districts. Detached villas and country houses are the standard dwelling types, other common houses are semi-detached buildings and three- or four-storey edifices with rental apartments. The three houses share some common features: all are two-storeys high, have hipped roofs, their windows sit flush with the façades, and are placed in rather generous gardens.[7]

The 1921 house for Ernst Maretzki, a lawyer and judge, and his wife Eva Liebrecht was a single-family home. One of the sons recalls that the interior was divided into the private quarters, like bedrooms for both parents and the two sons, located on the upper floor, whereas the more public rooms were on the ground floor: the living room, the dining room with a bay window, a loggia, and servicing rooms like the kitchen, pantry, hall, and entrance.[8]

The other two buildings each accommodated two sets of inhabitants. The semi-detached G. Levy and Adolf Hofer houses (1921–22, the western house has since been destroyed), erected for two gentlemen of private means, had exteriors made from exposed red brick. The rooms were organized within rectangular plans with the lower floors divided by central, load-bearing walls into two zones. One was for the kitchen, entrance, and auxiliary rooms, and the other for living and dining rooms. Bedrooms and bathrooms were on the upper floors, accessible through open halls with curved stairs.[9]

The Schimeck house (1922, now demolished; fig. 5.1) was built for the families of the two daughters of an industrialist who was in the paper-producing business. Each of the young families occupied one floor of the building with its T-shaped plan. The stem stretched into the depth of the lot while the crossbar followed the street front. A low

Figure 5.1. Garden façade of the Schimek house, Berlin, 1922. Used with permission of the RIBA Library Photographs Collection.

hipped roof that disappeared from sight near the house emphasized the mass of the stem. The crossbar accommodated a hall, gentleman's room, sitting room, dining room, and kitchen and pantry. From the hall, a few steps lead into the stem where the bedrooms, bathrooms, dressing rooms, and maid's chamber were located. The upper apartment had a similar arrangement.[10]

Outside, a raised terrace, partially covered by a balcony for the upper apartment, was placed along one side of the stem. A flight of steps lead to a pergola-covered seating area in the garden. Receding, segmental arches structured the facades just above the level of the soil. At the street façade bow windows on each floor were placed on top of each other within a vertical strip of exposed brick laid in a diamond-shaped decorative pattern. At the end of the stem a basement apartment offered accommodation for the gardener of the property. Additional rooms for maids and other personnel were located in the attic.

These earliest houses by Freud were conventional in both form and plan. Different in size, each house grouped rooms according to their more private or public character. The rooms were either separated by a load-bearing wall, located on different floors, or in different parts of a more complex configured plan. Built during the early 1920s, the houses continued domestic architectural traditions from before the Great War and even turn-of-the-century domestic architecture. The latter, in turn, had sought much of its inspiration in the bourgeois *Biedermeier* culture of the early nineteenth century. While Freud referenced this period, for example, with the segmental arches of the façade of the Schimek house, none of his designs show signs of an interest in the architectural Expressionism that had excited many architects in Berlin at the time the three homes were built.

Relationships with Clients

To start a career with three houses, even if conventional ones, was not a small success. That at least was Neutra's thought, who jotted down in his diary that Freud and his wife were 'full of happy expectations and in a wealthy household. He has two houses for three families under construction and is doing things cleverly.'[11] This remark expresses less a feeling of jealousy but more an anxiety that he might never experience a comparable success. Neutra wrote this in July 1921, after his move to Berlin in October 1920 when Freud had arranged for him to work in the office of Pinner & Neumann. While this job never came to fruition, Neutra eventually found employment as a municipal architect in the small town of Luckenwalde near Berlin in spring 1921. By October 1921, Neutra had already left this position to begin to work in Berlin with Mendelsohn.[12]

Freud shared some of his commissions with Neutra, who had designed gardens for the houses his friends had conceived or altered. At least three projects are documented: the Henneberg garden (1921),[13] the Maretzki garden, and a garden at the country estate of the Brasch family. The Henneberg house was a remodelling by Freud of an existing two-storey villa in Dahlem. Neutra reported that his garden had received the greatest appreciation.[14] The Maretzki garden was more difficult.[15] A point of contention was Eva Maretzki's preference for roses that could be cut for decorative uses over the sturdy *Erika*, a heather-type plant.[16] This was less an argument between plant lovers, but more over the issue of a useful garden versus a decorative one. Ultimately, the garden, as it is remembered today, was primarily the former with fruits and vegetables, but also with a decorative lawn and perennials.[17]

The most challenging commission was the garden for the Brasch family at their country estate in Großgaglow near Cottbus. There Neutra had to overcome the resistance of the manager of the agricultural estate who was paid by receiving a share of the profits. Neutra told in a letter how he patiently listened to Mrs. Brasch and two of her daughters while he dispensed advice ranging from the caretaking of small babies to that of Swiss and Dutch cows. At the end of a day-long visit, Neutra had mastered the domestic arrangements of the estate and the clients, but was also tired of arguing. Recalling his military experience, he eventually simply issued firm instructions to the village gardener to lay out a new feeding ground for one hundred chickens and to replant two pine trees closer to the house.[18] The ironic tone of his letter mocked both the clients and his work for them. Neutra made fun of the contradictions between his struggle for a living and the secure circumstances of the clients. He commented, for example, that the Brasch family was pleasant to deal with, especially as they were of established wealth.[19] At the same time, Neutra poked fun at the non-architectural aspects of his work, such as tending alike for babies and managers, chicken and cows, thus realizing that extended care for a client—including matters that were only slightly or not at all related to architecture—was part of the chosen profession. At stake was the relationship between architect and client.[20]

Freud went through similar experiences when he designed the interior of a new home for Max and Mirra Eitingon. In early 1921, the Eitingons began to communicate with Freud about a move into a new apartment in Rauchstraße 4, Berlin-Tiergarten, just ten minutes away from Ernst L. Freud's own home.[21] For example, Mirra Eitingon corresponded with Freud about the allocation of rooms.[22] She gently rebuked Freud when writing that she had been 'capable of understanding well the plan for the "expert".'[23]

Closer to the move-in date at the end of April her tone changed, and now she exclaimed: 'Ernst, dear good Ernst, I need you, I need you very much, urgently etc.'[24] She insisted on Freud making time to discuss with her various tasks that needed to be accomplished before both the move-in date and her departure for a spa about ten days later.

Max Eitingon expressed similar stressful feelings but in a more philosophically resigned language: 'I now learn quite forcefully what takes about as much time as the analyses of a solid structure of a neurosis, *viz.* the synthesis of a good home.'[25] If a psychoanalyst would eventually help a client master a neurosis, by analogy, an architect could help a client to surmount whatever anxieties a new home or house would cause. Freud apparently fulfilled this and other expectations with his timely and skilful refurbishment of the lower floor of the two-storey, townhouse-style apartment. Pleased with the results Eitingon wrote to Sigmund Freud: 'We only have him to thank for the cosiness that we have by now in our promising home.'[26] Much later in his career, when he was in exile in the United Kingdom, Freud returned to this relationship between architect and clients. In his only known written statements about modern architecture, Freud declared modern clients to be on par with modern architects when it comes to the successful creation of modern homes.[27]

The First Modern House

Apparently, Freud found such clients when he worked on a detached house for the psychoanalyst couple Hans Lampl (1889–1958) and Jeanne (i.e. Adriana) Lampl-de Groot (1895–1987). Lampl was from Vienna and had been a childhood friend of Freud's eldest brother Martin. De Groot had been in analysis with Sigmund Freud until she moved to Berlin in 1925 to take up work in the psychoanalytical clinic for which Eitingon had enrolled Freud as the interior designer in 1920. The couple married in 1925 and in the same year they commissioned their house in Dahlem (fig. 5.2).

The Lampl house was Freud's first design that was acknowledged as modern when it was included in Elisabeth M. Hajos and Leopold Zahn's *Berliner Architektur der Nachkriegszeit,* one of the earliest surveys of modern post-war architecture in Berlin.[28] Freud worked on this project at a time when modernist domestic architecture just began to appear in and around Berlin. Mies van der Rohe had published in 1923 his famous designs for a country house made from concrete, and his design for a brick country house followed in 1924. In 1923, a small suburban estate of several detached houses, which Neutra had designed the preceding year for the Mendelsohn office, had been completed in Berlin-Zehlendorf.[29] These houses were of cubic volumes, with flat roofs, stucco facades with brick dressing around some windows, while other openings stretched around corners giving the impression of ribbon windows, and cantilevered balconies and horizontal slabs shading the facades below (fig. 5.3). These houses further developed the modern architectural language that Mendelsohn had used for the semi-detached villas at Karolingerplatz in Berlin (1921–22) and again at the Dr. Sternefeld house in Berlin's Westend (1923–24). Other architects like, for example, the Luckhardt brothers also began to deploy a more modern, almost modernist style in their terraced townhouses in Berlin Zehlendorf's Schorlemmer Allee (1925). Erwin Gutkind conceived a house for two clients in Berlin Staaken (1923–24) as rigid geometrical cubic masses of brick and stucco, and Mies

Figure 5.2. Garden façade of the Lampl house, Berlin, 1925–26. Photograph from *Die Pyramide*, July 1928, used with permission from the Collection Centre Canadien d'Architecture / Canadian Centre for Architecture, Montréal.

Houses in and around Berlin 75

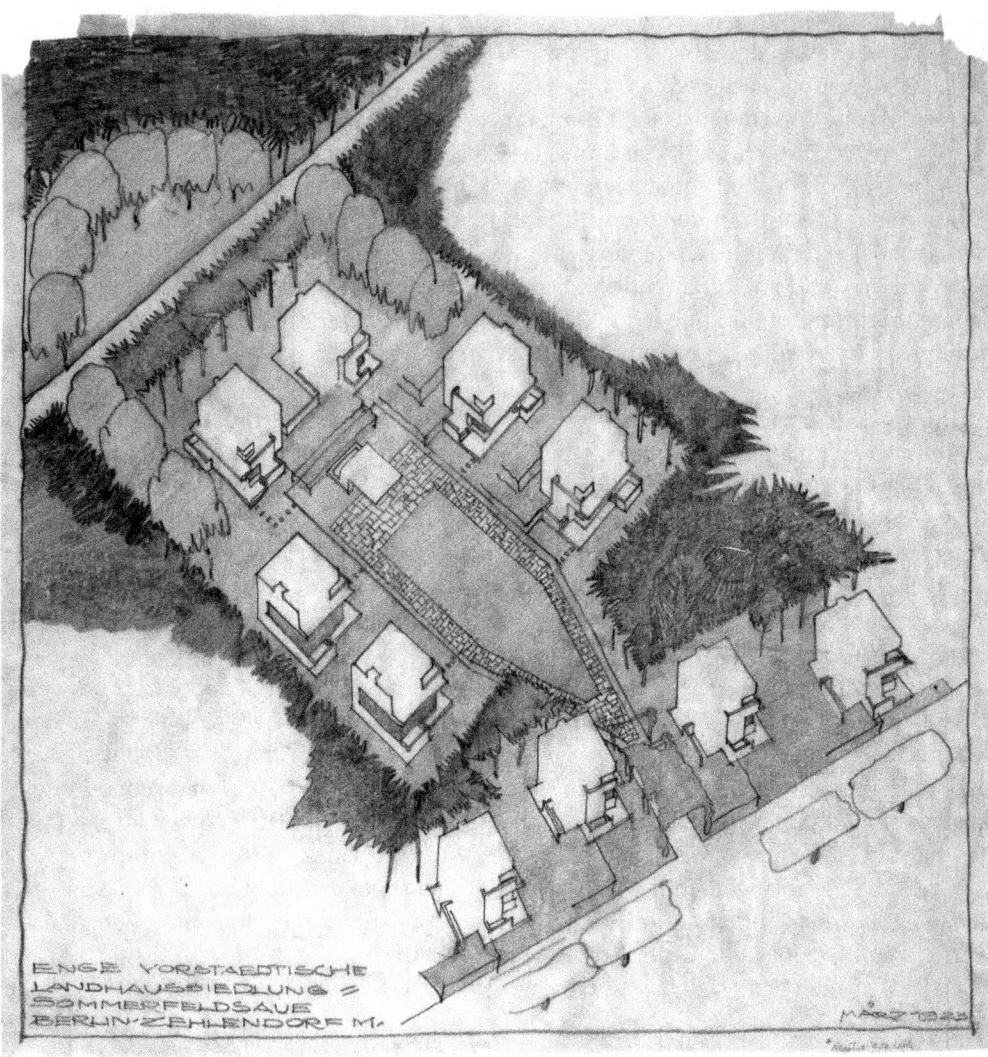

Figure 5.3. Sommerfeld housing scheme, Berlin-Zehlendorf, 1923, by Erich Mendelsohn and Richard Neutra. Used with permission of Dion Neutra, Architect © and Richard and Dion Neutra papers, Department of Special Collections, Charles E. Young Research Library, University of California at Los Angeles.

van der Rohe designed his Wolf country house in Guben (1925–26) as a composition of flat-roofed cubes.[30]

Accordingly, the overall cubic form and volume of the detached Lampl house indicate a modern building by the standards of the time. The building is two storeys high, though a sunken garage and cellar lift the main floors above ground level.[31] A flat roof is accessible from a low attic space built on top of half of the upper floor, making the northwest façade almost four storeys tall. The exterior is made of dark aubergine-coloured clinker brick: perhaps a reference to Lampl-de Groot's Dutch background, but in any case a popular contemporary building material. Alternating protruding layers of clinker brick around openings in the façade add a strong rhythm of shadow to the surface and recall similar detailing of houses designed by Mendelsohn and Neutra. The brick and the projecting courses may be considered as faint remnants of the architectural Expressionism that had been popular in Berlin until well into the 1920s, in the same way as this earlier modern style had still influenced some Mendelsohn houses from that period. However, Freud's Lampl house is better understood through its references to Loos and the latter's ideas about modern domestic architecture. The stepped silhouette, the tight vertically oriented cubic volume, and Freud's intention to contain all rooms within a clearly defined, almost square footprint, remind one strongly of such modern domestic designs by Loos like, for example, the unrealized Moissi house (1923) and, even more, the Rufer house (1922) in Vienna.[32]

The interior arrangements were more complex than in the three earlier houses. In addition to being a family home, the building accommodated a psychoanalytic practice (fig. 5.4). The consulting room, a waiting room, and the living and dining rooms and kitchen are all on the lower floor. In order to separate the private from the professional quarters, Freud installed a hall behind the main entrance. From there, five doors lead, clockwise, into the cloakroom, waiting room, consulting room cum study (fig. 5.5), living room, and, finally, to the stairs. Upstairs are the bedrooms for the parents and the children, a bathroom, and two chambers for maids.

One characteristic of the interior was built-in, floor-to-ceiling cupboards and wardrobes, for example, in the lady's bedroom (fig. 5.6). The length of the wall was divided into five glass doors framed in dark wood. Curtains behind the glasspanes hid the inside. Indirect lighting, wall-to-wall carpeting, and the occasional Oriental rug were other elements of Freud's interior that conveyed the impression of a tasteful and solid design. The house's modern exterior was combined with a conventional floor plan regarding types of rooms and their arrangements. This was not a lack of modernity, but such a split was not unusual for homes of that period; after all, the era of experimentation with open plans in German and European domestic architecture was still to come.

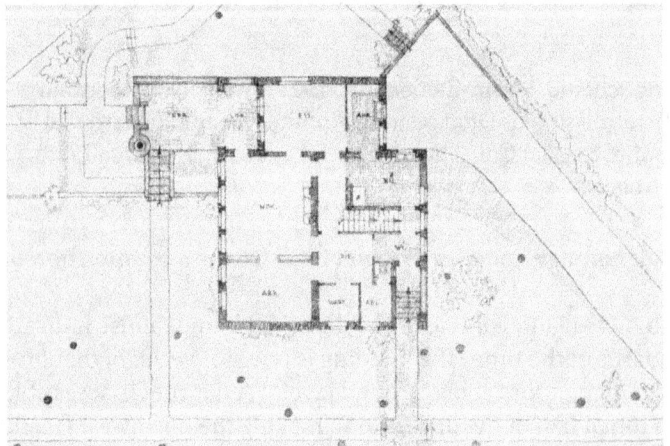
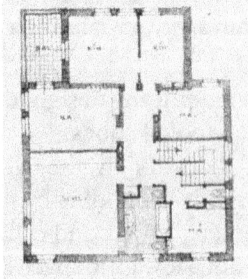

Figure 5.4. Lower- and upper-level plans of the Lampl house, Berlin, 1925–26. Photograph from H. Hoffmann. 1929. *Neue Villen*. Stuttgart: Julius Hoffmann, used with permission of the Collection Centre Canadien d'Architecture / Canadian Centre for Architecture, Montréal.

Figure 5.5. Desk and chair in the study in the Lampl house, Berlin, 1925–26. Photograph from *Die Pyramide*, July 1928, used with permission of the Collection Centre Canadien d'Architecture / Canadian Centre for Architecture, Montréal.

Figure 5.6. Built-in wardrobe, dressing table, and chair in a bedroom in the Lampl house, Berlin, 1925–26. Photograph from H. Hoffmann. 1929. *Neue Villen.* Stuttgart: Julius Hoffmann, used with permission of the Collection Centre Canadien d'Architecture / Canadian Centre for Architecture, Montréal.

The Frank Country House near Berlin

While the Lampl house was the first of Freud's domestic designs that received widespread publicity, the Frank country house was his greatest publicity success, especially later in England. Freud began to work on the project in 1928, the same year in which two seminal masterpieces of modern domestic architecture were conceived: the Tugendhat villa in Brno by Mies van der Rohe and Mendelsohn's own house, Am Rupenhorn, in Berlin's Westend. Freud's client, Dr. Theodor Frank (1871–1953; fig. 5.7), was a director of the Deutsche Bank, a position to which he had risen when in 1929 the Disconto-Gesellschaft, of which he had been an owner, was taken over. Dr. Frank and his wife, Margot Frank (1889–1942; fig. 5.8), wished their country house to be both a weekend retreat for their family and a representative home in which to entertain clients and business partners. To this end they purchased in Geltow, between Berlin and Potsdam, a site that was stunningly located on a cliff above Lake Schwielow (fig. 5.9); the Tugendhat villa and the Mendelsohn house also shared this setting on the high end of a steeply declining site.

Figure 5.7. Dr. Theodor Frank in front of his country house. Used with permission of Robert Gelber and Christopher Gelber.

Figure 5.8. Margot Frank (centre) among guests at a Deutsche Bank event in 1930. Used with permission of the Historisches Institut, Deutsche Bank AG.

Houses in and around Berlin   79

Figure 5.9. Lakeside terraces of the Frank country house, Geltow, 1928–30. Used with permission of the RIBA Library Photographs Collection.

The Frank country house was a departure for both the clients and the architect. For the Franks it was a move into modernity, especially when compared with their traditional city home in Lützowplatz, Berlin-Tiergarten.[33] There the family occupied a luxurious inner-city apartment with two living rooms, a dining hall, seven bedrooms, and three or four bathrooms, all arranged around a corridor of almost fifty yards.[34] Now they were to move into a purpose-built modern home. For Freud, this house was his largest domestic project thus far. Work started in 1928 and lasted well into 1930. It was also his most modern dwelling. He pushed the house extremely close to the edge of the land so that its southern façade enfronts the lake view yet is far enough away from the edge in order to provide space for a large terrace in front of the house (fig. 5.10). From there the building rises to a height of three storeys with each floor receding from the lower one, thus creating stepped terraces with metal tube railings. The northern entrance façade and the two smaller sides are compositions of interlocking cubes and rectangular solids (fig. 5.11). All facades are made from exposed, dark brown clinker brick. Freud's attempt to eliminate all corridor spaces is particularly remarkable. This succeeded only partially on the upper level, but created a neatly arranged, spacious ground floor plan (fig. 5.12).

80   Ernst L. Freud, Architect

Figure 5.10. Lakeside façade of the Frank country house, Geltow, 1928–30. Used with permission of the Collection Centre Canadien d'Architecture / Canadian Centre for Architecture, Montréal.

Figure 5.11. Entrance façade of the Frank country house, Geltow, 1928–30. Photograph from 1992, used with permission of Volker M. Welter.

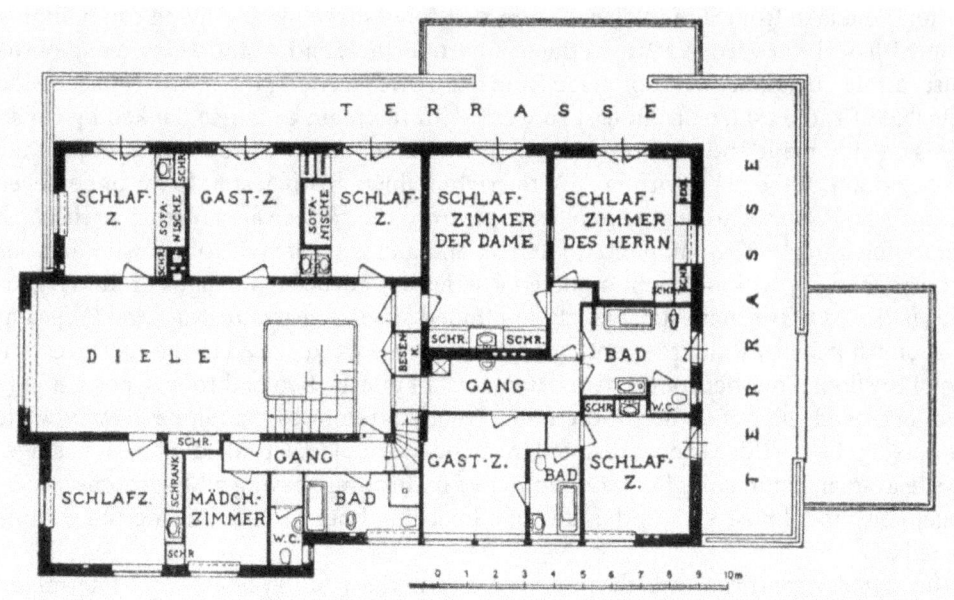

Figure 5.12. Lower- and upper-level plans of the Frank country house, Geltow, 1928–30. Photograph from G. A. Platz. 1933. *Wohnräume der Gegenwart.* Berlin: Propyläen, used with permission of the Collection Centre Canadien d'Architecture / Canadian Centre for Architecture, Montréal.

Along the lake front, Freud placed from east to west the library, living room, dining room with a winter garden towards the southern terrace, and, at the western end of the house, a small loggia with a roof made from glass bricks. Along the northern façade the sequence of rooms starts, from east to west, with the main entrance flanked by cloakrooms on either side and a central hall ahead with an open fireplace at the far end of the axis beginning at the main entrance. To the right follows an open stair to the upper level. This stair hall also separates the public rooms from the service area further to the west comprising a porter's room, pantry, kitchen, and a cluster of staff rooms with a goods entrance. The upper floor accommodated a series of bedrooms arranged around a generous hall, east of the main stair, which functioned as a living area on this level. Adjacent bedrooms for the lady and the gentleman of the house were placed in the southwestern area of the floor. Four bedrooms, two day rooms for guests, two bathrooms, and a maid's room occupied the remainder of the floor. Freud's attempt to guarantee privacy while minimising the corridor spaces resulted in an awkward plan. Crooked internal passageways lead to an astonishingly small number of bathrooms serving all bedrooms; an arrangement that almost evokes the idea of a boarding house squeezed into the volume of a villa.

The spatial organization and the interior design of this country house were determined by the two-fold need to create a relaxing environment for the 'weekend' as it was called in Weimar Germany using the then fashionable English term, and to offer a representative home for a manager of a leading bank. Because the clients did not give up their city home, Freud designed most built-in furniture and moveable furniture and advised the owners on what items to purchase. The double function of the home is perhaps best captured in the large-scale informal asymmetry of the overall plan, which Freud then filled in with small-scale symmetries, especially within individual rooms on the lower level. For example, two vertical terracotta reliefs glazed in Persian blue flank the door underneath a large canopy with integrated illumination. Possibly created by the sculptor Alfred Hüttenbach (1897–1960),[35] they depict idyllic scenes with animals and musicians thus hinting at the relaxed, but therefore not informal environment one was about to enter. A narrow passageway leads into the main hall. Halfway along, two steps interrupt this corridor, thereby forcing an entering visitor to pay attention to his steps and enter the house in an orderly manner. The main hall could also be entered from the cloakrooms at either side of the corridor. Accordingly, three symmetrically placed doors gave access to this central space. Similarly, at both sides of the brick fireplace on the opposite wall two doors were placed symmetrically—the left leading to the library, the right to the drawing room.

In front of the fireplace stood three comfort chairs, upholstered with cushions made from a light-coloured fabric with a bold print, around a circular table on which Hajos and Zahn's *Berliner Architektur der Nachkriegszeit* was placed (fig. 5.13). The construction of the house had only begun by the year of the book's publication, yet its use indicates the modern context in which Freud saw the largest domestic commission of his career. More comfort chairs and a sofa offered further seating in front of a panorama window at the eastern end of the hall (fig. 5.14). The furniture pieces were made from cherry wood stained to an ebony colour; the cubic wooden frames filled with cane that ensured a light rather than heavy impression. Black-green English rubber flooring and green upholstery and cushions contrasted with red curtains over light sheers. A ceiling grid of slender wooden slats intersected perpendicularly with stronger-dimensioned beams complemented the country house look. Yet a bowl to leave visiting cards was placed prominently

Figure 5.13. Lower-level hall of the Frank country house, Geltow, 1928–30. Used with permission of the RIBA Library Photographs Collection.

Figure 5.14. Panorama window in lower level hall of the Frank country house, Geltow, 1928–30. Photograph from G. A. Platz. 1933. *Wohnräume der Gegenwart*. Berlin: Propyläen, used with permission of the Collection Centre Canadien d'Architecture / Canadian Centre for Architecture, Montréal.

84 *Ernst L. Freud, Architect*

on the sofa table as a reminder that this hall was part of the ritual of calling formally on the inhabitants.

To the west, the hall merged with the open staircase to the upper floor (fig. 5.15). A strongly dimensioned bronze railing on a low wall separated the stairs from the hall without obstructing an oblique view into the upper part of the house. A light box on top of the dividing wall between the two flights of stairs provided a visual accent for the view from

Figure 5.15. Stair hall of the Frank country house, Geltow, 1928–30. Used with permission of the RIBA Library Photographs Collection.

the adjacent hall; this view axis was further emphasized by a niche for formal flower arrangements. The arrangement of the stair, its visual and spatial intersection of upper and lower floor and the flower niche, are somewhat reminiscent of the central hall in Adolf Loos's Müller house in Prague, likewise begun in 1928 (see chapter 3, fig. 3.3).

The door on the left of the fireplace opened into the library whose walls were covered by a wainscoting of near black Makassar ebony with lighter bands of brown to golden hues. The panels reached up to about two thirds of the walls; only around the windows did they touch the ceiling. Here, as elsewhere in the house, Freud used horizontally oriented sash windows, which were unusual in Germany but lend an elegant look.

The door to the right of the fireplace led to the drawing room with two symmetrically placed windows ahead, and two doors in either corner of the western wall. From the far corner the winter garden was accessible; from the near one the dining room. This door, together with a second one from the stair hall, gave Freud another opportunity for a small symmetrical arrangement within the dining room, as did two niches on either side of a window looking out to the western-most loggia. Towards the south the view went through a floor-to-ceiling window into the winter garden and from there through a six-winged foldable glass door towards the lake. The window could be lowered into the basement and the glass door could be folded away in order to give unobstructed access to the terrace and the view. Two tables with twelve chairs furnished the dining room; all pieces were made from Makassar ebony with lightly coloured stripped-silk upholstery that were matched by the pale-yellow colour of the plaster (fig. 5.16). The tables were either placed together for a larger formal dinner or set apart for two more intimate groups.

Figure 5.16. Dining room with lowered glass window to the winter garden, Frank country house, Geltow, 1928–30. Photograph from G. A. Platz. 1933. *Wohnräume der Gegenwart.* Berlin: Propyläen, used with permission of the Collection Centre Canadien d'Architecture / Canadian Centre for Architecture, Montréal.

This floor plan was a genuine achievement for Freud, as a brief comparison with the plans of the Tugendhat villa and the Mendelsohn house shows. Mies van der Rohe organized the villa with an open plan on the lower living floor (see chapter 1, fig. 1.6). Mendelsohn adopted a linear flow of spaces that started in the entrance hall with a dining room on the one side and a large living space to the other. The latter accommodated also a drawing room and music area with a piano (fig. 5.17). A third and more traditional possibility for arranging formal spaces to entertain a dinner party was, for example, Klein's enfilade of rooms in the townhouses in Berlin (see chapter 1, figs. 1.4 and 1.5).

Freud's plan offered a sequence of social spaces that could be deployed on appropriate occasions. This sequence began with the entrance hall, followed by either the library as the gentlemen's room or the drawing room as the ladies' room. From there, both groups could unite briefly in the drawing room before entering the dining room. After the dinner, the party could split with the ladies occupying the winter garden and the terrace, whereas the gentlemen could retire to the library as a smoking room before they would join the other half of the party on the terrace. This sequence Freud inscribed into an arrangement of the rooms that on first sight appears informal, for example when rooms were accessible through doors in a corner; the off-axis arrangements, however, were balanced by the symmetrical layout of individual spaces and elevations of walls within each room.

On the upper level, only the hall was regularly published (fig. 5.18). The space was more rustic than its counterpart below, an effect achieved by mixing bright colours like

Figure 5.17. Living room in Erich Mendelsohn's own house, Berlin, 1929–30. Photograph from G. A. Platz. 1933. *Wohnräume der Gegenwart.* Berlin: Propyläen, used with permission of the Collection Centre Canadien d'Architecture / Canadian Centre for Architecture, Montréal.

Figure 5.18. Upper-level hall, sofas designed by Ernst L. Freud, tubular steel chairs by Ludwig Mies van der Rohe and Lilly Reich, Frank country house, Geltow, 1928–30. Photograph from G. A. Platz. 1933. *Wohnräume der Gegenwart*. Berlin: Propyläen, used with permission of the Collection Centre Canadien d'Architecture / Canadian Centre for Architecture, Montréal.

grey-violet and yellow and bold patterns like broad tartans.[36] Freud underlined the relaxed impression by combining furniture of his own design with tubular steel furniture, for example MR 10 chairs which Mies van der Rohe and Lilly Reich (1885–1947) had designed for the Werkbund exhibition in Stuttgart in 1927. Metal chairs were also used in the more functional settings of the upper-level outdoor terraces and in the small guest rooms with their bunk-like beds in recessed niches which recall attempts by some modernist architects to replace bedrooms with mere sleeping cabins. Thus, the interior of the upper level shows that Freud was not only aware of the most recent developments in modernist interior design and architecture; but that he used modernist designs such as the metal chairs in order to differentiate the more private, and therefore more relaxed, upper-level rooms from the more formal rooms on the lower level.

In May 1933, Dr. Frank was forced to resign from his position as director of the bank; five years later he was forced to give up the last official position he held within the bank. The family fled initially to Brussels and later emigrated to the south of France. In 1942, Margot Frank was arrested under unknown circumstances. Some family sources state that she was kidnapped by the Gestapo in Nice while her husband was in the hospital, others that she was arrested in Cannes or that the couple had been captured on a trip to the north of France. What is certain is that after her initial imprisonment at Camp Drancy, Mrs. Frank was transported with convoy number 27 to Auschwitz on 2 September 1942. The convoy of about 1000 people reached the concentration camp on 4 September 1942; 113 people were selected for forced labour while the others, including Mrs. Frank, were sent to the gas chambers. Dr. Frank survived National Socialism and passed away in Zurich in 1953.[37]

More Houses in and near Berlin

The Frank country house was the climax of Freud's career in Berlin. Never again would he build such a large and lavishly equipped private home, but his next project—the conversion of a recently built detached private house in Berlin-Westend—continued his engagement with modern houses. The Buchthal house was just a few plots away from the Schimek house. Originally, the building was designed in 1922–23 by the brothers Hans (1890–1954) and Wassili (1899–1972) Luckhardt together with Hans Hoffmann (1884–1952; fig. 5.19). The client was the businessman Eugen Buchthal (1878–1954), father of the art historian Hugo Buchthal (1909–96). It was one of the few buildings that was built in the Expressionist architectural style when it had flourished in the aftermath of the Great War. The house even included an Expressionist garden full of sharp-angled and star-shaped flowerbeds designed by garden architect Eryk Pepinski (born 1886). Located at an intersection, the building was L-shaped with wings of equal length. The corner was occupied on the inside by a music salon with a large window in front of which stood an

Figure 5.19. Buchthal house, Berlin, 1922–23, by Hans and Wassili Luckhardt with Franz Hoffmann. Used with permission of the Akademie der Künste Berlin, Hans-und Wassili-Luckhardt und Alfons-Anker Archiv: WV29.

Expressionist fountain underneath a zigzag gable. The entrance was squeezed to one side of this monumental corner on Halmstraße.

Apparently, Buchthal grew quickly tired of Berliners on Sunday outings poking their sharp-witted fun at his residence. Responsive to his client's needs, Freud stripped the entire house, inside and out, of all traces of architectural Expressionism, flattened the sculptural qualities of the street facades by making the second storey fully visible above the corner and roughly along half of each side wing, and aligned the entrance with the axis of the street crossing in a traditional manner. At the rear of the building he added a covered patio from which a terrace paved with irregular cut natural stone extended into the garden (fig. 5.20). Freud did not turn the Buchthal house into a document of *Neue Sachlichkeit*;[38] instead he ensured that an exceptionally visible house was turned into an inconspicuous piece of domestic architecture.

Almost ironically, Freud's next client, the perfume manufacturer Ludwig Scherk, was a patron of both avant-garde and younger architects. For example, in 1926–27 Scherk commissioned from the Expressionist architect Fritz Höger (1877–1949) new premises for his business in Berlin-Steglitz. In 1927, Salvisberg redesigned a Scherk shop on Berlin's Kurfürstendamm. For his private residence, Scherk turned to Freud who conceived a two-storey building with the familiar division into public rooms on the lower floor and private rooms upstairs (fig. 5.21). A central load-bearing wall further divided each floor into two bands of rooms. The lower floor accommodated in the first band an entrance

Figure 5.20. Buchthal house after the refurbishment by Ernst L. Freud. Used with permission of the RIBA Library Photographs Collection.

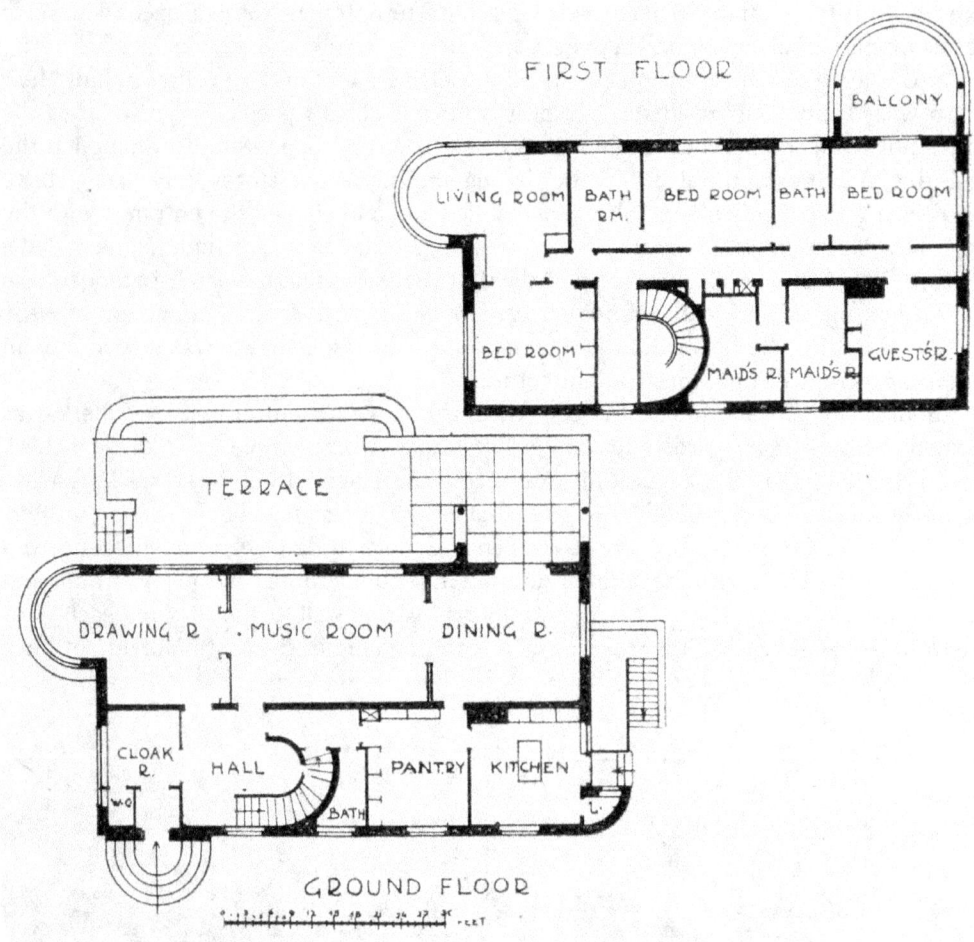

Figure 5.21. Lower- and upper-level plans of the Scherk house, Berlin, 1930–31. Photograph from *Homes and Gardens,* April 1934, used with permission of the National Library of Scotland, Edinburgh.

hall with curved stairs towards the upper level, followed by workspaces for the domestic servants and the kitchen. Opposite the entrance hall was the drawing room leading to a central music room and a dining room opposite the kitchen. The dining room extended onto a terrace with a half-circular balcony above. Upstairs were bedrooms for the owner of the house, guests, and the maid. The half-circular bay window, which extended below the drawing room, belonged upstairs to an intimate living room. The exterior of the house is dominated by the curves of the bay windows, balconies, and an entrance canopy—features perhaps inspired by Mendelsohn's architecture but lacking its elegance. A strongly profiled window surrounds on the ground floor and broad stucco bands of a dark shade, holding together the upper-floor windows, lend a generally heavy-handed appearance to the exterior.

The completion of Freud's last project in Germany was overtaken by the rise to power of National Socialism that forced both the architect and his clients into exile. In 1932, Freud had begun to plan a country house for Carl Mosse and Gerda Mosse (née Brasch), a sister of Lucie Freud. Carl Mosse was a paediatrician who taught at the Charité and who stemmed from the Berlin Mosse publishing family. About a decade earlier, Mendelsohn and Neutra had redesigned the editorial offices of the daily *Berliner Tageblatt* when they added several floors and a dramatically curved corner to the existing building. The Mosse house was located in Krampnitz to the southwest of Berlin. Work began with a small building that accommodated a garage and a chauffeur's apartment (fig. 5.22). Plans for the entire project have never been found, but if the chauffeur's house is representative of the main building, then Freud conceived the Mosse country house in a different architectural language than the Frank house. While the latter played off elements of modernism, especially with its cubic, flat-roofed exterior, the high-pitched roof of the small building in Krampnitz suggests that Freud envisioned this country house in a vernacular-inspired architectural language.

Only the small building was completed before works stopped in early 1933. Hitler had been sworn in as Reich Chancellor on 30 January 1933, an event that the National Socialists celebrated with a five-hour, torch-lit march through Berlin; an indication that this was not just another change of government. The violence against Social Democrats and Communists in the aftermath of the burning of the Reichstag building on 27 Febru-

Figure 5.22. Garage and chauffeur building of the never completed Mosse country house, Krampnitz, begun in 1932. Used with permission of the RIBA Library Photographs Collection.

ary 1933 conveyed a similar message. On paper, Germany remained a democracy for at least a little longer. National elections were held on 5 March 1933, but they gave the Nazi party only 43.9 per cent of the votes, though 'nearly two-thirds of the voters had lent their support to parties—the Nazis, the Nationalists, and the Communists—who were open enemies of Weimar democracy'.[39] Thus the final slide of Weimar Germany into a dictatorship had begun. While the initial Nazi violence was directed against the political enemies—especially the Social Democrats, trade unions, and the Communist party—Jewish citizens soon were targeted as well. On 1 April 1933, a nationwide public boycott of Jewish businesses was held. This was only the first of many acts of violence and increasing legal restrictions against the Jewish population of Germany.

For Carl and Gerda Mosse, 1 April 1933 brought home with tragic personal consequences the great dangers that they were to face in a National-Socialist Germany. On that Saturday, a brother of Carl Mosse undertook his routine weekly trip to Berlin from which he never returned. He was murdered while taking an after-lunch coffee on a terrace of a café on Kurfürstendamm. Subsequently, Carl Mosse immigrated to Shanghai, leaving behind his wife and their children, and thus breaking up his marriage and his family.[40] Gerda Mosse lived for a few more years in the chauffeur's building in Krampnitz, before her and her children managed to join Ernst L. and Lucie Freud in London.

The latter had not waited to see if developments were to calm down or even to be reversed. Like many Jews living in Germany, they had many reasons to stay, not least their new apartment at Matthäikirchstraße 4, a residential street lined with townhouses and villas from the early nineteenth century, which was even more elegant than nearby Regentenstraße where they had lived until c. 1932. Their decision to leave Berlin must have been taken within months of Hitler coming to power because from the end of June until late August 1933, Freud was in London in order to explore work possibilities, research schools for his three sons, and prepare for the family's exile. On 22 September, Lucie Freud and the three boys left Berlin by train. Freud remained to wind down his business,[41] sort out financial issues, and deal with the chicaneries of the state bureaucracy that had begun to make it harder, even though not yet impossible, to export personal possessions and financial resources. From 7 November onwards Freud supervised the dismantling of the interior of the new apartment for shipment to the United Kingdom. He expected to finally leave Berlin on 10 or 11 November but last-minute bureaucratic difficulties delayed his departure until after 13 November, the date of the last letter Freud sent from Berlin to his wife in London.[42] The couple never returned to Berlin. Later, his career in Weimar Germany would occasionally weigh on his mind. In February 1945 he wrote to his cousin Harry Freud (1909–69) in Canada, who as a soldier of the Army was about to be deployed in Germany: 'Should you be allowed to enter the area, please find out what has happened to my house at Lake Schwielow. If it is still standing, surely an important animal lives there.'[43] Unfortunately, it is not known whether Harry Freud was ever able to see the house.

Notes

1. This figure (as well as all following ones) comprises only projects that have been identified. Unidentified projects have not been counted.
2. See the entry for Anna Freud 1931 in the 'Selected List of Works'.

3. Letter from Richard Neutra to Dione Neutra, 26 November 1921 (Box 36, Folder 5, Richard J. Neutra collection, Archives-Special Collection, College of Environmental Design, Cal Poly Pomona).
4. Table 'Bautätigkeit in deutschen Städten von über 100 000 Einwohnern ...', Statistisches Reichsamt (ed.). 1924/25–929. *Statistisches Jahrbuch für das Deutsche Reich* 44 (1924/25)–49 (1929).
5. Single family dwellings in Berlin constituted 78.75 per cent of all new buildings for dwellings in 1923, 62.70 per cent in 1924, 58.80 per cent in 1925, 54.50 per cent in 1926, 47.30 per cent in 1927, 32.60 per cent in 1928, and 27.80 per cent in 1929, the last year this building type was listed as a separate category (Statistisches Reichsamt (ed.). 1924/25–1929. *Statistisches Jahrbuch für das Deutsche Reich* 44 (1924/25)–49 (1929)).
6. Not all of these commissions went to architects nor do the figures tell us anything about the projects' size and locations within Berlin.
7. Ilka (1894–1968) and Paul Schimek fled Germany and lived in San Francisco, California (Claims Tribunal Conference, http://www.crt-ii.org/_awards/_apdfs/Schimek_Ilka.pdf, accessed 24 March 2004).
8. Email from Thomas Maretzki to author, 6 June 2004.
9. Dietrich Worbs. 1997. 'Ernst Ludwig Freud in Berlin', *Bauwelt* 88 (issue 42): 2398–2403, (2399).
10. Building file Halmstraße 10/11a, Charlottenburg, Berlin, Landesarchiv Berlin, Rep 207, Acc 2372.
11. Diary entry for 18 July 1921 (R. J. Neutra, diary, vol 9, 1920–22, box 335, Richard and Dion Neutra Papers, Department of Special Collections, Charles E. Young Research Library, University of California at Los Angeles). Most likely, the houses will have been the Maretzki house and the Levy/Hofer house.
12. T. S. Hines. 1982. *Richard Neutra and the Search for Modern Architecture: A Biography and History.* New York: Oxford University Press, 30–37. It is not known if Pinner & Neumann were related to Dr. Pinner, Detmolder Straße 3, Berlin, at whose address Ernst Freud received correspondence between December 1919 and May 1920.
13. Letter from Richard Neutra to Dione Neutra, 26 November 1921 (Box 36, Folder 5, Richard J Neutra collection, Archives-Special Collection, College of Environmental Design, Cal Poly Pomona). The letter speaks to two commissions for garden designs; the second may have been the Maretzki garden.
14. Letter from Richard Neutra to anonymous recipient, not dated (Box 36, Folder 11, Richard J Neutra collection, Archives-Special Collection, College of Environmental Design, Cal Poly Pomona).
15. In contractual negotiations with Erich Mendelsohn Neutra was represented by Ernst Maretzki who had met Louise Mendelsohn via the Mosse family; see letter from Erich Mendelsohn to Louise Mendelsohn, 11 August 1922 (Erich and Louise Mendelsohn Papers, Series 1, Box 1, Letters Erich Mendelsohn to Louise Mendelsohn 1910-1928, Special Collections, Getty Research Institute)
16. Letter from Richard Neutra to anonymous recipient, not dated (Box 36, Folder 11, Richard J Neutra collection, Archives-Special Collection, College of Environmental Design, Cal Poly Pomona).
17. Email from Thomas Maretzki to author, 6 June 2004.
18. Letter from Richard Neutra to anonymous recipient, not dated (Box 36, Folder 11, Richard J Neutra collection, Archives-Special Collection, College of Environmental Design, Cal Poly Pomona).
19. Letter from Richard Neutra to anonymous recipient, not dated (Box 36, Folder 11, Richard J Neutra collection, Archives-Special Collection, College of Environmental Design, Cal Poly Pomona).

20. For Neutra's handling of this issue once he was in the US, see S. Lavin. 2004. *Form Follows Libido: Architecture and Richard Neutra in a Psychoanalytic Culture*. Cambridge, MA: MIT Press, 47–52.
21. Letter from Max Eitingon to Sigmund Freud, 17 April 1921 (M. Schröter [ed.]. 2004. *Sigmund Freud Max Eitingon, Briefwechsel 1906–1939*, 2 vols. Tübingen: Edition Diskord, vol. 1, letter 207E, 249–250).
22. Letters from Mirra Eitingon to Ernst L. Freud, 12 and 23 January 1921 (Freud Museum London, box Lux [i.e. Lucie Brasch] papers, A–K).
23. Letters from Mirra Eitingon to Ernst L. Freud, 12 January 1921, (Freud Museum London, box Lux papers, A–K, my translation).
24. Letter from Mirra Eitingon to Ernst Freud, 7 April 1921 (Dr. Michael Schröter, Berlin, my translation).
25. Letter from Max Eitingon to Sigmund Freud, 7 June 1921 (Schröter, *Sigmund Freud Max Eitingon, Briefwechsel 1906–1939*, vol. 1, letter 211E, 255–256 (255)).
26. Letter from Max Eitingon to Sigmund Freud, 9 August 1921 (Schröter, *Sigmund Freud Max Eitingon, Briefwechsel 1906–1939*, vol. 1, letter 213E, 257–258).
27. Ernst L. Freud. 1934. 'A Foreign Architects observes England', *Design for To-day* 2 (October): 394–395
28. E. M. Hajos and L. Zahn. 1928. *Berliner Architektur der Nachkriegszeit*. Berlin: Albertus, 45, 113.
29. Hines, *Neutra*, 34–36.
30. W. Müller-Wulckow. 1928. *Wohnbauten und Siedlungen*. Königstein i. Taunus: Karl Robert Langewiesche, 61, 53, 59, 60, 47.
31. H. Hoffmann. 1929. *Neue Villen*. Stuttgart: Julius Hoffmann, 100–101.
32. M. Risselada. 1991. 'Documentation of 16 houses', in M. Risselada (ed.). 1991. *Raumplan versus Plan Libre. Adolf Loos and le Corbusier, 1919–1930*. Delft: Delft University Press, 78–134 (83–85).
33. The address was either Lützowplatz number 7 or 13, depending on the source (the former, for example, G. Wenzel (ed.). 1929. *Deutsche Wirtschaftsführer: Lebensgänge deutscher Wirtschaftspersönlichkeiten Ein Nachschlagewerk über 13000 Wirtschaftspersönlichkeiten unserer Zeit*. Hamburg: Hanseatische Verlagsanstalt, 642; the latter in 1994. *Jüdische Adressbuch für Gross-Berlin: Ausgabe 1931*. Berlin: Arani, 101). In 1935 Dr. Frank was living at Wielandstraße 25–26, Berlin-Charlottenburg (H. A. L. Degener [ed]. 1935. *Degeners Wer ist's?*, 10th ed. Berlin: Herrmann Degener, 431).
34. Autobiography of Ruth Gelber, a daughter of Theodor and Margot Frank, cited in an email from Robert Gelber, Santa Barbara, CA, to the author, 29 October 2005.
35. G. Bönnen. 2007. *Wormers jüdische Künstler, Kunstleben und Kunstförderung um 1900–1933—Berta Strauß und Alfred Hüttenbach*. Worms: Worms-Verlag.
36. G. A. Platz. 1933. *Wohnräume der Gegenwart*. Berlin: Propyläen, 74–75, 237, 252, 352. A later, British publication listed the ceiling and wall as painted light grey, the floor as dark-blue linoleum, the doors Oregon pine with the panels covered in bright blue linoleum ('Country House on a Lake near Berlin. Designed by Ernst L. Freud', *Architects' Journal* 79 [21 June 1934]: 892–893 [893]).
37. Letter from International Tracing Service to the author, Bad Arolsen, Germany, 7 January 2008. S. Klarsfeld. N.d. *Le Memorial de la Deportation des Juifs de France*. Paris: Centre de Documentation Juive Contemporaine de Paris, entry convoy number 27; Yad Vashem, *The Central Database of Shoa Victims' Names*, entry Margot Frank, née Kaufmann, submitted by her daughter Ruth Gelber, 28 February 1980, www.yadvashem.org, accessed 3 November, 2005. Email and letter correspondences and personal conversations with Robert Gelber and

Christopher Gelber, California, 2003–8. Email correspondence with Reinhold Frost, Historisches Institut, Deutsche Bank, September 2005.
38. J. Lowden. 2000. 'Hugo Herbert Buchthal 1909–1996', *1999 Lectures and Memoirs Proceedings of the British Academy* 105: 308–336 (312).
39. R. J. Evans. 2005. *The Coming of the Third Reich*. London: Penguin, 340.
40. A. Stevens. 1975. *The Dispossessed*. London: Barrie & Jenkins, 36–40; conversation with Carola Zentner, London, 12 July 2002.
41. In July 1934, when Freud already lived in England, he stamped a letter with 'Ernst Freud Dipl. Ing. Architekt Berlin W. 9 Potsdamerstr. 129/130'. This Berlin address may suggest that the office was not dissolved but run by an unknown colleague on behalf of Freud. I have not been able to solve this riddle (letter from Ernst L. Freud to Frau Dr. Harald Wolf, Leipzig, 19 July 1934 [Collection Florian Hülsen]).
42. Letters from Ernst L. Freud, Berlin, to Lucie Freud, London, 26 June, 17 August, 22 September, 7 November, 8 November, and 13 November 1933 (Collection Esther Freud, London). Ernst L. Freud and the three sons were naturalized on 4 September 1939 (Certificate of Naturalization, collection Stephen Freud, London).
43. Letter from Ernst Freud to Harry Freud (9 February 1945, folder Ernst Freud / Lucie Freud 1938–49, box 5, Harry Freud papers, Manuscript Division, Library of Congress, Washington DC).

Chapter 6

Couches, Consulting Rooms, and Clinics

On 14 February 1920, the world's first 'Policlinic for the Psychoanalytic Treatment of Nervous Diseases' opened at Potsdamer Straße 29 (today no. 74) in Berlin. Located just to the south of the Landwehrkanal, the policlinic was slightly inconvenient for visitors, who had to make their way up to the fourth floor. Regardless, Eitingon and Karl Abraham were satisfied with the premises. Both men spoke highly of Freud's interior design for the institution, which was, incidentally, within walking distance of Freud's apartment at Regentenstraße 11 on the other side of the canal. Eitingon had financed the enterprise and as part of his support for Freud, the latter was asked to refurbish the interior. While the work was underway, Eitingon commented that Freud has helped 'us very thoroughly with the furnishing of the policlinic, he designed for us the furniture, found good craftsmen, and supervises all the work'.[1] After the opening, Abraham wrote that 'Ernst … has won lasting recognition for himself in his designing of the policlinic, which is admired by everyone'.[2] A contemporary source describes the clinic as comprising 'four rooms … located on the fourth floor of an unassuming apartment house near the center of Berlin' with each room 'furnished only with a simple cane couch, a chair and table'.[3] Photographs seem not to have survived, if they were ever taken, nor do we have any information about the colour scheme.[4]

Together with his older sister Mathilde (1887–1978) and her husband Robert Hollitscher Freud attended the opening. The program of speeches, recitations, and music mixed bourgeois taste in classical music with a nod towards Viennese avant-garde compositions. After an opening speech by Abraham, the psychoanalyst Ernst Simmel (1882–1947) recited Rilke and the singer Therese Bardas performed Schubert songs accompanied by her husband, the pianist Willi Bardas (1887–1924).[5] The singer Gronsky-Heidenreich presented songs by Gottfried Keller set by Arnold Schönberg (1874–1951), Eduard Mörike set by Hugo Wolff (1860–1903), and from Christian Morgenstern's *Palmström* poems. The evening ended with Simmel reading from the 'catastrophic stories' by Oskar H. Schmitz and Abraham reflecting about the 'rise of the policlinic from the unconscious'.[6] Comparable to his father, Freud was not known as a connoisseur of music, but he will have enjoyed the Rilke readings. In any case, the opening of the policlinic with Freud's interior design marked the beginning of his architectural career in Berlin. It was also the first of a small series of psychoanalytic spaces that Freud was asked to design in Berlin and London, though most of them have rarely been discussed in both the history of architecture and of psychoanalysis.

Historiography of Psychoanalytic Consulting Rooms

Concurrent with contemporary psychoanalytic practice, Freud conceived two types of consulting rooms. One was individual consulting rooms, usually attached to or located within a psychoanalyst's private home. This setup followed the tradition of psychoanalytic practice as established by Sigmund Freud. The other kind was consulting rooms in the new professional setting of psychoanalytic clinics where they could be used by several psychoanalysts.

Six designs by Freud for individual consulting rooms and four clinic settings in Berlin and London are currently known to us. None of the rooms from the first group can be reconstructed in its entirety from images and drawings; photographs either do not exist or have not survived. Freud's drawings of settings of consultation couches are mostly so little inscribed that they cannot be clearly identified. The lack of sources is one possible cause for the near total anonymity of this part of Freud's œuvre, but the integration of these rooms into the sphere of private homes provides another explanation that harks back to contemporary psychoanalytic practice.

The photographer and historian of psychoanalysis Claudia Guderian calls the secrecy that surrounded many consulting rooms 'one of the biggest taboos of psychoanalysis' when she set out to photograph these rooms in connection with her recent study of the couch and its settings.[7] A comparable attitude seems to have existed in the early history of psychoanalysis, when photographs of Sigmund Freud's consulting room were only taken when the room was about to be lost in 1938. Similarly, a picture of Melanie Klein's London consulting room, published in 1935 and identified for the first time here, was cropped to avoid showing the couch. Assuming the privacy of the consulting room was already a professional attitude among psychoanalysts during the 1920s and 1930s, today's dearth of archival material would be a consequence of the increasing professionalisation of a then still-young field. This last point also sheds light on the neglect of Ernst Freud's psychoanalytic spaces by architectural history, which is ironic considering that modern architectural history and theory have so often drawn on psychoanalytic ideas for their own historical analyses.

The physical location of Sigmund Freud's consulting room between the family apartment and the study ensured that the room has often been approached as an extension of a bourgeois home, rather than a strictly professional workplace. The many homely aspects of the interior of the consulting room and the study reinforced the perception of the rooms as belonging to the domestic sphere. Accordingly, architectural historical analysis of Sigmund Freud's workspaces is often embedded in larger interests such as, for example, developing notions of domesticity in nineteenth-century bourgeois culture, the interrelationships between interiority and the bourgeois self, or ideas of an architectural uncanny.[8]

This focus on the bourgeois individual and its domestic environment corresponds to the much earlier concern with the human body and architectural space that characterised early psychology.[9] For example, Robert Vischer's concept of empathy, developed in the 1870s, theorized the sense perception of space and artistic forms, and Heinrich Wölfflin's *Prolegomena to a Psychology of Architecture* (1886) argued for a psychological approach to architectural spaces and details. Both approaches are based on parallels between the body and architecture as exemplified in latter two's efforts to withstand gravity. Dream analysis, for example in Karl Albert Scherner's *Das Leben des Traums* (1861), had pointed to a potential congruence between architectural spaces and the inner spaces of the human mind as another analogy well before Sigmund Freud's *Die Traumdeutung* (1899). The interiorities of the mind and the home characterize also Walter Benjamin's reflections on the late nineteenth-century bourgeois life in which impressions in the physical surfaces of furnishings and objects in the home are understood as traces of human intentions and feelings.

While, thus, individual psychoanalytic consulting rooms became part of the realm of the private home, a similar privacy issue did not exist with regards to consulting rooms in clinical settings, the second type of rooms Freud designed. Existing photographs of consulting rooms show spaces of the Berlin policlinic and the private psychoanalytic Sanatorium Schloß Tegel. Included in contemporary promotional brochures, they are probably the earliest photographs of psychoanalytical consulting rooms that were ever published. Apparently, the privacy of consulting rooms in a clinical setting was considered differently from the other type of room. Clinical consulting rooms were not, in general, associated with single psychoanalysts; thus the treatment room with couch and chair began to develop into the symbol of properly conducted treatment. Professionalization in this case resulted in much more visible consulting rooms, which was also important for the potential economic success. For example, the Tegel sanatorium relied on patients who paid for treatment, which it hoped to attract with an illustrated brochure showing images of Freud's interior designs.

Accordingly, some consulting rooms have always been publicly visible, and issues of privacy surrounding the couch do not fully explain psychoanalysis's long neglect of architectural designs of consulting rooms. Instead, this seems to have been grounded in the allegedly passive placement of the patients on the couch and the methodological focus on the inner spaces of the mind. Both points made it easy to consider the couch and the chair as the location of the psychoanalytic process which apparently happened independently from any other spatial environment.

Harold Stern's study of the couch was among the first to ask after the significance of the couch, but architecturally his questioning rarely ventured beyond that furniture.[10] A more recent study argues for a link between Freudian psychoanalysis and so-called 'social justice' movements in early twentieth-century Vienna and Berlin. It also describes some of Freud's clinical consulting rooms. Yet it is more an attempt to tie, via Freud's architecture, psychoanalysis to the radical avant-garde modernism of, for example, the Bauhaus than to discuss possible implications of Freud's designs for psychoanalysis.[11] Guderian's publication addresses the spatial context of the couch in psychoanalysis in history and present. She develops a model of interlocking psychoanalytical spaces influencing the analytic process with the couch at the centre and approaches to buildings housing the consulting rooms at the periphery. But Ernst Freud's psychoanalytical spaces do not feature in her study.

The Primeval Consulting Room at Berggasse 19

When in the later 1900s Sigmund Freud moved his practice back from the ground floor of Berggasse 19 to the first-level apartment number 6 adjacent to the family home in number 5, the consulting room was installed towards the rear of the building where it overlooked the courtyard. To the one side of the new consulting room, in the main building, was the waiting room and to the other side, in a side wing, was Freud's private study. Photographs and descriptions of the consulting room as it had existed on the ground floor from 1896 onwards, or even of the earlier practice rooms when they were still integrated within apartment number 5, seem not to exist. The interior of the new consulting room is preserved thanks to the photographs by Edmund Engelman (1907–2000).[12] These were taken when Freud and the majority of his large family were forced into exile to London in the aftermath of the German occupation of Vienna in 1938.

Throughout his career, Freud practiced in many different consulting rooms. Beside those at Berggasse 19 and his study cum consulting room in the English exile, he possibly used up to thirty temporary rooms, for example, when he was on holidays.[13] Yet, it is the Vienna room, used for almost thirty years, that constitutes the primeval consulting room. It is centred on the couch that stood alongside the wall opposite the only window. Sigmund Freud owned this couch since 1890 or 1891 when it was given to him by a patient.[14] It moved with the family into Berggasse 19 when the young Freud couple settled there in September 1891.[15] Covered with an oriental rug and a second rug hung behind it at the wall, the couch is asymmetrically upholstered with a cylinder-shaped bolster on one side (fig. 6.1). A wedge-shaped and moveable second bolster stuffed underneath the rug further heightens the head end. On top of this already high headrest additional cushions are placed to offer adjustable support. Behind the head end of the couch stands Freud's chair. It is cubic overall, covered in green velvet with armrests and a backrest of level height,

Figure 6.1 Sigmund Freud's consulting room, Vienna. Used with permission of Sigmund Freud Museum, Vienna © Edmund Engelman.

with the wall behind the low chair offering an improvised headrest.[16] A square footstool, whose lower horizontal braces show signs of its use as footrest, is placed in front of the chair. This arrangement existed since 1934 when increasing hearing difficulties forced Freud 'to re-verse the position of his couch and chair to hear his patients' with his left ear.[17]

The couch and the chair are the core elements of the spatial setting of psychoanalysis. In his own writings, Freud referred only occasionally to the spatial arrangements of consulting rooms, most notably in his 1913 paper 'On Beginning the Treatment'.[18] There Freud identified his earlier practice of medical hypnosis as the origin of the patient's horizontal position. In addition, the analyst's position behind the couch, and thus invisible to the patient, is described as a professional discretion that hides the potentially influential facial reactions of the psychoanalyst from the patient.

Significantly, Freud called the relationship between patient and psychoanalyst, respectively of couch and chair, 'a certain ceremonial of the situation in which the treatment is carried out'.[19] *Ceremonial* implies movement through and within space, however restrained either may be; accordingly, psychoanalysis is determined at least in parts by the interaction between two people within the spatial setting as circumscribed by the positioning of chair and couch to each other.[20] This recalls Plessner's discussion of social interactions in formalized spatial settings in order to safeguard the soul; the difference is that the practice of psychoanalysis is aimed at lifting the veil that Plessner had hoped would protect the soul.[21]

Freud's focus on the setting of couch and chair made psychoanalysis independent from the larger room that contained the smaller spatial setting. The latter is essential, precisely defined, and therefore transferable. Whereas for the former no specific arrangements were demanded, regardless of any influence the larger spaces may have had on the psychoanalytic process. For example, one temporary consulting room that Freud used in late 1929 was 'very plain, the floor bare save for a small rug'. Beside a desk near the window, only the couch and the chair were noted: 'To the right of the desk and against the wall was a comfortable couch with blankets on it and a shawl or soft woollen blanket folded on the head end. Behind the couch was a leather-covered chair with a straight back.'[22]

While thus the surrounding room was not of immediate concern for Freud as far as the psychoanalytic treatment was concerned, he was not oblivious to this space, especially in his home in Vienna. Comparable to the spatial setting of psychoanalysis, this larger space was also determined by the objects inside of it. The former was defined, first, by the couch and the chair at its centre and, second, by the ceremony unfolding around these objects; in short, the space was conceived from the objects outwards, to paraphrase the modernist architectural claim to plan from the inside out. Within the latter, the larger room, the objects that filled it over time had a similar effect.

Looking from the couch at the entire consulting room of Sigmund Freud, the surrounding walls are covered with framed artwork, etchings and drawings, fragments of antique paintings and reliefs, and photographs of colleagues. Moreover, display cases hold antique statues behind glass while others are placed in front of the leather and cloth spines of the books on the shelves. Descriptions of Freud's consulting room usually recall the objects that were in it: the couch, the chair, and the large number of artwork and antique statues. They define the space of the room which itself always remains on the edges of perception, comparable to the street space in Rilke's poem 'The Meeting in the

Chestnut Avenue' that was evoked solely by describing two approaching humans. Accordingly, the objects in Freud's consulting room and also his study can be considered as an assembly of Rilkean household gods stimulating new insights when pondered without, necessarily, expressing the owner's inner feelings. It remains doubtful if these objects had a similar effect on the patients, or that Freud had wished for them to have such an impact. One of his patients, for example, kept his eyes covered with a handkerchief while associating freely on the couch. Freud had to invite him explicitly to open his eyes to see a portrait bust during an analytical session in 1937; otherwise the diary of this analysis never refers to an object inside the Viennese consulting room.[23]

Next to the window, a two-winged double door opens into the consulting room from the waiting room.[24] A second such door along the wall perpendicular to the window gives access to Freud's study. At the opposite wall, a small exit door concealed by the same narrowly striped wallpaper that covered all the other walls leads back into a corridor from where the main entrance door into the apartment can be reached (see chapter 2, fig. 2.2). Spatially, this arrangement looks as awkward in plan as any description may read. The consulting room was essentially an anteroom to Freud's study. Functionally, the sequence of rooms enforced a circular movement that helped to avoid encounters between departing and arriving patients.[25]

Yet when the interiors of the consulting room and study and the circulatory pattern between them and the adjacent spaces are looked at through the eyes of an architect, the former will have appeared cluttered, the latter clumsy, and both in need of improvement. When Ernst L. Freud visited home in May 1923, Anna Freud complained about his attempts at rearranging Berggasse 19:

> In the short time he was here, he wanted to make all sorts of improvements in order to demonstrate to all of us what we should do in an improved manner. And because I did not want to follow at all, he found that I had lost my youth, had no courage and had become conservative, exactly as I should not be. But I believe that he is wrong. Because I live here I know that everything came about somehow over the course of time according to the essence of the humans around us, and I orient myself accordingly. I don't know if this is that bad.[26]

The remark about interiors of rooms maturing over time is best illustrated by Anna Freud's own consulting room at Berggasse 19 (fig. 6.2). Everything that is needed is inside the room—for example, a couch with her father's portrait on the wall above, a chair, a ceramic stove, a rug, side boards, and even a bookshelf designed by Augenfeld.[27] Yet while Sigmund Freud's room, even in images, radiates the personality of the occupant, Anna Freud's consulting room seems not to. For example, the furniture along the walls are isolated individual pieces rather than an ensemble with an atmosphere. The difference appears to be a consequence of a lack of time; not just of past time that was lost with the exile, but also of future time that was cut off by the enforced departure. Thus the close bond between an inhabitant of a home and his possessions to which, as discussed in chapter 3, Rilke referred to when he reflected on memory as it attached to objects—his household gods—never developed in the case of Anna Freud's consulting room in Vienna. While Freud was not allowed to change his father's and his sister's consulting rooms, he designed many such rooms—including the couches—in Berlin and London.

Figure 6.2. Anna Freud's consulting room, Vienna, with a shelf designed by Felix Augenfeld. Used with the permission of Sigmund Freud Museum, Vienna © Edmund Engelman.

Consulting Rooms and Couches in Berlin

Consulting rooms designed by Ernst L. Freud were free from visual clutter, abundant artwork, and oriental rugs—a visual clarity that, however, was perhaps not entirely the result of the architect's imagination. In the mid 1920s the Santa Barbara psychoanalyst Pryns Hopkins (1885–1970) described the London room of Ernest Jones as 'large, but unlike that of his mentor, Freud, it was nearly bare of furniture and gloomy'.[28] On first glance, the rooms by Ernst L. Freud appear as if he had deliberately sought to separate himself architecturally from his father's legacy. He conceived couches with clear geometrical lines, experimented with their position within the rooms, and developed purpose-made chairs for the psychoanalysts. Yet on second glance, the consulting rooms show that despite all differences, Freud had studied closely the settings of his father's consulting room and adapted those elements that the elder Freud had identified as essential for the psychoanalytic space.

In autumn 1928 Freud was asked to design for the second time an interior for the Berlin policlinic when it moved from its original premises at Potsdamer Straße 29 into new ones on Wichmannstraße 10. When the policlinic celebrated its tenth anniversary in 1930, a *Festschrift* was published that was illustrated with photographs of some of Freud's interiors.[29] One of the images shows a treatment room (fig. 6.3); its polished wooden floor was not covered by a rug and the walls seemed to be painted directly on the plaster. Next to the window with a net curtain a small desk and a bentwood chair are placed at a 45-degree angle in the corner of the room. The chair has curved armrests and a circular seat and appears to be the Thonet B3 model that was derived from a design by Otto Wagner for the Postal Savings Bank in Vienna.[30] To the left, a plant is just visible; to the right, in front of a door behind a dark curtain stands an upholstered comfort chair turned slightly towards the viewer. It follows, parallel to the wall, the couch with the upholstered head end closest to the chair. A small portrait photograph of Sigmund Freud hangs to the left of the dark curtain almost above the desk.[31]

Another photograph gives a glimpse into the consulting room for the doctor on duty, a large room with a bow window towards the street (fig. 6.4). A cupboard with glass doors in the upper half and wooden doors below takes up the left wall. Towards the bow window four chairs surround a small table. To the right stands the analyst's chair followed by the couch placed parallel to the wall, though partially hidden by a projecting pillar. The chair and couch are of the same type as those in the smaller treatment room. A picture hangs above the couch and three others are above the cupboard; the centre one is identifiable as an engraving of Sigmund Freud after a portrait by Ferdinand Schmutzer (1870–1928) from 1926.

Figure 6.3. Consulting room, Berlin policlinic, 1928. Photograph from Deutsche Psychoanalytische Gesellschaft (ed.). 1930. *Zehn Jahre Berliner Psychoanalytisches Institut (Poliklinik und Lehranstalt)*. Vienna: Psychoanalytischer Verlag.

Figure 6.4. Doctors' room, Berlin policlinic, 1928. Photograph from Deutsche Psychoanalytische Gesellschaft (ed.). 1930. *Zehn Jahre Berliner Psychoanalytisches Institut (Poliklinik und Lehranstalt).* Vienna: Psychoanalytischer Verlag.

Freud also arranged a lecture room and a meeting room. The former occupied the socalled *Berliner Zimmer*, an often awkwardly shaped and badly lit through-room between the main building and the side wings of a typical Berlin apartment building. This lecture room was furnished with several rows of bentwood chairs oriented towards a blackboard and a lecture podium. Again, a net curtain hangs in front of the window and some pictures decorate the walls. For the meeting room Freud designed a long conference table made from heavy, rectangular slabs of wood (fig. 6.5). Along either side are lined-up bentwood chairs with both square and circular seats. At the far end a bookshelf with fullheight glass doors is built into the wall, above which a portrait of Sigmund Freud is given a place of honour.[32]

The settings of couch and chair in the consulting rooms of the policlinic follow closely Sigmund Freud's instructions about their placement with respect to each other. They also illustrate my earlier remark about the transferability of the spatial setting of psychoanalysis into different locations. New were the portraits of Sigmund Freud that hung above or near to the couch, a practice also seen in the later photographs of Anna Freud's Berggasse 19 consulting room. These portraits gained additional visual importance due to the otherwise uncluttered and orderly character of the rooms. With the exemption of the conference table, Freud used mass-produced, modern bentwood chairs and light fittings. The latter added a distinct modernist, if not to say avant-garde, note to the interiors because Freud chose a lamp by the Danish designer Poul Henningsen (1894–1967).[33] Whether or not Freud designed the couches and the chairs of the policlinic is not known. He was, however, in charge of the design of nearly all furniture—including couches and

Figure 6.5. Meeting room, Berlin policlinic, 1928. Photograph from Deutsche Psychoanalytische Gesellschaft (ed.). 1930. *Zehn Jahre Berliner Psychoanalytisches Institut (Poliklinik und Lehranstalt).* Vienna: Psychoanalytischer Verlag.

chairs—for a psychoanalytic sanatorium that had been founded in Berlin-Tegel the year before.

Sanatorium Schloß Tegel

When the Sanatorium Schloß Tegel opened on 11 April 1927, it represented the most ambitious endeavour of the fledgling psychoanalytic movement in Berlin. It was the brain child of Simmel, who had gathered his first experiences with psychoanalysis when he treated war neuroses during the Great War. The clinic was born out of his particular interest in stationary psychoanalysis which would remove the patient from daily life in order to recover.[34] It was located within the grounds of the Humboldt-Schloß, also known as Schloß Tegel, the property of the von Humboldt family. Even though the sanatorium took its name from Schloß Tegel, it was not in the manor house designed by Karl Friedrich Schinkel. Rather, in 1906 a private medical clinic, Kurhaus Schloß Tegel, was established on the edge both of the Schloßpark and the adjacent Tegel Lake (fig. 6.6). It offered medical treatments, physical therapy, and psychological advice, especially for chronic illnesses and nervous diseases.[35] Kurhaus Schloß Tegel was a new, four-storey tall, sprawling compound, whose many towers, turrets, balconies, bow and oriel windows, and partially exposed timberwork evoked romanticized notions of medieval German buildings. Nearby outbuildings with water basins and surrounding gardens allowed the patients to take in both the waters and fresh air while performing healthy gymnastics. Freud refurbished

Figure 6.6. Kurhaus Schloß Tegel, Berlin, built in 1906, later demolished. Photograph from Volker M. Welter.

this building extensively in order to create an environment conducive to the psychoanalytical, physical, and dietary treatments that were offered in Simmel's sanatorium.

Simmel's plans for the Sanatorium Schloß Tegel were indicative of the positive economic mood of the mid 1920s that allowed such an endeavour to go forward. Yet in the aftermath of the economic crisis from autumn 1929, the company that had leased the sanatorium folded in September 1931.[36] Initially, Simmel had inquired about a purchase of the building—to which end Freud surveyed it, concluding that 'a significant expense of money will be necessary to refurbish and modernize both the building and the furniture'.[37] The extent of the interior works can be gleaned from an inventory that was drawn up when the sanatorium collapsed financially.[38] For example, the department store N. Israel, a specialist supplier to hospitals and hotels, built from Freud's designs twenty-five day beds, twenty-four cupboards, and twenty-two (of each) bedsteads, night stands, writing desks, and shelves. Three treatment rooms were equipped with couches, chairs, and small tables with glass tops. Other furniture was for a villa for Simmel and the medical staff—communal dining rooms, lounge, waiting rooms, and office spaces. A Citroën car completes the inventory.[39]

A promotional brochure for the sanatorium is illustrated with Freud's interiors, in particular those of a single bedroom (fig. 6.7), a double bedroom (fig. 6.8), and a treatment room. The two private rooms show fully developed Freudian interiors, even though they were located in an institutional rather than a domestic setting. The floors are linoleum, covered partially with rugs with geometric patterns. All furniture is made from wood with the occasional cane filling and is composed of clear-cut geometric forms. The furnishing program was conventional with beds, nightstands, day bed, desk and chair, sheers to filter

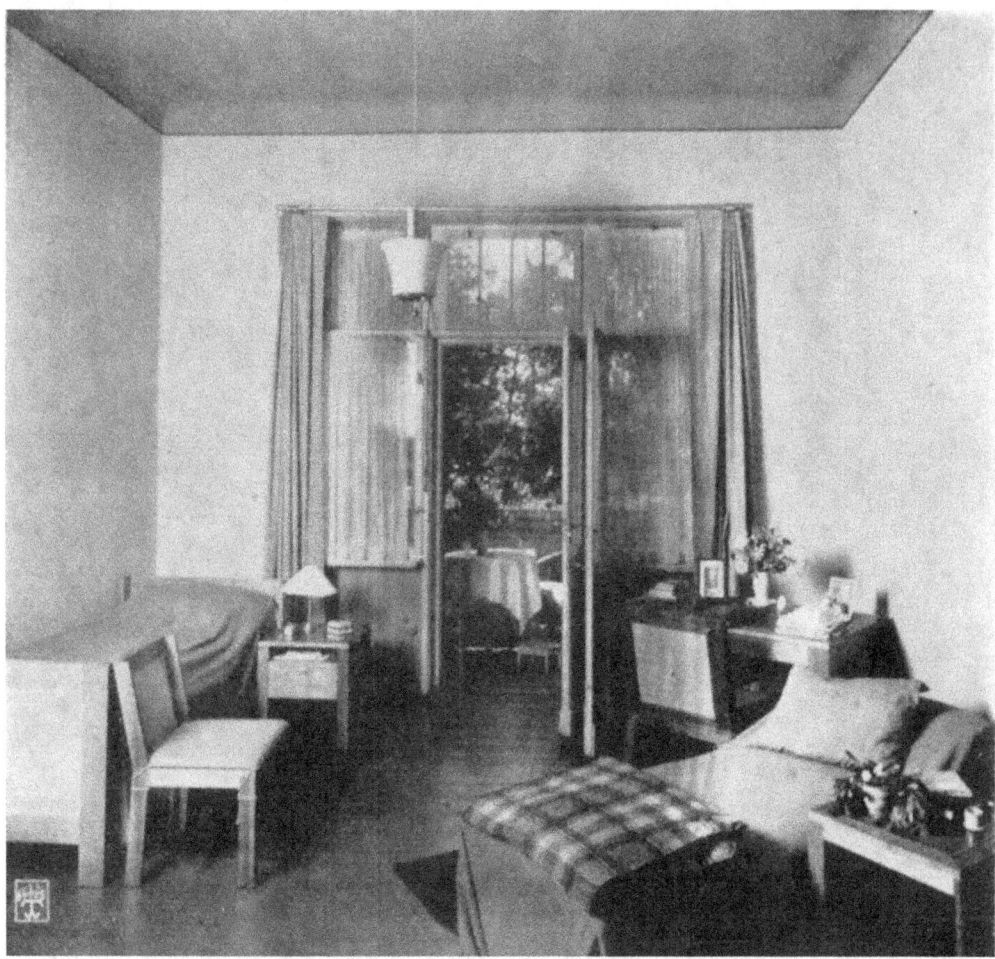

Figure 6.7. Single bedroom, Sanatorium Tegel, Berlin, 1927. Photograph from Anonymous. 1927. *Sanatorium Schloß Tegel Psychoanalytische Klinik Berlin Tegel*, s.l. No publisher, in Library of Congress, Manuscript Division, Ernst Simmel Papers.

the light, and curtains to keep it out entirely. The rooms were designed with an emphasis on creating 'the impression of a comfortable living space and work room' thanks to 'the inconspicuous posture of the form of the bed'. The description continues: 'A simple rectilinearity of the architectonics of the furniture combines their colours and the large, differently hued expanses of walls, ceilings, and curtains into a comforting, harmonious overall picture. Accordingly, each room is tuned into its own colour, while also being integrated into the atmosphere that results from the yellow and brown of the foyer and the corridors' mixed daylight that streams freely everywhere'.[40] Remarkable is the emphasis placed on the colours and the straight, geometrical forms of the furniture; both are considered to contribute to the healing process. The latter is further supported by the design of the private rooms that simulates at once living rooms, studies, and home offices—domestic spaces that thrive on activity—rather than bedroom settings more typically associated with passive forms of relaxation.

Figure 6.8. Double bedroom, Sanatorium Tegel, Berlin, 1927. Photograph from Anonymous. 1927. *Sanatorium Schloß Tegel Psychoanalytische Klinik Berlin Tegel*, s.l. No publisher, in Library of Congress, Manuscript Division, Ernst Simmel Papers.

The treatment room that is pictured in the brochure is much more serene (fig. 6.9). The most prominent feature is the couch that stands freely in the centre with a small square side table adjacent to the head end. Sigmund Freud as well as Anna Freud had their couches aligned with one of the walls of their consulting rooms. Ernst L. Freud had adopted this placement when he designed the second Berlin policlinic, the precise arrangements in the original location are not known. But in the Sanatorium Schloß Tegel the couch was put in a much more exposed position in the centre of the room. Too few images of contemporary consulting rooms exist to decide if this position was new or widely accepted. When in 1938 the British architect Christopher Nicholson (1904–48) designed a consulting room for Rosemary (Molly) Pritchard (1900–85), he proposed a comparable location for the couch.[41] Pritchard's couch was placed diagonally in front of a fireplace with the head end oriented towards a free-standing, curved screen that prevented views of the couch from the door (figs. 6.10 and 6.11). Also, in the English context, the position of the couch in relation to the larger room was theorized by psychoanalyst John Rickman (1891–1951). During the 1940s, when training students, Rickman used a small model of a couch and paper strips symbolizing the walls of a consulting room in order to discuss different positions of both couch and patients in space.[42] As late as the 1950s, to push the couch into a free-standing position within the consulting room was referred to as a 'break with tradition'.[43]

Figure 6.9. Consulting room, Sanatorium Tegel, Berlin, 1927. Photograph from Anonymous. 1927. *Sanatorium Schloß Tegel Psychoanalytische Klinik Berlin Tegel*, s.l. No publisher, in Library of Congress, Manuscript Division, Ernst Simmel Papers.

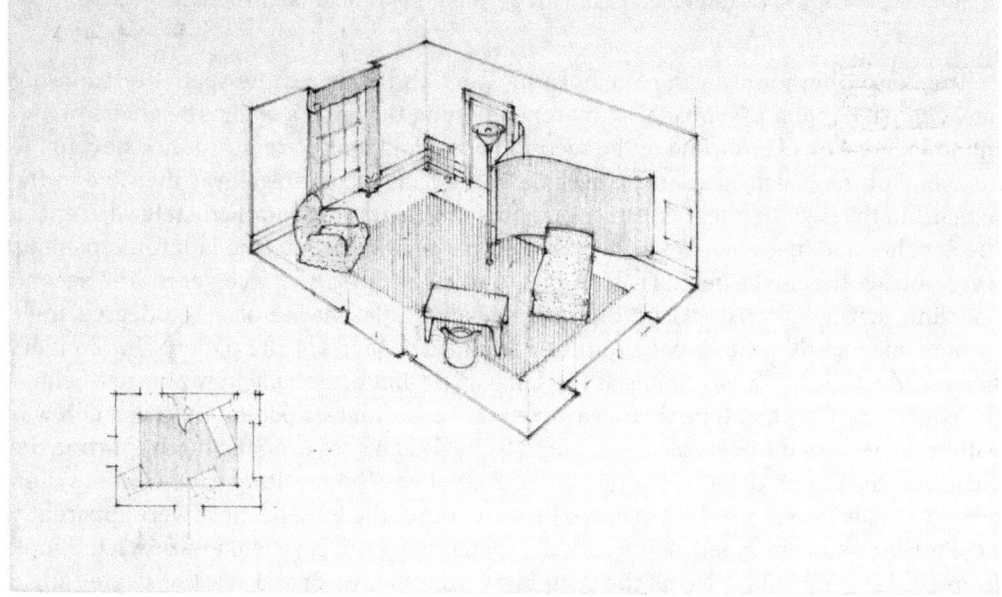

Figure 6.10. Design for Rosemary (Molly) Pritchard's consulting room, London, by Christopher Nicholson, 1938. Used with permission of the RIBA Library Drawings & Archives Collections.

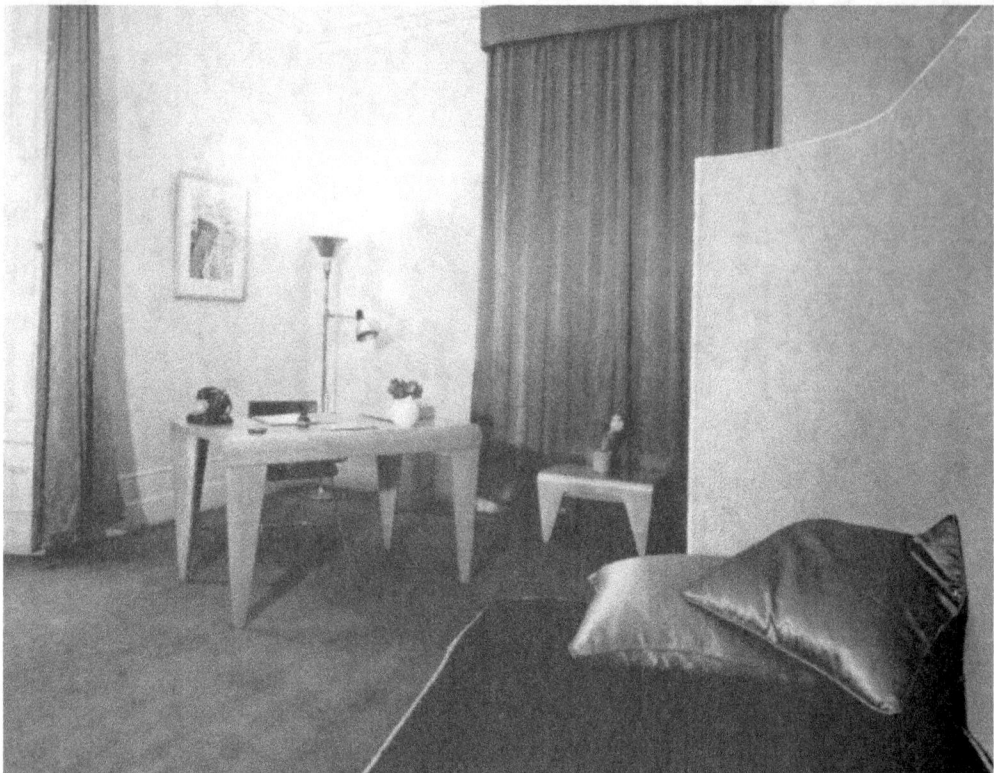

Figure 6.11. Interior of Rosemary (Molly) Pritchard's consulting room, London, 1938. Photograph from J. Pritchard, 1984. *View from a Long Chair. The Memoirs of Jack Pritchard.* London: Routledge & Kegan Paul, used with permission of Jonathan Pritchard.

The consulting room in the Sanatorium Tegel also changed the spatial relationship between patient and psychoanalyst by repositioning the latter's chair. The chairs of Sigmund Freud, Anna Freud, and of the second Berlin Poliklinik were positioned next to the head end of the couch; similarly, the chair in the Sanatorium Tegel was invisible to the patient. In the two Viennese consulting rooms the chairs stood immediately adjacent to the couches and, because they were oriented perpendicularly to the latter, the patients were outside the direct field of vision of the psychoanalyst and vice versa. The second policlinic setting likewise placed the psychoanalyst adjacent but at a 120-degree angle to the couch so that the direct sightline still faced away from the patient. In Simmel's sanatorium, the chair's position is at the same angle, but diagonally in the corner behind the couch and thus much further away from it. Accordingly, a patient on the couch was within full view of the psychoanalyst. Nicholson's design goes even further by putting the chair into the corner diagonally opposite to the couch. The resulting wide field of vision from the chair is somewhat interrupted by the curve of the screen. These were apparently isolated, little-known experiments with the spatial setting of psychoanalysis. A handbook from 1954 recommends placing the chair away from the couch and at a 120-degree angle to it in order to ensure both aural and visual contact with a patient; fellow psychoanalysts reacted to this proposal fearing 'a revolution or complete turnabout of their position.'[44]

The couch Freud designed for the Sanatorium Tegel followed the Viennese original while modernizing and abstracting it (fig. 6.12). It was 2.20 m long, 52 cm tall at the foot end, and 80 cm at the other. The head end bent steeply upwards, recalling the very high head end of the original couch in Vienna. Two hinges underneath the cylindrical footrest indicate that the vertical end board could be lifted, perhaps to access storage space. The drawing does not indicate colours and material other than that the base was covered with linoleum. A bulky chair, another Freud design, accompanied the couch. Two square frames made from wood form the sides and armrests of the chair with a thickly cushioned seat in between. The upholstered backrest inclines slightly backwards. Underneath the seat a pull-out footrest is installed that recalls a similar feature of the wicker basket chairs that were (and still are) popular at beaches along the German Baltic Sea. Freud will have been familiar with these beach chairs as he owned a holiday home on the island of Hiddensee.

The setting in the Sanatorium Tegel is the only one known to us in which Freud designed a couch and a chair that were made-to-measure for psychoanalysis. None of the two pieces of furniture survived the course of history, even though one couch from the sanatorium made its way to England when its owner fled Germany. The son of Eva Rosenfeld (1892–1977), a Berlin-born psychoanalyst who had worked in the sanatorium, writes that his 'mother was not paid her final salary but received a prophetic gift instead—a

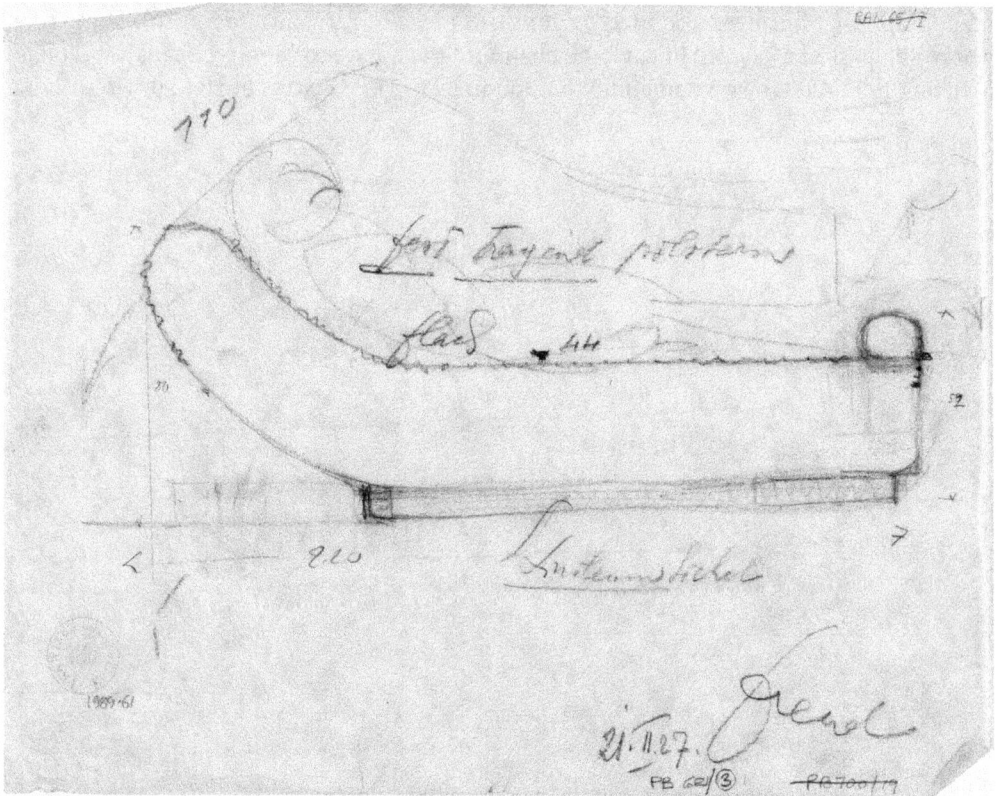

Figure 6.12. Sketch of the consulting couch, Sanatorium Tegel, Berlin, 1927. Used with permission of the RIBA Library Drawings & Archives Collections.

beautiful couch, designed by Freud's architect son Ernst—which was to serve as her patient's couch for the next forty years'.⁴⁵ It was, however, not the treatment couch with its pronounced head end as depicted in the photographs. Instead, Rosenfeld's couch was flat, rectangular, and covered in green rep.⁴⁶ The son summed up his recollections of his mother's couch by comparing it to a simple bed. He thus described exactly Freud's approach to designing psychoanalytic couches *other* than the ones designed for the Sanatorium Schloß Tegel. Usually, his couches were rectangular and low with cylindrical armrests at one or both short ends. Depending on the intended use, the drawings are labelled 'couch' or 'treatment couch', presumably in an attempt to economize time and creative efforts (figs. 6.13 and 6.14). For example, Freud used very similar designs for couches in the lower-level hall of the Frank country house and in the consulting room for Melanie Klein in London.

Psychoanalytic Spaces in London

When Klein asked Freud to refurbish her house in St John's Wood in 1933, Freud divided an L-shaped drawing room into a smaller waiting room and the consulting cum living room. The latter was furnished with bulky comfort chairs, a sofa, and various Freud-designed tables. The couch stood next to the single comfort chair at the right edge of the photograph that has been cropped to omit this piece of furniture (fig. 6.15). Some time before she passed away, Klein gave the chair and the couch to the psychoanalyst Donald Meltzer (1922–2004) who had come to London in 1954.⁴⁷ Klein's couch had two wooden

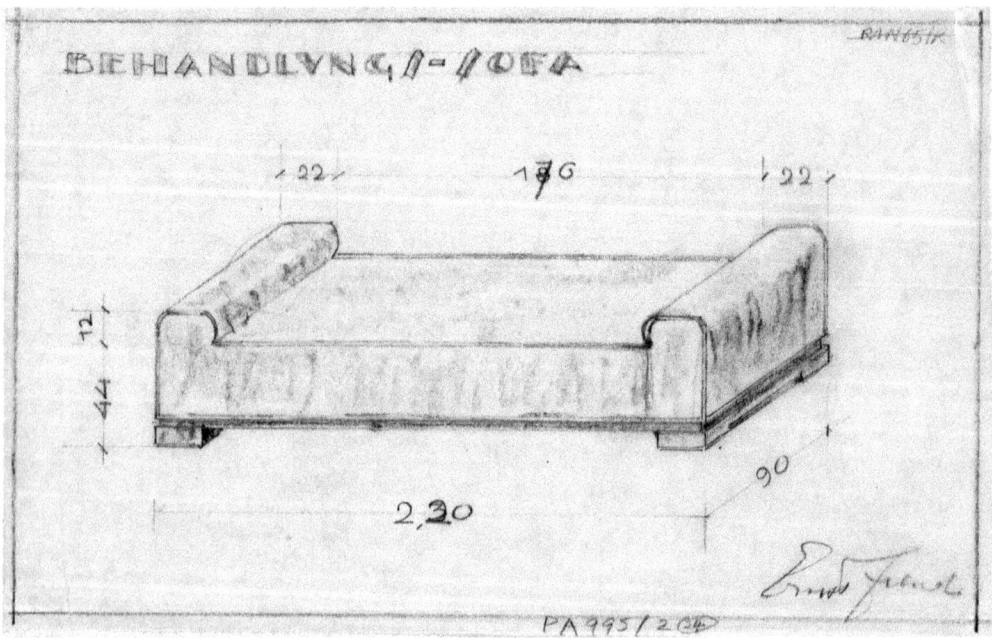

Figure 6.13. Sketch of a consulting couch. Used with permission of the RIBA Library Drawings & Archives Collections.

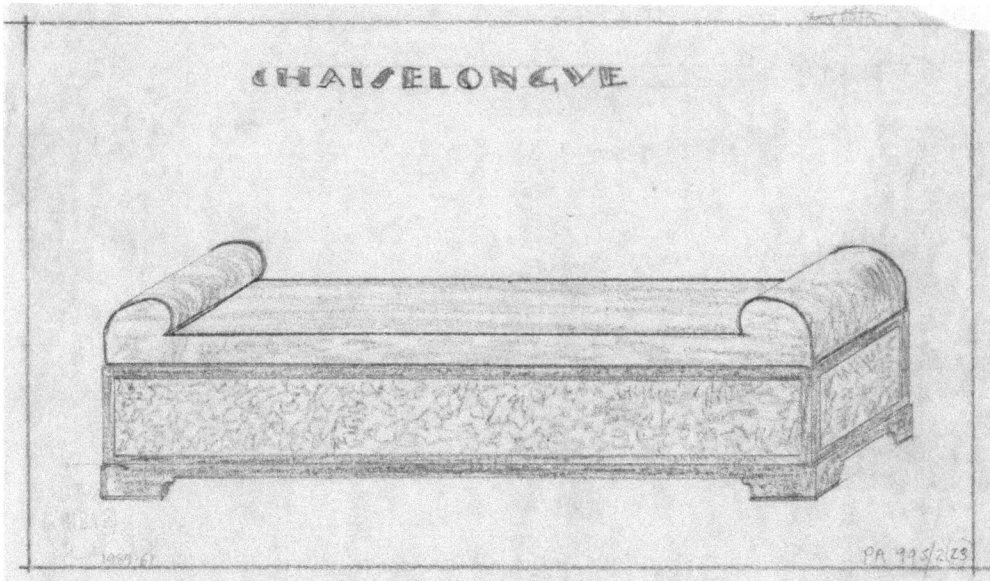

Figure 6.14. Sketch of a bed couch. Used with permission of the RIBA Library Drawings & Archives Collections.

armrests filled with a double layer of cane. It was upholstered with pale green, narrowly striped rep. Cylindrical cushions from the same material could be used as temporary back support if the couch was placed alongside a wall. Most likely it was a Freud design, as a couch in the lower-floor hall of Freud's Frank country house was of a similar size and with similarly shaped armrests. The latter, however extended into a permanent backrest holding rectangular cushions of green colour. Neighbours of Klein recall other features of Freud's design—a glass-plated front door, a striking copper surround for a fireplace lit by two brass lamp holders—that gave the refurbishment a distinct modern character.

Klein was one the earliest clients of Freud after he had immigrated to England in the autumn of 1933; commissions from other psychoanalysts followed soon. Already during an exploratory visit to London in the summer of 1933, Freud had discussed possible projects with fellow immigrants who, like he, tried to establish a new economic basis for their lives in exile. One such client was Kate (Käthe) Friedlaender (1903–49, née Frankl, divorced Misch), the first female medical student at the University of Innsbruck. After she had studied briefly with Sigmund Freud in Vienna, she married Dr. Walter Misch (1889–1941) in 1929, with whom she lived in Berlin where both worked at the Charité. They fled Germany in 1933, first to Paris and then to London. Subsequently, Friedlaender opened a psychoanalytic practice for which Freud designed the consulting room in c. 1934. Initially, the room occupied a space in a house in St. Anne's Terrace, but around 1939 or 1940 it was transferred to a new family apartment in Harley House. Her niece describes the 'consulting room [as] sleek and very modern, though that was mainly confined to the furniture. The Harley House consulting room was a large rather square plain room, the interior design input mainly by the way of furniture. There was a bent plywood armchair which was ... probably [by Alvar] Aalto.' From 1938 onwards, Friedlaender worked

Figure 6.15. Melanie Klein's consulting cum living room, London, 1933. Used with permission of the RIBA Library Photographs Collection.

with Anna Freud and was one of the co-founders of the Hampstead clinics; professional differences forced both women to eventually go their own ways.[48]

Shortly before Friedlaender, now Misch, established her own psychoanalytic practice, she had joined the efforts of Hilde Maas, another exiled psychoanalyst, to found a psychoanalytic sanatorium in London. The goal was to employ exiled doctors and psychoanalysts from Berlin; they were joined, for example, by Richard Hamburger, professor of paediatrics at the Charité and a Freud client in Berlin and London. Mass approached Freud in July 1933 regarding the refurbishment of an unidentified building in Hampstead. By mid March 1934, the sanatorium idea had generated interest from an adjacent hospital and Maas told them that Freud was her architect. Later that month Freud wrote that his 'patron is charming and … the foundation of the new place will happen, so I've been doing more work on the drawings'. By early April, £15,000 had been raised for the project; accordingly, Freud prepared more concrete plans. Sadly, these have not been located. However, an insurmountable hurdle arose when Dr. Misch and '70% of the remaining doctors failed an exam' that they were obliged to take in order to be able to practice in Great Britain; the project subsequently faltered in April 1934. Until then, Freud had been enthusiastic; at some point he even wrote to his wife that the sanatorium was to become his first building in England.[49]

Similar to the year 1919 when Freud was about to move to Berlin, the circumstances of his exile in 1933 forced him again to pin his hopes on speculative projects that turned out to be elusive. Then it had been dreams about building in Palestine, now it was psychoanalytic buildings in England. But as before, Freud would eventually overcome all difficulties and as a 41-year-old man he found his home in England. To this phase of his life the next chapter will now turn.

Notes

1. Letter from Max Eitingon to Sigmund Freud, 13 January 1920 (M. Schröter [ed.]. 2004. *Sigmund Freud Max Eitingon, Briefwechsel 1906–1939*, 2 vols. Tübingen: Edition Diskord, vol. 1, letter 161E, 184–185).
2. Letter from Karl Abraham to Sigmund Freud, 13 March 1920 (E. Falzeder [ed]. 2002. *The Complete Correspondence of Sigmund Freud and Karl Abraham 1907–1925*, trans. by C. Schwarzacher. London: Karnac, letter 317A).
3. C. P. Oberndorf. 1926. 'The Berlin Psychoanalytic Policlinic', *The Psychoanalytic Review* XIII: 318–322 (318).
4. E. A. Danto. 1999. 'The Berlin Poliklinik: Psychoanalytic Innovation in Weimar Germany', *Journal of the American Psychoanalytic Association* 47 (4): 1269–1292; E. A. Danto. 2005. *Freud's Free Clinics: Psychoanalysis & Social Justice, 1918–1938*. New York: Columbia University Press.
5. G. Fischer. 1966. *Dienstboten, Brecht und Andere: Zeitgenossen in Prag, Berlin, London*. Olten: Walter-Verlag, 203. Therese and Willi Bardas were clients of Freud who designed for them in early 1925 a new bedstead (Notebook Inventory Regentenstraße 11, reverse end of notebook: list of events from 17/03-[illegible]/04/1925 while Ernst Freud in Rome, Lux Papers L–Z, Freud Museum London).
6. K. Brecht et al. (eds.). 1985. *'Hier geht das Leben auf eine merkwürdige Weise weiter …' Zur Geschichte der Psychoanalyse in Deutschland*, s.l.: Michael Keller, 30.
7. C. Guderian. 2004. *Magie der Couch: Bilder und Gespräche über Raum und Setting in der Psychoanalyse*. Stuttgart: W. Kohlhammer, 7, my translation.
8. For example: A. Vidler, 1992. *The Architectural Uncanny: Essays in the Modern Unhomely*. Cambridge, MA: MIT Press; D. Fuss. 2004. *The Sense of an Interior: Four Writers and the Rooms that shaped them*. New York: Routledge; C. Rice. 2007. *The Emergence of the Interior: Architecture, Modernity, Domesticity*. London: Routledge.

9. In the following I rely on H. F. Mallgrave and E. Ikonomou. 1994. *Empathy, Form, and Space: Problems in German Aesthetics, 1873–1893*. Santa Monica, CA: The Getty.
10. H. R. Stern. 1978. *The Couch, Its Use and Meaning in Psychotherapy*. New York: Human Sciences Press.
11. Danto, *Freud's Free Clinics*.
12. E. Engelman. 1993. *Sigmund Freud: Wien IX. Berggasse 19*. Vienna: Christian Brandstätter.
13. C. Guderian. 2004. *Die Couch in der Psychoanalyse: Geschichte und Gegenwart von Setting und Raum*. Stuttgart: W. Kohlhammer, 20.
14. L. Marinelli. 2006. 'Vorstellungen eines Möbels', in L. Marinelli (ed.). 2006. *Die Couch: Vom Denken im Liegen*. Munich: Prestel, 7–29 (10).
15. P. Gay. 1998. *Freud: A Life for Our Time*. New York: W.W. Norton, 103.
16. Colour information from Guderian, *Die Couch*, 20.
17. M. Molnar (ed.). 1992. *The Diary of Sigmund Freud 1929–1939: A Record of the Final Decade*, trans. M. Molnar. London: Freud Museum Publications, 234.
18. S. Freud. 1913. 'On Beginning the Treatment', in J. Strachey et al. (eds.). *The Standard Edition of the Complete Psychological Works of Sigmund Freud*, trans. by J. Strachey. London: Hogarth Press, vol. 12, 121–144.
19. Freud, 'On Beginning the Treatment', 133. Strachey translation reads 'a certain ceremonial which concerns the position in which the treatment is carried out'. I have amended this in order to come closer to the German original which reads 'ein gewisses Zeremoniell der Situation, in welcher die Kur ausgeführt wird' (S. Freud. 1913. 'Zur Einleitung der Behandlung', in S. Freud. 1955. *Gesammelte Werke*. London: Imago, vol. 8: *Werke aus den Jahren 1909–1913*, 454–478 [467]).
20. Occasionally, a third person was briefly involved when, for example, Freud's maid made up the couch when the patient was apparently already in the consulting room (S. Blanton. 1971. *Diary of My Analysis with Sigmund Freud*. New York: Hawthorn Books, 103).
21. See chapter 1, endnote 52.
22. Blanton, *Diary*, 20.
23. Blanton, *Diary*, 88. The rule to keep one's eyes closed during a psychoanalytic session can be traced back to a remark in *The Interpretation of Dreams* (S. Freud. 1909. *The Interpretation of Dreams*, trans. J. Strachey. London: Hogarth, 101).
24. Blanton, *Diary*, 44.
25. Occasionally, the spatial arrangement of waiting room and consulting room in Vienna did not have the desired effect; see Blanton, *Diary*, 56.
26. Letter from Anna Freud to Lou Andreas-Salomé, 10 May 1923 (D. A. Rothe and I. Weber [eds.]. 2001. '… als käm ich heim zu Vater und Schwester' Lou Andreas-Salomé —Anna Freud Briefwechsel 1919–1937, 2 vols. Göttingen: Wallstein Verlag, vol. 1, 184–185 [185], my translation).
27. Engelman, *Sigmund Freud*, 73.
28. P. Hopkins. 1962. *Both Hands before the Fire*. Penobscot, ME: Traversity Press, 94.
29. Deutsche Psychoanalytische Gesellschaft (ed.). 1930. *Zehn Jahre Berliner Psychoanalytisches Institut (Poliklinik und Lehranstalt)*. Vienna: Internationaler Psychoanalytischer Verlag, 1930.
30. K. Mang. 1982. *Thonet Bugholzmöbel: Von der handwerklichen Fertigung zur industriellen Produktion*. Vienna: Christian Brandstätter, 108, 118.
31. The photograph is too small to allow identification of the picture on the wall.
32. As far as one can see on the reproduction of the photograph, the portrait of Sigmund Freud is from roughly 1921; see E. Freud, L. Freud, and I. Grubrich-Simitris (eds.). 1989. *Sigmund Freud: Sein Leben in Bildern und Texten*. Frankfurt: Insel, 222.
33. T. Jørstian and P. E. Munk Nielsen (eds). 1994. *Light Years Ahead: The Story of the PH Lamp*, s.l.: Louis Poulsen, 134.

34. U. Schultz and L. M. Hermanns. 1987. 'Das Sanatorium Schloß Tegel Ernst Simmels—Zur Geschichte und Konzeption der ersten Psychoanalytischen Klinik', *Psychotherapie, Psychosomatik, Medizinische Psychologie* 37 (2 February): 58–67; E. Simmel. 1927. 'Die psychoanaytische Behandlung in der Klinik', *Psychotherapie, Psychosomatik, Medizinische Psychologie* 47 (3 March–4 April 1997): 137–144.
35. J. Marcinowski. 1906. *Kurhaus Schloß Tegel bei Berlin: Sanatorium für physikalische und diätetische Behandlung von chronischen Erkrankungen und Erschöpfungszuständen. Spezialanstalt für die psychische Behandlung nervöser Leiden. Arbeits- und Beschäftigungskuren (Psycho-Pädagogik)*. Halle: Gebauer-Schwetschke.
36. Schultz, Hermanns, 'Das Sanatorium Schloß Tegel', 61. A lease was signed on 6 November 1926 with a duration until 1936. The company had a capital of 90,000 Reichsmark (RM) and the rental costs were to increase annually from initially 12,000 RM to 20,000 RM by the end of the lease (File Ernst Simmel Schloß Tegel, Archiv zu Schloß Tegel, Fach XII, Einzelne Grundstücke, Nr. 40 Kurhaus (Stiftung Simmel), Heft 1926–31).
37. Letter from Ernst Simmel to Geheimrat von Heinz, my translation (File Ernst Simmel Schloß Tegel, Archiv zu Schloß Tegel, Fach XII, Einzelne Grundstücke, Nr. 40 Kurhaus [Stiftung Simmel], Heft 1926–31).
38. The inventory was drawn up by the lawyer Karl Selowski (1889–1949), a client of Ernst Freud; S. Ladwig-Winters. 1998. *Anwalt ohne Recht: Das Schicksal jüdischer Rechtsanwälte in Berlin nach 1933*. Berlin: Be.bra, 207.
39. File Ernst Simmel Schloß Tegel, Archiv zu Schloß Tegel, Fach XII, Einzelne Grundstücke, Nr. 40 Kurhaus (Stiftung Simmel), Heft 1926–31.
40. Anonymous. 1927. *Sanatorium Schloß Tegel: Psychoanalytische Klinik*. Berlin: Sternfeld, 13–14, my translation.
41. N. Bingham. 1996. *Christopher Nicholson*. London: Academy Editions, 72. Rosemary Pritchard was married to Jack Pritchard (1899–1992), the founder of Isokon, the British modern furniture producer. Isokon tables were selected for the consulting room that was located on 4 Upper Harley Street, London (J. Pritchard. 1984. *View from a Long Chair: The Memoirs of Jack Pritchard*. London: Routledge & Kegan Paul, 114).
42. P. King. 2003. 'Introduction: The Rediscovery of John Rickman and his work', in P. King (ed.). 2003. *No Ordinary Psychoanalyst: The Exceptional Contributions of John Rickman*. London: Karnac, 1–68 (61).
43. J. D. Lichtenberg. 1995. 'Forty-five Years of Psychoanalytic Experiences On, Behind, and Without the Couch', *Psychoanalytic Inquiry* 15 (3); 284.
44. T. Braatøy. 1954. *Fundamentals of Psychoanalytic Technique*. New York: John Wiley & Sons, 111.
45. P. Heller (ed.). 1992. *Anna Freud's Letters to Eva Rosenfeld*. Madison, WI: International University, 40.
46. Letter from Victor Ross to author, 30 July 2002.
47. Conversation with Donald Meltzer, Oxford, October 2002. He stilled used both pieces in his home in Oxford in late 2002; it is not known what happened to the couch after D. Meltzer passed away in 2004. Attempts to contact the Donald Meltzer Psychoanalytic Atelier (www.psa-atelier.org) and the Donald Meltzer Development Fund have been unsuccessful.
48. Email correspondence with Gerda Flöckinger CBE, November 2006 to January 2007; *Psychoanalytikerinnen in Europa. Biografisches Lexikon*, www.psychoanalytikerinnen.de/, ad vocem, accessed 15th January 2007.
49. Letters from Ernst Freud to Lucie Freud, 12 July 1933; 13, 14, and 22 March 1934; 9 and 11 April 1934 (collection Esther Freud).

Chapter 7

At Home in England

In October 1934, almost a year after his arrival, Freud summarized his impressions on the state of modern architecture in England in a letter to the editor of *Design for To-Day:* 'Sir, ... it is most surprising to a continental observer how very few modern buildings are to be found and that on the whole the idea of modern architecture has not yet begun to influence the features of English towns. This clearly shows that for the erection of modern buildings the existence of modern architects is not sufficient. Important above all are clients, inclined to accept and appreciate the principles of modern architecture.'[1] By depicting English towns as bereft of modern buildings Freud tapped into a common prejudice about Great Britain held by many foreign architects and some British modernists. However, by underlining the role of modern clients, Freud at the same time rejected the assumption that modern architecture was primarily the result of the works of an architectural-artistic avant-garde. Both points were potentially of great concern for émigré architects. The apparent lack of modern architecture was understood—or often misunderstood—as indicating a need for the services of the exiled modern architects. And in order to re-establish their practices, beside all legal and professional hurdles that had to be overcome, exiled architects needed modern clients.[2] Among the hurdles were especially admission to the country, work permits, the search for the required professional British partner, and the language. Other obstacles were professional qualifications as demanded by, for example, the Royal Institute of British Architects and stipulations as imposed by regulations like the Architects Registration Act (1938).[3]

Going into Exile

The moment the Nazis were officially in power, thoughts about exile and the search for a new home country began for many German citizens and foreigners who lived in Germany. Ernst L. and Lucie Freud decided to leave Berlin during the first months of National-Socialist rule. If this thought did not cross their minds earlier, then it certainly at least began after the murder of a member of the Mosse family, their closest relatives in Berlin. Even before that, the Freud family experienced German anti-Semitism, when, for example, in the summer of 1932 Lucie Freud was verbally attacked by a neighbour when she played with her own and other children outside their holiday home on the island of Hiddensee.[4] By the end of June 1933 Freud was in London to prepare for the family's exile.[5] Lucie Freud and the sons left Berlin in late September 1933 and Freud followed in mid November after the shipment of the family apartment's furniture was on its way to England.[6]

Even though potentially exposed to Nazi terror as both a Jew and the son of Sigmund Freud, Freud's Austrian citizenship will have initially offered some protection as far as official government measurements against Germany's Jewish population were concerned.[7] Other colleagues were in more immediate danger. Bruno Taut, a prominent anarcho-socialist and architect of social-housing estates, was forced to flee Germany within a day when he learned on 1 March 1933 that his name appeared on a blacklist.[8] Mendelsohn, a German-Jewish citizen famous in cultural-architectural circles, likewise had to leave suddenly in March 1933. His political opinions, but even more so his successful career as a modern architect who counted among his clients many large businesses, made him a prime subject for any Nazi demagogue.[9] Other architects needed much more time to make the decision for exile and then to see it through. Freud's former boss in Munich, the architect Fritz Landauer, travelled back and forth between Munich and London from 1933 until 1937, when he finally settled in the British capital.[10]

While on his own in England during the summer of 1933, Freud wrote almost daily, sometimes twice a day, to his wife. The earliest two letters date from 26 and 27 June 1933.[11] They describe the first days in London and capture the purpose of the trip: to make contacts with British architects and to arrange for work, schooling for the boys, and possible housing. At the turnstile of the Berlin-Zoologischer Garten train station Freud accidentally met the lawyer Harry Cohn (1896–1981),[12] an acquaintance who was fleeing to Holland on the same train. During the journey, Freud obtained legal advice most likely concerning the need for a partnership with a British architect, a requirement for émigré architects seeking work in England. One plan, suggested by Edwin Herbert Samuel (1898–1978),[13] was for Freud to team up with the architect Robert Lutyens (1901–1971), a son of Sir Edwin Landseer Lutyens (1869–1944). It is not known if the plan was put into practice or, indeed, with which architect Freud partnered during the first years in England.[14]

Freud also made use of his father's contacts among British Zionists and psychoanalysts, for example, when in order to be permitted to the United Kingdom in 1933 he gave as reason for the trip some business he had with Ernest Jones. Shortly after his arrival, Freud met with David Eder, another of his father's friends who had helped to arrange the commission for the Weizmann house in Jerusalem in 1926. Eder tried to facilitate meetings with the younger Samuel and also with Simon Marks (1888–1964) of the department-store chain Marks & Spencer.

Continental Europeans, many of them fellow émigrés, were another important social network during Freud's exploratory stay. In his first two letters, Freud reported a rigorous schedule of appointments. On day one, he lunched with Jones and afterwards, for example, travelled to Dulwich to meet art dealers from Berlin and Vienna.[15] Day two began with a meeting with Eder, followed by visits to boarding houses to find a room, and in between an appointment with a Frau Geheimrat Blume. Then Freud lunched with Melanie Klein's daughter, Melitta, and her husband, Dr. Walter Schmideberg,[16] an occasion at which he met the latter's English teacher and instantly arranged lessons for himself. In the afternoon, Freud contacted further names from a list he had brought with him. Among them, for example, was fellow refugee Melchior Palyi (1892–1970), professor of economics and chief economist of the Deutsche Bank, a connection that came possibly through Theodor and Margot Frank.

The remainder of the second day was reserved for meetings with architects. Freud saw Francis Rowland Yerbury (1885–1970), the secretary of the Architectural Association, who offered help with publishing Freud's buildings; Serge Chermayeff (1900–96), the British partner of Mendelsohn, who was also in London during June 1933;[17] and a third, unidentified architect, a recommendation of Adolf Platz who had illustrated some of Freud's designs in his book on modern German interiors.[18] Chermayeff asked Freud back for cocktails and supper the next day when they were joined by Mendelsohn, his wife Louise (1894–1980), and the Dutch architect Hendrik Theodorus Wijdeveld (1885–1989). This encounter was one of the few occasions where Freud hinted at the stress the exile caused him. He called the evening lovely, but then noted in the understated manner so typical of him that no time had been spent on himself, meaning on discussing his future in exile.

Freud also looked actively for architectural experiences that would dovetail with his own work and would thus establish some familiarity in unfamiliar surroundings. Upon visiting an exhibition of modern furniture, most likely 'British Industrial Art in Relation to the Home',[19] Freud found that English design had progressed in parallel with continental European developments because much of the furniture displayed detailing comparable to that he had used for many years.[20]

A children's parlour, however, aroused his objection and he arranged for the publication of his design for the Bermann-Fischer nursery in Berlin.[21] This was the first of a number of Freud projects that were published in British journals between 1933 and 1937, including three detached three houses,[22] a bank office,[23] and a children's waiting room designed for the paediatrician Professor Richard Hamburger.[24] Freud contacted most of the journals during his initial stay in England.[25] How much of this publicity was dependent on the family name is difficult to assess, though only some of the articles referred to Freud's father.

With the selection of projects presented to the magazines Freud positioned himself as a modern architect. His modernity, however, was built around the bourgeois single-family house as a contemporary design task rather than its dissolution into new forms of either experimental architecture or living. A comparison of the Willow House (1932), Cambridge, by George Checkley (1893–1960), with Freud's Scherk house in Berlin, published by *Homes and Gardens* in March 1934,[26] emphasized this distinction between modernist and modern houses.

In opposition to the modernist cubic forms and horizontal windows of the house in Cambridge (fig. 7.1), the appeal of Freud's building rested on its skilful fusion of modern forms—like, for example, the semi-circular bay windows and the flat roof—with more traditional aspects of bourgeois houses and life. The readers were informed that the Scherk house was carefully integrated into an existing birch wood; that the latter was on an adjacent, not-yet-built-upon lot the photograph did not give away (fig. 7.2). Reassuringly, traditional brick had been used instead of unconventional materials like, for example, concrete. That Freud preferred sash windows—typical for British architecture while unusual in Germany—now gave his house a more familiar face. Finally, the series of rooms—for example, drawing room, music room, dining room, and wine cellar—invited identification with a bourgeois way of domestic life: 'The [Scherk] family being musical, the reception rooms were connected by wide openings to enable a large assembly to listen to concerts given from time to time.'[27] Freud's modern house affirmed rather than questioned bourgeois life in the suburbs of the modern city.

Figure 7.1. Willow house, Cambridge, by George Checkley, 1932. Used with permission of the Collection Centre Canadien d'Architecture / Canadian Centre for Architecture, Montréal.

Figure 7.2. Garden facade of the Scherk house, Berlin, 1930–31. Used with permission of the RIBA Library Photographs Collection.

By the time Freud returned to Berlin in late August 1933 important groundwork for a new life had been laid. The schooling of the children was solved with the decision to send them to the pedagogically experimental boarding school Dartington Hall near Totnes in Devon. Moreover, as a reduced annual fee had been offered, Freud had calculated that he and his wife could live in cheaper accommodation that would include his office as another cost-saving measure.[28] With regard to his architectural career, Freud had launched a small, but impressive publicity campaign. In addition, he had made contacts with potential clients from both émigré and psychoanalytic circles so that he could hope to have work the moment he would settle in England for good. While there was no guarantee that the accidental and arbitrary reality of exile would be overcome, Freud's pre-exile architectural work formed an important element of the foundation on which to base attempts to re-establish his practice. Once in London, Freud could continue both to build single-family houses and to design interiors even if his practice never grew back to its former size. He also ventured successfully into the design of multi-apartment buildings, for him a new area of expertise.

Setting up Office in London

Freud's first clients in England were mainly drawn from the circle of fellow refugees. Among them were Berlin acquaintances that turned to their former architect to obtain designs for their new homes and interiors. In addition, Freud acquired new clients from among the German-Jewish refugees. While the number of commissions and the size of individual projects were smaller than before, the early London projects constituted a surprising continuity between both phases of Freud's professional life.

Many of the émigré clients had left Germany during early 1933 and had been, to different degrees, able to take with them material possessions like furniture and financial resources.[29] That they turned to a German-speaking architect avoided any possible language barrier. To establish oneself in exile with an architect-designed interior, or even a house, was, moreover, symbolic of the wish to regain normality in one's new life. Occasionally, it may have indicated the financial possibilities of some émigrés, but for most the commission of a new home or interior meant financial hardship, which explains the often small scale of these projects. For example, in 1934 a refugee couple, Fritz and Ann Hess, asked Freud to advise them on the interior of a rental apartment in the Highgate area of London Hampstead. The entire job comprised the design of two fitted cupboards, the order of some other furniture, and to find suitable curtains.[30] But even such a small architect-designed project made a statement about creating a new home in new surroundings.

With regard to Freud himself, these early works may have suggested to him that his English career might continue basically along lines familiar to his Berlin career, an impression that was reinforced by the commissions he received from psychoanalysts. Among the latter were émigrés like, for example, Dr. Hilde Maass and Dr. Kate Friedländer who planned the already mentioned sanatorium project for London. Freud also designed a consulting room for Friedländer in the St. John's Wood area of London.

Freud's first British clients were likewise psychoanalysts. Beside Austrian-born Melanie Klein, who had lived in England since 1926, Ernest Jones was another early Freud client. In 1935–36, Freud enlarged for Jones a seventeenth-century cottage in Elsted, Midhurst, Sussex, by adding a new wing with several rooms. A separate entrance allowed for the use of these lower-floor rooms as consulting rooms. Two years later, Freud redesigned a cottage in Sandon, near Baldock, Hertfordshire, for a colleague of Jones, the psychoanalyst John Rickman.

Chronologically, however, projects for fellow refugees who had already been clients in Berlin launched Freud's English career. The majority of the projects were conversions of existing houses. For example, Freud worked on the various British homes of his Berlin friends, the art historian Wolfgang Herrmann (1899–1995) and Annie Herrmann (née Marx, died 1995). In 1927, Freud had designed for the Herrmanns twenty-six pieces of furniture for a new house in Berlin-Dahlem to which the couple moved in that year.[31] The Herrmanns left for England on 20 October 1933[32] and could take at least some of the Freud-designed furniture with them. Initially they lived at 89 Kingsley Way in London Hampstead, until they moved to 11 Pilgrim's Lane in the same borough in 1963. On each occasion, Freud was called upon to plan and decorate the new home.[33]

Another such commission came from Richard Hamburger who had run in Berlin, beside his professorship at the Charité, the private *Gartenhausklinik* for children with waiting room furniture designed by Freud. When forced into exile,[34] Hamburger exported to London his consulting room—the material basis of his medical career—including tubular steel medical furniture, the cork flooring, and the Freud furniture.[35] Apparently, Freud reinstalled the room in the new family home in London's St John's Wood area and again in another home in Maida Vale after the first family home had been damaged.

Houses in and around London

In 1935, Freud was commissioned to design a detached house for Dr. Adolf (died 1940s) and Heide Marx (died 1962), the parents of Annie Herrmann; this was Freud's first new single-family home in England. Dr. Adolf Marx had been a banker with Singer & Friedländer Bank in Berlin but the couple left Germany probably as early as 1932. Adolf and Heide Marx were active art collectors who owned many paintings by such artist friends as Otto Müller, Max Pechstein, Martin Bloch, Erich Heckel, and Anton Kerschbaumer. Contemporary photographs show the walls of the London home filled with mainly German Expressionist paintings combined with old-fashioned furniture (fig. 7.3).[36]

Between July and November 1935, Freud produced three plans for the house that varied the distribution of rooms on both the ground and upper floors in relation to the shifting location of the main entrance.[37] The final interior of the house unfolds in typical Freudian manner with a load-bearing wall separating the vestibule, stair hall, cloakroom, and kitchen along the front of the house from the dining and sitting room that face Hampstead Heath on the other side. Private and guest rooms were upstairs, a maids' rooms and a lead-lined storage cabinet for fur coats were in the attic.

The exterior of the Marx house is made of brownish-red, exposed bricks with metal windows from the Crittall Company sitting flush in the surface; Freud was friendly with Walter Francis Crittall (1887–1956), called 'Pink' Crittall, for whom he refurbished a farmhouse in Great Easton, Essex.[38] Towards the garden, Freud staggered on the ground floor tri-partite metal windows and slender mullions in a continuous band (fig. 7.4). The

Figure 7.3. Paintings and furniture brought over from Berlin and installed in the Marx house, London, 1935–36. Used with permission of Harry Weinberger.

Figure 7.4. Garden façade the Marx house, London, 1935–36. Used with permission of the RIBA Library Photographs Collection.

horizontality of this asymmetrical arrangement is further emphasized by a narrowly protruding lintel that extends without interruption into the flat concrete roof covering an adjacent loggia. On the upper level, three window openings are cut symmetrically into the wall without emphasizing a central middle axis.

This façade treatment recalls similarly arranged garden facades of, for example, the Charlton house (1928–29; fig. 7.5) and the Wiertz house (1928), both in Berlin-Dahlem, which were designed by Otto Salvisberg. Should Freud not have seen these houses in situ, he may have studied the Charlton house in the 1932 book *Neue Wohnbauten*.[39] Perhaps Freud even knew the house that Salvisberg had erected in Dahlem in 1928–29 for the art dealer Alfred Flechtheim (1878–1937), another refugee in London. While different in size, the ground floor plan of the Marx house bears similarities with that of the Flechtheim house including the positioning of the covered terraces. For Salvisberg, these houses were steps towards accepting formal principles of modernist architecture—like the cubic volume and horizontally banded windows in plain facades, but not the open plan—for his bourgeois domestic architecture. For Freud, the Marx house meant a step towards adjusting his domestic architecture to local conventions perhaps best visualized in the rather steep hipped roof.

A similar adjustment to building traditions guided Freud's design from 1936 for a music room for Pine House, an existing country house in Churt, near Hindhead, Surrey (fig. 7.6). The client was Nellie Muriel Gill (1881–1970), a prominent figure in the Hindhead and Haslemere music society, who occupied the house with her life partner, Ruby Davison. In the late 1930s and 1940s, Benjamin Britten and Peter Pears, the Amadeus quartet, Jennifer Vyvyan, Evelyn Rothwell, and others performed in the new music room.[40]

Placed perpendicular to the main house, only the garden façade and the wall at the far end of the music room have window openings. The latter is pierced by three stained-glass windows designed by Ernst von Leyden (1892–1969). The former is a sequence of slender brick piers alternating with slightly recessed, tall French metal windows. This garden fa-

Figure 7.5. Garden façade of the Charlton house, Berlin, by Otto Salvisberg, 1928–29. Used with permission of the Collection Centre Canadien d'Architecture / Canadian Centre for Architecture, Montréal.

Figure 7.6. Exterior of the music room, Pine House, Churt, Surrey, 1936. Used with permission of the RIBA Library Photographs Collection.

çade appears like a modernized version of a traditional English building. Designed without any decorative features, the garden façade evokes a faint echo of the main façade of Christopher Wren and Nicholas Hawksmoor's King's Gallery (1695–96) at Kensington Palace, in particular the proportions of the narrow windows between rising brick piers that give the impression of pilasters.[41]

The interior of the music room was modern with regards to forms and materials. Freud designed a long wooden sideboard that functioned as bookcase, storage space for music scores, and cocktail cabinet; all these were built by furniture maker Ian Henderson. A low room divider made from travertine marked the passageway to the main house (fig. 7.7). Integrated into the divider was an open fireplace in front of which lay a rug designed by Marion Dorn (1896–1964). Light fittings made of bronze with pale silk shades, wall coverings from Japanese grass cloth, and an oak wood mosaic floor completed the elegant room.

Whether the client for the music room was the same Mrs. M. M. Gill, who occupied a terraced house at 8 Alexander Place in South Kensington, London, from 1937–42, could not be ascertained. A certain similarity, however, exists between the music room interior and the refurbishment of the terraced house from 1937 to 1938. Freud placed the dining room on the ground floor and combined two first-floor rooms into a large drawing room. The main focus of the latter was a low sideboard made from waxed Australian walnut that integrated a travertine fireplace, a bookshelf, a radio recess, and other practical storage

Figure 7.7. Fireplace in the music room, Pine House, Churt, Surrey, 1936. Used with permission of the RIBA Library Photographs Collection.

spaces (fig. 7.8).[42] This piece recalls the music room, with its built-in furniture, as do the light fittings, again made from bronze with cream silk shades, and a dark brown rug by Dorn. Taken together, these details suggest either the same client or a practically minded architect who used similar details and comparable interior designs on projects he worked on in parallel.

The 1937 refurbishment of a semi-detached house, designed in 1910 by Barry Parker and Raymond Unwin in Hampstead Garden Suburb, took Freud into one of the centres of bourgeois life in London. Moreover, the project is remarkable because both émigré and British artists were engaged by the clients Dr. David Matthew, a psychiatrist, and his wife, A. A. Matthew. Freud radically transformed the interior by merging two rooms on the ground floor into one sitting room with a writing corner, a seating area with a fireplace, and a small library. Murals depicting Diana among wild animals were painted by the exiled German artist Hans Feibusch (1898–1998) and decorated the enlarged room that faced Hampstead Heath (fig. 7.9).[43] Dorn and Riette Sturge Moore (1907–95) contributed curtains and soft furnishings for the sitting room and the upstairs bedrooms.

In the same year Freud began to work on a speculative development of townhouses and a multi-apartment building. The first project comprised six single-family houses, arranged in three semi-detached pairs, in Frognal Close in Hampstead. The second was the design of fifty-six apartments in a four-storey building along Lyttelton Road, again in Hampstead.

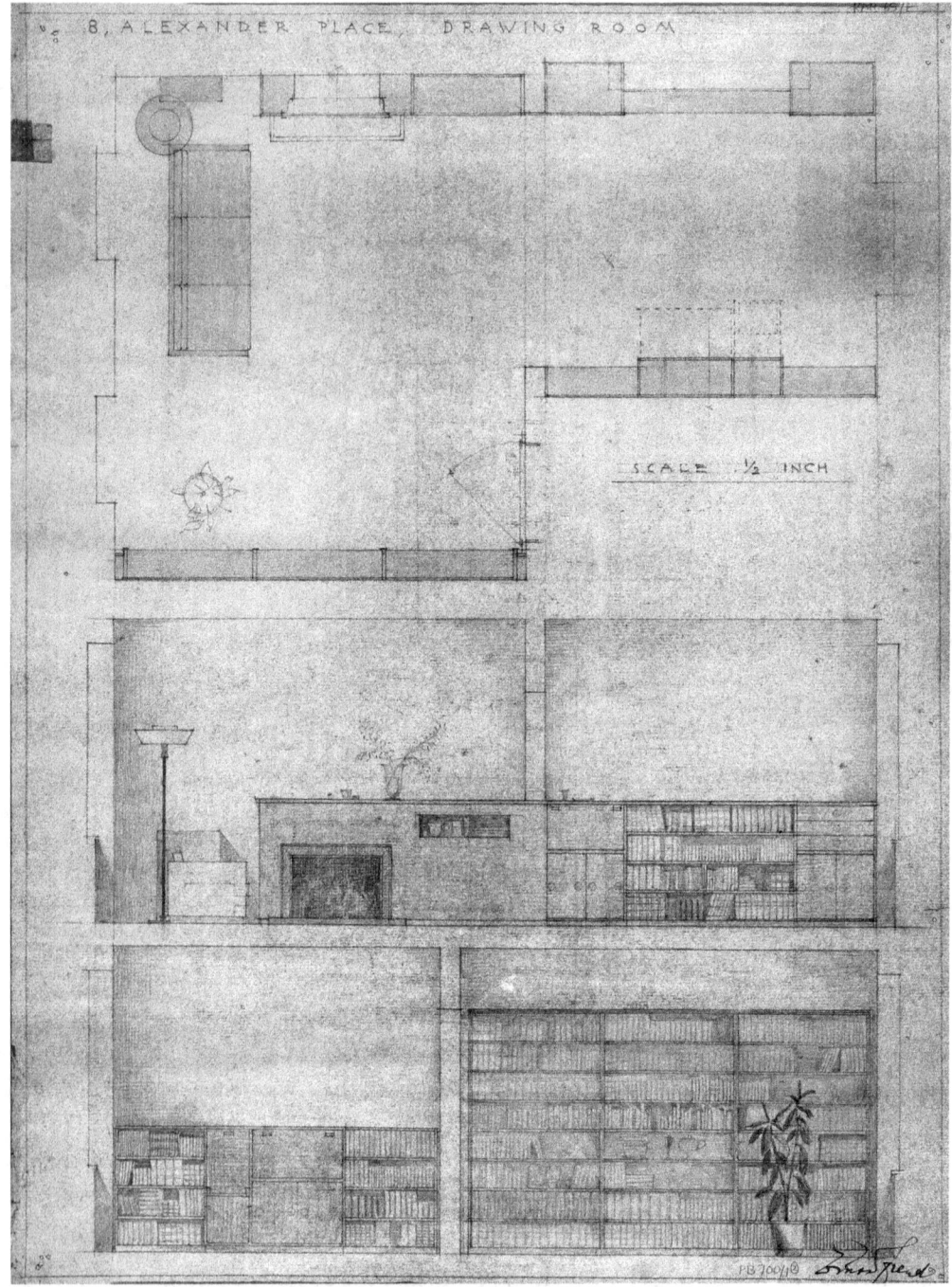

Figure 7.8. Interior design of 8 Alexander Place, London, 1937–38. Used with permission of the RIBA Library Drawings & Archives Collections.

Figure 7.9. Living room, with murals by Hans Feibusch, of the Matthew House, London, 1937–38. Used with permission of the Architectural Press Archive / RIBA Library Photographs Collection.

The Frognal Close project developed around a cul-de-sac that ensured privacy whilst maintaining 'a proper urban unity'.[44] The project recalls a Berlin scheme that was possibly on Freud's mind when he designed the original plan, now lost, for the group in London. Initially, Freud had envisioned two detached houses on either side of the cul-de-sac and two semi-detached ones at the far end; the number of houses and their placement were similar to the scheme by Neutra and Mendelsohn for Berlin-Zehlendorf from 1923 mentioned in chapter 5 (see fig. 5.3) In that case the builder Adolf Sommerfeld (1886–1964)[45]—from 1939 onwards also an émigré in England—had commissioned a suburban development of ten detached houses. Four were placed along Onkel-Tom-Straße with the remaining six grouped behind them around a cul-de-sac, two to either side and two at the end; these six were never realized.

Planning stipulations forced Freud to amend his design to three pairs of semi-detached buildings. Due to the sloping site the front-most two homes are a storey taller than the two-storey houses located in the rear. Freud kept all rooflines at the same height and thus achieved a strong visual unity. The buildings are cubic with flat roofs, the exposed brick relieved with some stone dressing, and the metal windows are framed horizontally by projecting bricklayers (fig. 7.10). Another reference to the Berlin scheme is the manner with which, at the houses flanking the entrance into the cul-de-sac, the window-cum-

Figure 7.10. Street corner of Frognal Lane townhouses, London, 1937–38. Used with permission of the Collection Centre Canadien d'Architecture / Canadian Centre for Architecture, Montréal.

brick bands on the first floor are pulled around the corner brick pillars that rise above thin, horizontally protruding roofs protecting the entrances below (fig. 7.11).[46]

While working on the Frognal scheme, Freud also designed Belvedere Court, a block of fifty-six rental apartments (fig. 7.12). Freud divided the large volume into three slabs linked with perpendicular stair towers with curved endings. Each of the seven staircases leads to two apartments on each floor. The four to five bedrooms and the living room of most apartments face south, and kitchens with a small utility balcony and bathrooms are strung along the northern façade.

The exterior is made of brownish, exposed bricks with reconstituted stone trimmings that frame the windows just above and below the openings. These whitish bands add a strong horizontal note to the complex. Freud pulled the bands across the curves of the towers and thus prevented any of the aerodynamic effects that characterized often similarly rounded corners at modernist buildings in Berlin. The three slabs follow the natural slope of the ground by stepping down half a level at each stair tower with the window sill bands of the one block becoming the window head bands of the next higher one. Like Frognal Lane, this development shows that Freud was very skilled in inserting modern volumes into the urban environment in an elegant manner.

Before the outbreak of the Second World War, Freud completed one more new building that was an attempt to create a deliberately modernist home. The client was Mrs. Dorothy Daisy Cottington-Taylor (née Gale, died 1944), from 1924–40 the director of the Good Housekeeping Institute for which Freud would execute a number of designs during the war. 'The Weald' was located in Betchworth, Surrey (fig. 7.13). Unusual for

At Home in England 131

Figure 7.11. Street corner of Sommerfeld housing, Berlin-Zehlendorf, by E. Mendelsohn and R. Neutra. Used with permission of Dion Neutra, Architect © and Richard and Dion Neutra papers, Department of Special Collections, Charles E. Young Research Library, University of California at Los Angeles.

Figure 7.12. Exterior of Belvedere housing block, London, 1937–38. Photograph from *The Builder*, February 1939, used with permission of the Collection Centre Canadien d'Architecture / Canadian Centre for Architecture, Montréal.

Figure 7.13. Exterior of 'The Weald', Betchworth, Surrey, 1937–39. Photograph from © The Courtauld Institute of Art, London.

Freud, the detached building shows an L-shaped plan. A one-storey tall wing accommodates a garage that doubled up as a home cinema, and parts of a servant's flat. The main body of the house was two storeys tall. The most remarkable feature is a half-circular bay window extending the dining room on the ground floor and the master bedroom above. This bay window and, indeed, the exterior recall modernist German dwellings. Alternating horizontal white stucco bands and strip windows structure the appearance of the curved extension. The flat roof accommodates a roof terrace and while there is no open plan, the spacious living room and an adjacent study, separated with foldable glass doors, occupy nearly half of the ground floor. Dreams of domesticity clothed in a modernist shell were the agenda for this commission, for the new home was to square the owner's wish to live modern and simple with the pursuit of her favourite pastime, viz. 'matters domestic—home-making, furnishing, cooking, catering, cleaning, sewing and decorating.'[47] When the house went on sale in 1948, significantly, the sales brochure censured carefully all images of the modernist bay window while emphasizing the practicality of the domestic spaces.[48]

The Second World War and its Aftermath

The townhouses project, the large apartment complex, and the modernist Cottington-Taylor house were all for clients with no known earlier connection to Freud, thus indicating that he was beginning to attract clients from outside the circles of fellow refugees and psychoanalysts. The outbreak of the Second World War on 1 September 1939 changed all this. On 30 August 1939, a certificate of naturalization was issued for Freud and his sons.[49] This Freud signed on 4 September 1939, just three days after the war had begun and a day after the United Kingdom had entered it. Because of his new citizenship Freud was not treated as an enemy alien as was his Berlin office partner Alexander Kurz.[50] When the British government began to intern German and Austrian citizens from May 1940 onwards, Kurz was working as a servant in Scotland.[51] He was interned at least until the end of January 1940.[52]

While Freud avoided this fate, the war brought economic hardship and suffering to his family. At some point, possibly during early 1940, Ernst L. and Lucie Freud moved into rented quarters at 2 Maresfield Gardens, London Hampstead.[53] This allowed them to rent out their home at 32 St. John's Wood Terrace in London Westminster, a terraced house that will be portrayed in the next chapter. The rented apartment was on the ground floor of a building into whose attic flat Natasha (born 1921) and Stephen Spender (1909–95), friends of the Freuds, moved after September 1941.[54] The Freuds temporarily left their rented apartment in June 1941 to live with their three children in their own home, but by October they were back at 2 Maresfield Gardens.[55]

With the outbreak of the war private commissions for domestic architecture ceased almost immediately as Lucie Freud reported in a letter from the beginning of October 1939.[56] This was not a temporary situation, but a condition that extended well into the post-war era as the couple commented upon repeatedly in letters to family members and friends as late as the end of 1947.[57] In late January 1941, Freud wrote that he did not foresee his profession being revived before the end of the war. He stated further that 'bombed buildings are no consolation for the architect',[58] because repairing damage done by German air raids earned him some money but did not satisfy professional aspirations. Other than repair jobs, the protection of his family and friends was on Freud's mind. He converted the rented ground floor apartment into a strong room; it was perhaps when working on this homemade pill-box shelter that Freud recalled his experience during the Great War when his comrades died the moment their shelter took a hit. Freud's endeavours were never directly put to the test, but the durability of the home shelter was proven when in mid February 1944 the house opposite theirs was destroyed and on 13 March 1945 a nunnery adjacent to 2 Maresfield Gardens was hit by a German V-2 rocket.[59] Finally, Freud also mentioned occasionally his work for a firm in the city.[60] Possibly this refers to his work for an acquaintance, Franz Böhm, an engineer who ran a company for air compressors for pneumatic hammers. While Böhm was interned Freud kept the company going.[61]

Architectural work had not entirely come to an end during the war. Freud's contact with the director of the Good Housekeeping Institute resulted in a small series of projects centring on the institute's premises at 30 Grosvenor Gardens, London Westminster. Freud designed in 1940 a test kitchen and laundry rooms, followed by further kitchens for a cookery school in 1941, and a reorganization of the office spaces in 1943.[62] The newly won expertise in institutional kitchen design may have helped the parental decision, taken during 1940, to send their son Clement to work as an apprentice to a hotel kitchen.[63] It may also have helped Freud to obtain in July 1945 the commission for a new kitchen in the fourteenth-century Old Hall at Corpus Christi College, Cambridge.[64] While

Freud's war-time kitchens were celebrated in *Good Housekeeping*, the post-war kitchen in Cambridge was a less-happy project. After a prolonged construction period that lasted a full three years the bursar wrote rather dryly to Freud in 1949 that irrespective of 'certain snags with the present kitchen arrangement, nonetheless, taking it as a whole everyone is of the opinion that it has been a success'. He thanked Freud and expressed his hope that 'we shall not loose touch with you altogether'.[65] This, however, happened soon because Freud was not consulted when the kitchen was replanned already in 1951.

Back in November 1942, Freud expressed hope that building work was picking up again,[66] but in January 1945 Lucie Freud wrote that her husband was prevented from working as an architect 'as private building has been restricted to £10,-,- a year for the time being'.[67] Eventually, Freud returned to work as architect but the type of work was a far cry from his pre-war projects. Instead, once again he faced the task of setting up practice after he had already done so in Berlin in 1920 and in London in 1933. Now, in 1945, Freud was asked to repair structural damages and work on the interior decorations. Among his clients were the Spenders and, a year later, the actress Peggy Ashcroft (1907–91). For the former, Freud worked on their new home at 15 Loudoun Road, in St John's Wood, and for the latter he did similar work on a home at 40 Manor Lodge, Frognal Lane, in the Hampstead area, just around the corner from his pre-war townhouse development.[68] Freud also converted townhouses into apartments in, for example, Hampstead in London and in Littlehampton.[69]

Government-imposed economic restrictions contributed to this change of the focus of Freud's work, but more important was that post-war Britain focused on building large-scale urban reconstruction and social housing. Accordingly, architects who could design mass housing for institutional and municipal clients were required. Freud was aware of this near-seismic shift of his profession when he participated in the 1951 competition for the Golden Lane Social Housing Estate in London; in retrospect a key competition of the era that helped to launch a new generation of modern architects. To draw up the entry, Freud employed the young Arthur Erickson (1924–2009).[70] Both architects' work in the office, which was located in the garage of Freud's home, was only interrupted by regular afternoon teas taken inside the main house. As the drawings are missing, it remains unknown what, if any, input Erickson had on Freud's ideas for a social-housing estate; in the end it didn't matter as Freud's was not among the winning entries.

The exile reduced Freud's work as a domestic architect, but the consequences of the Second World War nearly destroyed this focus. Table 7.1 sets out Freud's English commissions for single-family domestic designs between 1933 and 1965 with multi-apartment buildings counted separately. The figures for the six years from his arrival in late 1933 to 1939 show that the exile was a dramatic junction in Freud's career but not the end of his emphasis on domestic architecture. The latter came after 1940 when during the next twenty-five years Freud worked on only eleven single-family houses. Moreover, the division of his English domestic works according to commissions by émigrés or non-émigré clients indicates that from 1940–65 the number of émigré clients declined significantly, especially when compared with the years from 1933 to 1939. Parallel to this decline, Freud did acquire a larger number of domestic commissions from non-émigré clients. This relative decline in domestic projects did not mean the end of Freud's career as an architect. Rather, as the next chapter will show, works for his extended family in and around London kept him busy. Moreover, in the post-war period Freud picked up non-domestic architectural projects, some of which were of prestigious character, indicating that Freud once again had become a society architect.

Table 7.1. Houses designed, built, and refurbished by Freud in England between 1933 and c. 1965 (excluding houses for his own and extended family)

number of projects	1933–39 (6 years)		1940–65 (25 years)	
	new	refurbished	new	refurbished
Émigré clients	1	4	1	1
Non-émigré clients	1	8	2	7
Total		14		11
Multi-apartment buildings	2	1	4	3

Notes

1. E. L. Freud. 1934. 'A Foreign Architect observes England', *Design for To-Day* 2 (October): 394–395.
2. See C. Benton. 1995. *A Different World: Émigré Architects in Britain 1928–1958*. London: Heinz Gallery, 45–76.
3. Benton, *A Different World*, 45–76.
4. M. Faust. 2001. *Das Capri von Pommern: Geschichte der Insel Hiddensee von den Anfänge bis 1990*. Rostock: Ingo Koch Verlag, 217.
5. There may have been already an earlier trip, as in the first letter from 26 June 1933 Ernst Freud wrote to his wife he is remembered at the hotel (letter from Ernst Freud to Lucie Freud, 26 June 1933 [collection Esther Freud]; I have only seen English translations of these letters).
6. Letters from Ernst Freud to Lucie Freud, 22 September 1933 and 13 November 1933 (collection Esther Freud). Clement Freud states that the family arrived in the UK in early spring 1933 (C. Freud, *Freud Ego*, London: BBC, 13.)
7. Ernst held Austrian citizenship until 1939 when he and the three boys were naturalized. Two Austrian passports exist for Lucie Freud. The first one was valid until 11 December 1933. The second passport was valid from 4 January 1934 until the same day in 1939. This suggests that she had Austrian citizenship already while she was living in Berlin. I was unable to establish if and when she obtained British citizenship (for all documents: collection Stephen Freud, London).
8. M. Speidel. 2003. 'Bruno Taut in Japan. Exil und Kulturkritik', in B. Nicolai (ed.). 2003. *Architektur und Exil: Kulturtransfer und architektonische Emigration von 1930 bis 1950*. Trier: Porta Alba Verlag, 199–225 (202–203).
9. C. Benton. 1995. 'Biographies', in Benton, *A Different World*, 187–190 (188–189).
10. S. Klotz. 2001. *Fritz Landauer: Leben und Werk eines jüdischen Architekten*. Berlin: Dietrich Reimer, 189–194.
11. Letters from Ernst Freud to Lucie Freud, 26 and 27 June 1933 (collection Esther Freud). Unless otherwise noted, all information in the following is drawn from these two letters.
12. S. Ladwig-Winters. 1998. *Anwalt ohne Recht: Das Schicksal jüdischer Rechstanwälte in Berlin nach 1933*. Berlin: be.bra Verlag, 113. The same year, Cohn escaped to Argentina (http://www.brak.de/anwalt-ohne-recht/Panel_LA_Stein_u_Cohn.pdf, accessed March 21, 2008).
13. Letter from Ernst Freud to Lucie Freud, evening of 30 June 1933 (collection Esther Freud).
14. In 1933, Freud did, however, have a chance to show the elder Lutyens some photographs of his work (letter from Ernst Freud to Lucie Freud, 9 March 1934 [collection Esther Freud]).

When in 1934 the Home Office requested references from local architects about the benefits of Freud's work for the country in order to renew his permit for another year Freud contacted again the elder Lutyens. As of September 1939 Ernst Freud had British citizenship and thus no longer needed a work permit. On 29 November 1940 he registered for the first time with the Architects' Registration Council for the United Kingdom (ARCUK; email from Architects' Registration Board, London, 6 April 2004).

15. Letter from Ernst Freud to Lucie Freud, 10 July 1933 (collection Esther Freud).
16. Melitta Schmideberg (née Klein) had lived on and off in the United Kingdom from 1928 onwards. Walter Schmideberg could secure a visa only in 1932. P. Grosskurth. 1986. *Melanie Klein: Her World and her Work*. New York: Alfred A. Knopf, 183–184.
17. Benton, *A Different World*, 188.
18. G. A. Platz. 1933. *Wohnräume der Gegenwart*. Berlin: Propyläen.
19. The exhibition was shown at Dorland Hall, Lower Regent Street, 20 June to 12 July 1933, and sponsored by *Country Life*. Information about the exhibition was kindly supplied by Alan Powers, London.
20. Letter from Ernst Freud to Lucie Freud, evening 30 June 1933 (collection Esther Freud).
21. Letter from Ernst Freud to Lucie Freud, 12 July 1933 (collection Esther Freud); Anonymous. 1933. [no title], *Design for To-Day* 1 (October): 237.
22. These were the Lampl house (1925), the Frank country house (1928–30), and the Scherk house (1930).
23. Richard Ginsberg director's office (1930) at the Mitteldeutsche Bodencredit-Anstalt Berlin.
24. M. Speyer. 1935. 'Decoration—the Doctor's Dilemma', *Design for To-day* 3 (June): 228–230.
25. Letter from Ernst Freud to Lucie Freud, 17 August 1933 (collection Esther Freud).
26. 'Two Modern Houses'. 1934. *Home & Gardens* (March): 504–506.
27. 'Two Modern Houses'. 1934. *Home & Gardens* (March): 506.
28. Clement Freud states that he and his two brothers had been scholars at Dartington Hall who were not obliged to pay a school fee (Freud, *Freud Ego*, 14). Ernst Freud mentioned in one letter to his wife that the first invoice from Dartington Hall had arrived (letter from Ernst Freud to Lucie Freud, 7 October 1933 [collection Esther Freud]). See also letters from Ernst Freud to Lucie Freud, 5 July 1933 and 10 July 1933 (collection Esther Freud).
29. In 1931, Germany enacted laws that controlled foreign exchange and the flow of the Mark into foreign countries—among them the Reichsfluchtsteuergesetz. This law, for example, taxed everything a resident who planned to leave the country—German or foreigner—owned. Initially, the Nazis used such existing laws selectively in order both to terrorize fleeing German-Jewish citizens and to extort money. Subsequently enacted Nazi laws made the transfer of material possessions and financial resources increasingly difficult until it became impossible. Initially, however, to transfer property was feasible even if it meant the partial loss of one's possessions due to excessive taxation. See B. Schreiber. 2007. '"Arisierung" in Berlin 1933–1945. Eine Einführung', in C. Biggeleben, B. Schreiber, and K. J. L. Steiner (eds.). 2007. *'Arisierung' in Berlin*. Berlin: Metropol, 13–53, especially 19–28.
30. Letters from Ernst Freud to Lucie Freud, 27 March 1934, 28 March 1934 (collection Esther Freud).
31. Letter from F. Herrmann, London, to author, 17 July 2001.
32. Letter from Ernst Freud to Lucie Freud, 19 October 1933 (collection Esther Freud).
33. Letter from F. Herrmann, London, to author, 14 August 2002. Conversation with H. Weinberger, Leamington Spa, 18 October 2002.
34. Richard Hamburger was already in exile in Edinburgh to retake his medical exam when Ernst Freud stayed in London in summer 1933 (letter from Ernst Freud to Lucie Freud, 10 July 1933 [collection Esther Freud]). The rest of the family apparently left Berlin on 8 November 1933 (letter from Ernst Freud to Lucie Freud, 7 November 1933 [collection Esther Freud]).

35. Letters from M. Hamburger to the author, 31 July 2002, 10 August 2002, and 8 October 2002.
36. Letter from F. Herrmann, London, to author, 14 August 2002. Conversation with H. Weinberger, Leamington Spa, 18 October 2002
37. London Metropolitan Archives, Acc/3816/P/02/644/A-C.
38. Conversation with C. Zentner, London, 12 July 2002. Freud refurbished the Maysland farmhouse when Crittall offered it to Gerda Mosse and her children, who lived there until 1946. On W. F. (Pink) Crittall see A. Crittall. 1989. 'The Story of the Crittall Family', in D. J. Blake. *Window Vision*, s.l.: Crittall Windows, 107–97 (184–86).
39. H. Eckstein. 1932. *Neue Wohnbauten*. Munich: F. Bruckmann, 9–11.
40. Correspondence and conversation with J. Penticost, Churt, August 2002.
41. K. Downes. 1966. *English Baroque Architecture*. London: Zwemmer, 43, plate 83.
42. M. Whirter. 1939. 'New Rooms for Old', *The Ideal Home* (March): 164–165.
43. 'Replanning of a House in Hampstead'. 1939. *Architectural Review* 86 (November): supplement 221–222.
44. 'A Group of Houses in Hampstead'. 1938. *Architectural Review* 84 (August): 54–56 (54).
45. C. Kress. 2007. 'Frühe "Arisierung" in der Bauindustrie: Adolf Sommerfeld und seine Firmengruppe', in C. Biggeleben, *'Arisierung' in Berlin*, 151–181.
46. See T. S. Hines. 1982. *Richard Neutra and the Search for Modern Architecture*. Oxford: Oxford University Press, 37.
47. D. D. Cottington Taylor and E. L. Freud. 1937. 'To buy or to build? Mrs. Taylor's long years of experience at Good Housekeeping Institute are being turned to good account now that she is building a house for herself', *Good Housekeeping* (June): 76–77, 146–148.
48. 'The Weald, Betchworth near Reigate' (sales particulars, c. 1948), Surrey History Centre, Woking, 2173/3/84.
49. Collection Stephen and Ann Freud, London.
50. Benton, *A Different World*, 79–83.
51. Letter from Lucie Freud to Grockchen, 2 October 1939 (folder 55 Lux to Augenfeld, box 12, Sigmund Freud papers, Sigmund Freud Collection, Manuscript Division, Library of Congress, Washington DC).
52. Letter from Marion Kurz (the daughter of Alexander Kurz), to [Alexander and Sophie Freud], 4 December 1940 (folder Kurz, Marion, 1940, box 6, Alexander and Sophie Freud papers, Manuscript Division, Library of Congress, Washington DC); letter from Ernst Freud to Alexander Freud, 25 January 1941 (folder Ernst Freud / Lucie Freud, 1938–53, box 1, Alexander and Sophie Freud papers, Manuscript Division, Library of Congress, Washington DC).
53. One of the earliest letter from this address is from Ernst Freud to Alexander Freud, 29 May 1940 (folder Ernst Freud / Lucie Freud, 1938–53, box 1, Alexander and Sophie Freud papers, Manuscript Division, Library of Congress, Washington DC).
54. J. Goldsmith (ed.). 1985. *Stephen Spender Journals 1939–1983*. London: Faber and Faber, 58. Clement Freud states that the Spenders lived a floor below the Freuds (C. Freud, *Freud Ego*, 33).
55. Letter from Ernst Freud to Harry Freud, 15 June 1941; letter from Ernst Freud to Harry Freud, 15 October 1941 (folder Ernst Freud / Lucie Freud, 1938–53, box 1, Alexander and Sophie Freud papers, Manuscript Division, Library of Congress, Washington DC).
56. Letter from Lucie Freud to Grockchen, 2 October 1939 (folder 55 Lux to Augenfeld, box 12, Sigmund Freud papers, Sigmund Freud Collection, Manuscript Division, Library of Congress, Washington DC).
57. Letter from Ernst Freud to Harry Freud, 15 November 1947 (folder Ernst Freud / Lucie Freud, 1938–49, box 5, Harry Freud papers, Manuscript Division, Library of Congress, Washington DC).

58. Letter from Ernst Freud to Alexander Freud, 25 January 1941 (folder Ernst Freud / Lucie Freud, 1938–53, box 1, Alexander and Sophie Freud papers, Manuscript Division, Library of Congress, Washington DC).
59. J. Sutherland. 2005. *Stephen Spender. A Literary Life*. Oxford: Oxford University Press, 286–287, 300.
60. Letter from Ernst Freud to Alexander Freud, 25 January 1941 (folder Ernst Freud / Lucie Freud, 1938–53, box 1, Alexander and Sophie Freud papers, Manuscript Division, Library of Congress, Washington DC).
61. Stephen Freud recalled that Franz Böhm, a refugee, had two companies, Contractor Services Ltd. and Compactor Engineering Ltd., for which he himself also worked at some point (conversation with Stephen Freud, 9 July 2002). See also C. Freud, *Freud Ego*, 68.
62. P. L. Garbutt. 1940. 'Once again The Institute leads the Way', *Good Housekeeping* (April): 36–37, 100; P. L. Garbutt. 1940. 'The New Institute opens its Doors', *Good Housekeeping* (September): 29–32; E. L. Freud. 1940. 'A Domestic Laboratory The Good Housekeeping Institute', *The National Builder* 20 (October): 49–51; P. L. Garbutt. 1942. 'The new Good Housekeeping School of Cookery approved by the Ministry of Food', *Good Housekeeping* (January): 28–29.
63. Freud, *Freud Ego*, 34.
64. 'Kitchen for Corpus Christi College, Cambridge'. 1949. *Architects' Journal* (6 January): 11–12.
65. Letter from Domestic Bursar to Ernst Freud, 11 February 1949 (box 'Kitchen Reconstruction 1945–49, Parker Library, Corpus Christi College, Cambridge).
66. Letter from Ernst Freud to Alexander Freud, 22 November 1942 (folder Ernst Freud / Lucie Freud, 1938–53, box 1, Alexander and Sophie Freud papers, Manuscript Division, Library of Congress, Washington DC).
67. Letter from Lucie Freud to Harry Freud 8 January 1945 (folder Ernst Freud / Lucie Freud, 1938–49, box 5, Harry Freud papers, Manuscript Division, Library of Congress, Washington DC).
68. Emails from Lady Spender to the author, 20 September 2004, 26 June 2005.
69. Letter from Ernst Freud to Harry Freud, 2 September 1945 (folder Ernst Freud / Lucie Freud, 1938–49, box 5, Harry Freud papers, Manuscript Division, Library of Congress, Washington DC); 'Conversion of Houses—Seaside Flats Little Hampton'. 1946. *The National House Builder and Building Digest* (November): 28–29.
70. Written answers by Arthur Erickson to a questionnaire by the author, 13 April 2005; *The Circle* newsletter, 18 March 1952 (RIBA archive); Corporation of London Record Office, List of Participants in the Competition; E. Iglauer. 1981. *Seven Stones, A Portrait of Arthur Erickson, Architect*. Madeira Park, British Columbia: Harbour Publishing, 54.

Chapter 8

Family Architect

Throughout his career in Berlin and London Freud worked on a large number of homes for both his immediate and extended family. In Berlin, Freud designed at least two interiors for his own family and the never-completed house for Carl and Gerda Mosse, already discussed in chapter 5. In London, Freud again created a home for his own family but also quickly became the architect for his wider family, most notably when he altered a house in Hampstead for his aging parents in 1938. He also completed jobs for his sisters Anna Freud and Mathilde Hollitscher, for example, and after the war for his son Stephen Freud and for members of the next generation of the Mosse family, his wife's relatives.

Along with a brief overview of this aspect of Freud's œuvre, this chapter focuses on both the family homes of Ernst L. and Lucie Freud in Germany and England and the home Ernst L. Freud created for his parents in London. In order to present an exemplary comparison between Freud's pre-exile and post-exile designs for the homes of his family, the narrative steps to some degree outside the chronology.

Berggasse in London

As the first family member who had fled to England in 1933, Freud was consulted by subsequently arriving relatives with regard to finding accommodation and even making investments into real estate. When his uncle Alexander Freud (1866–1943) left for England his exile in Switzerland, to where he had already fled in March 1938,[1] he lived in the seaside town of Hove in Sussex.[2] Alexander Freud relied on Freud to try to find suitable accommodation in London. He was specific that he wanted to live in both exile and old age in London close to Sigmund and Martha Freud's home, as it symbolized for him living in or at least being close to a new Berggasse.[3] Thus, even after Sigmund Freud had passed away on 23 September 1939, 21 Maresfield Gardens in Hampstead was elevated to the equivalent of Berggasse 19 in Vienna, the former centre for the extended family. With Freud's architectural help this new family centre was a reality for some time during and after the Second World War when many family members lived, worked, or owned property in the closer and wider vicinity of the last home of Sigmund Freud.

Alexander Freud himself purchased 4 Maresfield Gardens during the summer of 1939 as an investment property for which Freud drew up plans to divide the town house into rental flats.[4] Ernst L. and Lucie Freud moved into the adjacent building at 2 Maresfield Gardens in early 1940 in response to a deteriorating economic situation. Moreover, during 1941 Anna Freud and Dorothy Burlingham began to open various centres of the Hampstead War Nurseries in the vicinity of Maresfield Gardens. In January, the first children's rest centre was established at 13 Wedderburn Road,[5] with Freud having possibly been responsible for designing a bomb shelter in the structure. In the summer of that year, a babies' rest centre followed at 5 Netherhall Gardens, just a street over from Maresfield Gardens and refurbished by Freud. In 1951, Freud worked on 12 Maresfield Gardens, the first of three locations for the post-war Hampstead Child Therapy Course and Clinic on that street; the other two were number 21, acquired in 1955, and number 14, taken over in 1967.

More family properties were nearby in Belsize Park Gardens. Number 25 was owned by Gerda Mosse. During the war an apartment in the house was used to accommodate staff from the Hampstead War Nurseries.[6] Number 1 was owned by Gerda Mosse, Freud himself, and Mrs. Böhm, presumably the wife of Freud's friend and war-time employer Franz Böhm. Freud converted both houses into rental apartments. His sister Mathilde Hollitscher (1887–1978), for whom Freud had already designed a fashion store named 'Robell' on Baker Street in 1938, extended the Berggassen quarter to the north of Maresfield Gardens where she owned an investment property in Linfield Gardens.[7] And his son Lucian Freud pushed the borders of the Berggassen quarter to the south when he rented 28 Clifton Hill in c. 1948. Lucian Freud redecorated the interior in a way that earned his father's highest praise as Lucie Freud told in a letter:

> Lux [i.e. Lucian] painted the entire house in oil with his own hands and those of friends. I have never heard Ernst being so enthusiastic about the work of anybody else as he was about Lux's colours and his architectural and other ideas. The bedroom, for example, seems to be painted in a strangely matt green (Lux used paint for slate tablets) and Ernst said the effect of the colour is that one's eyes want to fall close as soon as one enters the room. Above the bathtub a stuffed fish is suspended in a glass box. One room, the conservatory accommodates Lux's drawing table and otherwise only plants and birds.[8]

Later the house was acquired by a member of the Mosse family and Freud again executed smaller architectural works.

Part of the new Berggassen quarter was of course also the London home of Ernst L. and Lucie Freud at 32 St John's Wood Terrace. That house is best understood in comparison with the family homes in Berlin; Freud himself drew such comparisons, for example during the exploratory visit to London in the summer of 1933 when he explored possible rental apartments.[9] Twice he described his experiences in London as a déjà vu taking him back to the time when his and Lucie Freud's life together began in Berlin. The first instance was when his temporary room in an English boarding house recalled his first rented room in Detmolder Straße in Berlin back in 1919.[10] The second came when Freud wrote to his wife that a new family home in London would not be quite as beautiful as the one in the Tiergarten quarter in Berlin, yet there were parts of London that were like the old West of Berlin.[11] After the couple was reunited in late 1933, they lived in an apartment at 36 Clarges Street in London's Westminster area.[12] In early 1935, their mail was addressed to 115 King Henry's Road in Hampstead.[13] Later that year, the Freuds moved into the terraced house at 32 St John's Wood Terrace in the same district[14]; this was to become the permanent family home in London. Disregarding differences in topography, urban layout, and architecture, some similarities between the St John's Wood area and the Tiergarten quarter exist. The latter was located to the west of the old royal hunting grounds that had been converted into a public park. The former was just to the north of Regent's Park which was of comparable royal background. In both cases, the city centre was within reach at the other side of the large park.

Family Homes in Berlin

From the three Berlin apartments, the only photographic records that exist are of the interior of Regentenstraße 23 where the family lived from c. 1924 until 1932. Some of the images were published in the August issue of *Die Pyramide* that was discussed in chapter 1.[15] They depict an interior whose design followed conventional ideas about bourgeois domesticity. The studio, or *Herrenzimmer*, was dominated by cubic furniture like, for example, a wooden wall-to-wall bookshelf surrounding a brick fireplace, a magazine cupboard made from polished pine stained in a shade of grey,[16] and Freud's desk and chair that stood nearby (fig. 8.1). In opposition to the serene and solid furniture, the beds and the daybed in the master bedroom were made from slender, wooden profiles lacquered in a light colour. Wardrobes with glazed doors and curtains behind the panes added to the gracile impression.[17]

Figure 8.1. Desk and chair in the study of Ernst L. Freud's second Berlin apartment, 1924–25. Photograph from *Die Pyramide*, August 1928, used with permission of the Collection Centre Canadien d'Architecture / Canadian Centre for Architecture, Montréal.

This architectural gendering of the rooms extended to a more conceptual level. The feminine furniture of the master bedroom reinterpreted Biedermeier furniture as exemplified in the curves of the endboards of the beds. Such seemingly simplistic furniture pieces were popular among the middle classes ever since the architect Paul Mebes (1872–1938) published his study *Um 1800* in 1908,[18] an evocation of bourgeois living that held great attraction for many German-Jewish citizens.[19]

While the bedroom looked towards the past, the studio established a subtle dialogue with contemporary modernist furniture and stylistic ideas. Freud's desk and chair were marked by a reduction of the wooden frames to functionally and structurally necessary elements, like, for example, the two open shelves that held up the writing surface and placed drawings and papers within easy reach. The chair was constructed from four vertical L-shaped profiles. The two rear profiles extended beyond the height of the upholstered seat in order to form with two horizontally inserted profiles the backrest. From the lower of the latter two armrests cantilevered towards the front edge of the seat. The chair displayed its structure, forwent ornament, and minimized the material needed to build it. At the same time, the reduction was not driven to the artistic extreme that, for example, transformed into abstract pieces of seating sculptures the Red-Blue chair (1918) and the Berlin chair (1923), both designed by Gerrit Rietveld (1888–1964) at around the same time. The profiles of the Red-Blue armchair pointed, so to speak, beyond their junctions towards modernist ideas about space and art. The profiles of the Freud chair did not protrude into such realms; his chair was modern, presumably comfortable, but it was not a signifier of modernism.

Similarly, the design of the magazine cupboard played on *De Stijl* principles with its front abstractly composed from the vertical planes of the doors, receding edges along the bottom and upwards on the right, and the open, upper-left quadrant structured by the rhythm of thick horizontal boards projecting from within the depth of the storage container (fig. 8.2). Finally, the bookshelf around the brick fireplace, in front of which two chairs that were similar to the desk chair were placed, recalled the domestic comfort of a library or smoking room in a bourgeois home. Within this cosy scene in front of a fireplace and spines of books signs of modern construction methods were visible but not displayed ostentatiously. For example, the continuous shelves

Figure 8.2. Journal cupboard in the study of Ernst L. Freud's second Berlin apartment, 1924–25. Photograph from *Die Pyramide*, August 1928, used with permission of the Collection Centre Canadien d'Architecture / Canadian Centre for Architecture, Montréal.

were extended along the length of the wall above the fireplace without any noticeable vertical support.

Freud's gendered understanding of modern interior and furniture modernized traditional forms of bourgeois domesticity and its spatial settings by combining the furniture with modern techniques and ideas. Beside such aesthetic statements, the furniture and interiors represented an investment into both material values and those associated with creating a home. Both paid off because when the family went into exile they could take their furniture with them to England where they eventually were fitted into their new home.[20]

A New Family Home in London

In London, the Freuds moved into 32 St John's Wood Terrace towards the end of 1935. The house was about a century old, three storeys tall, but only 15 ft and 9 in, or about 5 m, wide.[21] The transformation of the old house into a modern family home was an opportunity for Freud to redefine his ideas about modern architecture and interior design within the context of the new life in England. The focus now was on issues of efficiency with regard to the use of both space and limited economic means especially in comparison with some of Freud's Berlin projects. This shift in emphasis was an adjustment to the economic circumstances of exile and, possibly, a response to the lack of modernist architecture in English towns, circumstances in which Freud wanted to prove that he could modernize without resorting to modernist design.

The equation of modern architecture with efficiency was something Freud developed in the redesign of the house with regards to, first, the rational use of the small interior spaces and, second, the reliance on modern technology—in this case electricity—to efficiently operate the house. Concerning the first point, Freud created from two smaller rooms on the first floor a larger living room with a recessed dining area. Besides opening up the entire floor to more light, the arrangement put at the inhabitants' disposal traditional bourgeois spaces, even if on a much smaller scale than in Berlin apartments. Freud did not opt for an expressively open plan. Instead, he separated both areas with a purpose-designed hip-high sideboard towards the dining area with a shelf fitted at its rear towards the sitting area (fig. 8.3). The sideboard offered storage space and housed the shaft of a small service lift from the kitchen below. Both pieces were lifted off the floor by bent metal tube brackets fixed against the lower parts of the walls. Freud's Viennese friend Augenfeld had already used similar devices earlier, for example for a bar cupboard in an apartment in Vienna in c. 1930.[22] Another example for the considerate use of space was the master bedroom on the next floor up. There, bedroom furniture from the Berlin apartment was reinstalled in an intricate three-dimensional puzzle of built-in cupboards, wardrobes, and storage spaces along the upper parts of the interior walls (fig. 8.4).

More Berlin furniture could be found in the boys' bedroom where the chairs from the studio were put to use, and in the newly built study to the rear of the ground floor. From there Freud's view went over a new desk through a folding metal window into the garden (fig. 8.5). Along the wall a bookshelf again surrounded a fireplace in front of which the same fireplace screen was placed that can be seen on one of the photographs of the second Berlin apartment. (see chapter 1, fig. 1.3). The bookshelves, however, were different

Figure 8.3. Upper-level living room in Ernst L. Freud's London home, 1935. Used with permission of the RIBA Library Photographs Collection.

Figure 8.4. Bedroom furniture from the second Berlin apartment in Ernst L. Freud's London home, 1935. Used with permission of the RIBA Library Photographs Collection.

Figure 8.5. Ernst L. Freud at his desk in the study of his London home, 1935; on the shelf behind him is the portrait bust of Lucie Freud by Joachim Karsch. Used with permission of RIBA Library Photographs Collection.

this time, as Freud had taken to London the shelves from the Berlin apartment of Gustav Krojanker, his Zionist friend from days in Munich and his client in Berlin.[23]

With regard to the second point, the application of modern electric technology in the operation of the house, the intention was to increase the useable interior space.[24] To this end, Freud's house became an experiment in electrification with under-ceiling heating panels and an automated hot-water tank; similar appliances were used by Freud later, for example, in the remodelling of 8 Alexander Place in South Kensington as noted in the previous chapter. Consequently, in the St. John's Wood Terrace house most fireplaces and chimney flutes were removed, increasing the tight interior spaces and allowing Freud more freedom in changing the existing spatial division on the different levels.

Earlier in 1935, Freud made some architectural-philosophical observations about changes in a private home like his own. In a lecture on 'Modern Architecture in England?', of which a rudimentary record exists in a letter by Marshall McLuhan, Freud stated that 'the idea of the house centred around the hearth was gone' and that 'to break down the division between the house and out-of-doors' was one goal of recent architecture.[25] Both points were pragmatic adaptations to the much milder weather in England. In addition, the latter point was also a reference to modernist architectural principles that had already influenced the Frank country house near Berlin. There, the stepped terraces and the dining-room panorama window, which could be lowered into the basement, established close indoor-outdoor relationships without Freud therefore succumbing to modernist ideas aimed at a radically reshaped domestic architecture.

The Frank house, moreover, was centred on the open fireplace in the hall on the ground floor, an example of a Loosian emphasis on bourgeois domesticity in Freud's work that was reinforced in the case of the country house by other design elements like, for example, the slender wooden ceiling beams, more decorative than constructive, and the choreographed views into the upper level through the open stair hall. Regarding his English domestic interiors, Freud's radical-sounding rejection of the hearth as the centre of the home turned out eventually to be mostly a reduction in size and thus importance of this design feature. For example, the living room of the townhouse in South Kensington (fig. 8.6) and the music room for Mrs. Gill (see chapter 7, fig. 7.7) offered open fireplaces but both were much smaller and less prominent than those of Freud's Berlin designs.

While it lacked a fireplace, the main living room on the first floor of the St. John's Wood home was furnished with a combination of purpose-designed pieces and antique ones, another characteristic of the design that referred to Loos's ideas about domestic interiors. The origin of these pieces is unknown; they may have been in use already in Berlin, or perhaps they were heirlooms, or another example of the adjustments to English conventions that Freud made in his interior design ideas. The modernity of the home was unaffected by the parallel use of antique and modern pieces. The mixture triggered a

Figure 8.6. Living room with fireplace at 8 Alexander Place, London. Used with permission of the RIBA Library Photographs Collection.

comment about the house by the author Arnold Zweig (1887–1968), a fellow exile from Berlin and himself not a stranger to living in a modern house. Before Zweig had to flee Germany, he lived in Berlin in a house designed between 1930 and 1931 by Freud's colleague Harry Rosenthal.[26] Its centre was an all-glass writing room on the top level, an architectural attempt at helping Zweig to continue to write despite a progressively worsening eye ailment. After a visit to the Freud family house in London in October 1937, Zweig reported to his friend Sigmund Freud that the young family's new house 'is charming in its simple dignity and modernity'. That the older Freud didn't grasp the opportunity 'to sample the comfort of modern travel' in order to visit 'children and grandchildren in London'[27] Zweig regretted deeply.

From Hiddensee to Hidden House

During their time in Berlin the Freuds owned a holiday home on the island of Hiddensee adjacent to the island of Rügen off Germanys' Pomeranian coast along the Baltic Sea. From the nineteenth century onwards, Hiddensee was a destination for artists, writers, and intellectuals, many of whom harboured misgivings about modern metropolitan life and wanted to return to the bosom of nature.[28] During the Weimar Republic, the island developed into a popular holiday destination or, as the author Peter Squenz once quipped, an 'island of stars and the hopeful' including a 'furniture dealer, who read Bergson, lawyers who have dealings with the Völkerbund, daughters from well-looked-upon families who nevertheless dance or dabble in the arts and crafts, interior architects with factories, feuilleton editors, antiquarians'.[29] The property of the Freuds was one half of a fisherman's cottage that had been built in c. 1850 at the northern end of the Dorfstraße, the main street through the village of Vitte.[30] Photographs show a one-storey building huddled underneath a steep roof sheltering further rooms and covered by tiles rather than thatch. Freud had added two larger dormer windows to the roof, lifted the ceiling of one room to increase the available volume and installed a large sliding window (fig. 8.7).[31] After the Freuds had fled Germany, they sold their half in 1934 to a Leipzig-based lawyer and his wife.[32]

The loss of the holiday home must have been on the minds of Ernst and Lucie Freud in particular as they lived in London in much smaller surroundings than at their apartments in Berlin. By 1937 Freud had completed the extension of Ernest Jones's cottage, the house for the banker Marx, and the music room for Mrs. Gill. In the same year, he also received the commissions for the townhouses on Frognal Lane and the apartment complex Belvedere Court; accordingly, the Freuds may have felt that they could embark on again acquiring a cottage to make up for both the rather confined living situation in London and the former place on Hiddensee.

Sigmund Freud had comparable feelings when he congratulated his son early in 1938 on the 'opening of Hidden House' in Walberswick, Suffolk, on the east coast of England: 'It is typically Jewish not to renounce anything and to replace what has been lost. Moses, who in my opinion left a lasting imprint on the Jewish character, was the first to set an example. In our present difficult times your existence in England stands out boldly against all the misery around us. Whenever I think of your success I feel pleased and full of hope for the chances of the next generation.'[33] While Sigmund Freud identified the acquisition

Figure 8.7. Ernst L. Freud's cottage on the island of Hiddensee, Germany, 1924 or later. Used with permission of Florian Hülsen.

of the cottage as both an expression of a general Jewish character and as a return to normality in the life of his son, for Ernst L. and Lucie Freud the cottage constituted possibly an equally strong link with their life in Germany. Hidden House, the name of the new place, may have been a play on Hiddensee, the name of the German island.[34] In the early twentieth century some writers on the island speculated that the German word *Hidden* meant *Hütten* (huts),[35] in which case Hidden House would translate as *Hüttenhaus*, a small, simple house or, literally, a hut-house.

Compared with the Hiddensee cottage, the Hidden House was an improvement rather than a mere replacement, not least because the one-storey tall building was solely occupied by the Freud family. Architecturally, a circular bay with a multi-paned horizontal window that followed the curve at one corner of the living room distinguished the cottage (fig. 8.8). Together with the thatched roof, the modern bay window—most likely an addition by Freud—made the house reminiscent of modern cottages on Hiddensee and Rügen that were built during the early twentieth century by such architects as, for example, Rosenthal and Max Taut (1884–1967). The latter had designed in 1924 a summer house for Walter Pingel, an interior architect from Berlin. The Pingel house featured a steep thatched roof above a low-lying cube with horizontal, multi-paned corner windows along with slightly projecting oriel windows that stretched around the corners.[36] The curved bay window of the Hidden House appears almost like a comment on Taut's design. Inside the cottage the bay window opens up into the roof space with visible rafters, so that the interior recalls the one of the barn at the Northease country house that was illustrated in *Die Pyramide* together with Freud's second Berlin apartment.[37] In short, Hidden House is another example of Freud's English domestic architecture, fusing Freud's knowledge of recent buildings in Germany with his growing acquaintance with English architecture.

Economic considerations were most likely one reason to purchase a cottage in Walberswick, a small village on the Suffolk coast in an isolated corner of England and, accordingly, affordable even for a refugee family from Europe. The surrounding landscape may have been another incentive as the view from the dyke over both the North Sea and the hinterland is strongly reminiscent of the German coast along both the Baltic Sea and the North Sea. Walberswick lacks the steep cliffs of Hiddensee and the Pomeranian island is without tides going in and out, but both locations share 'the clarity of the air, the infinite magnitude of the land, the sea and the firmament, surrounded by the undivided line of the horizon—all that comes together and produces time and again a feeling as if one occupies infinite space,'[38] as one contemporary writer described the fascination of the landscape of Hiddensee.

Other German-Jewish and Continental exiles and refuges, some of them friends and relatives of the Freuds, likewise acquired properties in Walberswick. This was almost ironic considering that during the Great War, the Scottish architect Charles Rennie Mackintosh (1886–1925) had been arrested in the village because his Glaswegian accent was mistaken for that of a German spy.[39] Incidentally, it was Mackintosh's friend Patrick Geddes, with whom Freud was in contact when he planned the Weizmann house in 1926, and his wife Anna who helped to convince the authorities that the fellow Scotsman was

Figure 8.8. 'Hidden House' at Walberswick, England, with the addition of a glass bow window, 1937. Used with permission of Volker M. Welter.

an architect and not a spy. Now Freud became architect to an exile community in the village—most of them speaking English with variously strong accents—for which he refurbished and extended cottages, and after the end of the war even built new ones. Among his Walberswick clients were, for example, his sister Anna, the psychoanalyst Dr. Willi Hoffer (1897–1967), the engineer Franz Böhm, director of both Contractor Services Ltd. and Compactor Engineering Ltd.,[40] and yet again a Mrs. Gill who may or may not have been the very same owner of the music salon and the townhouse in South Kensington. The history of the exile community of Walberswick, the architectural history of their cottages, and the contribution Freud made to the architecture of the village remains to be written.

A Home for his Parents

When Arnold Zweig lamented in his letter from mid October 1937 that Sigmund Freud no longer travelled, little did he know that just over eight months later Sigmund and Martha Freud, Anna Freud, and various household members and friends would be on their way to England after the German occupation of Austria. The group left Vienna on 4 June 1938, stopped over in Paris the next day when Ernst L. Freud joined them, and arrived in Victoria Station on 6 June where Ernest Jones welcomed them. In 1923, in his architectural youth, Freud had longed to reorganize Berggasse 19, a wish that then, as cited in chapter 6, had solicited Anna Freud's sharp rebuttal. Fifteen years later as a mature architect of forty six years Freud suddenly not only had the opportunity but the responsibility to create a new home for his parents and other relatives.

Temporarily, the Freud family moved into rented accommodation at 39 Elsworthy Road close to Regent's Park. Comparable to his son's exploratory trip to London in mid 1933, Sigmund Freud made sense of the unfamiliar surroundings through a comparison with a familiar place, viz. his favourite location to spend the summers away from Vienna. On the same day that he had arrived in London Sigmund Freud explained in a letter to Eitingon, and apparently to himself, that from the 'window I see nothing but greenery which begins with a charming little garden surrounded by trees. So it is as though we were living in Grinzing.' Freud continued that the ground floor offered with bedroom, study, and sitting room sufficient spaces for the temporary stay in this house. He described it as 'elegantly furnished' for which he credited his son who 'really is what he has been called, a "tower of strength".'[41]

A few months later, Sigmund and Martha Freud moved into their last home at 20 Maresfield Gardens in London Hampstead. The purchase of the two-storey detached house had already taken place in July 1938,[42] but afterwards Freud 'transformed the house into a ruin in order to restore it anew in a more suitable state for us.'[43] Originally, the house was erected in the early 1920s by the local builders James Tomblin and Albert Hastilow. Its Queen Ann revival style, white windows with multiple panes, and red brick including quoins at the corners and other restrained decorative details illustrated well what British homeowners and house builders preferred over modernist architecture. Even though the Queen Ann revival style harked back to the early seventeenth century, it was the English equivalent to the revival of German bourgeois Biedermeier houses from around 1800.

The detached house had eight bedrooms, three reception rooms, two bathrooms, and two garages, all of which Freud began to adjust to the needs of the new occupants by, in the words of his father, 'making two rooms into one or the other way around, sheer witches' sorcery translated into architectural terms'.[44] On the ground floor, servicing rooms like a kitchen and scullery, and a small quarter for the housekeeper Paula Fichtl, were organized to the left of the main entrance, with a dining room straight ahead; and to the right was Freud's study and consulting room which occupied two rooms knocked together. On the upper level, Anna Freud gained privacy in the rooms above the service wing, a sitting room was located above the dining room, and two bedrooms, one to the front and one to the rear, were above Sigmund Freud's working quarters. Towards the garden, a new loggia was added on the lower level with a balcony above with circular Luxfer glass prism inserted into the floor to help light the loggia below—the only conscious use of a modernist detail in a visible but most inconspicuous manner. Finally, a newly built-in lift allowed Sigmund Freud and his wife's sister, Minna Bernays (1865–1946), to sample some of the comforts of modernity, not those of air travel Zweig had recommended in 1937, but of being electrically moved up and down simply by pushing a button.[45]

To recreate the interior of Sigmund Freud's Viennese study and consulting room was another goal of the remodelling of 20 Maresfield Gardens. Together with the couch and the adjacent chair those two rooms symbolized both psychoanalysis and Sigmund Freud's life, in particular because in his exile the original rooms had been lost. The Vienna rooms, however, had just been a shell for the couch, the chair, the library, the antiquities, and a number of other furniture pieces and personal possessions that Sigmund Freud could take with him into exile. To export personal property was still relatively easy, though not without anxieties and uncertainties, when Ernst L. Freud left Berlin in late 1933. By 1938, however, it had become a complicated chicanery that in Sigmund Freud's case was mastered successfully mainly because of diplomatic interventions by the United States and with the help of the loyal friends Jones in London and Marie Bonaparte in Paris. The latter paid most of the ransom money the Nazis demanded in exchange for both exit visas for the family and permission to export personal possessions.[46]

Any accurate and detailed recreation of the Viennese rooms in the English settings was made impossible by the combination of study and consulting room into a single space at 20 Maresfield Gardens. Initially, Freud tried to frame the placing of the couch between bookshelves, assuming a surviving sketch that shows a couch with a tall head-end was for his father's London home (fig. 8.9). The rescue, however, of many personal possessions, furniture, and Sigmund Freud's most beloved collection of antique statues and stone carvings provided a sufficient number of familiar objects to recreate the atmosphere and the visual impression of the Viennese rooms. Along one wall in the new home, Ernst L. Freud provided a floor-to-ceiling bookshelf that accommodated those books the older Freud had deemed worthwhile to be shipped to London. Integrated into the new shelf were two Biedermeier display cabinets that in Vienna had held parts of the collection of antiquities. More antiquities were placed on a rustic table in front of the shelf and in other display cabinets distributed throughout the room (fig. 8.10). Against another wall the couch was placed with the comfort chair standing perpendicular to the headend. Above the couch some of Sigmund Freud's art prints were hung and behind it a rug covered the wall. In front of the couch a desk was placed at which stood Freud's chair

Figure 8.9. Design for the setting of a consulting couch between bookshelves, possibly for 20 Maresfield Gardens, London. Used with permission of the RIBA Library Drawings & Archives Collections.

Figure 8.10. Bookshelves in S. Freud's consulting room cum study, London. Used with permission of the Freud Museum London.

(fig. 8.11). This had been designed in 1930 by Augenfeld as an order by Anna Freud who presented it to her father. More antiques were placed in a small recess behind the consulting chair and adjacent to the couch.

The ensemble was reminiscent of that in Vienna, yet it was not an accurate recreation. For example, the Abu Simble print that hung above the couch in Vienna now was above a fireplace. The room appeared as if it had been recreated from memory, by arranging the most important objects close to where they had been placed in the Vienna rooms. As I have argued in chapter 6, the setting of couch and chair as the sites of psychoanalysis was independent of whichever larger room contained the two essential pieces of furniture. The London consulting room cum study was another example of the principal transferability of the intimate spatial setting of psychoanalysis into different architectural spaces. At the same time, the orderly hand of Ernst L. Freud was visible in small design adjustments like, for example, the near symmetric integration of the display cases into the bookshelf or the lightly toned walls that made smaller groupings of furniture and objects stand out much more than in the darker spaces of the Berggassen apartment. This recalls a comparable procedure that Freud had used in the Marx house in London. There he had likewise combined into small ensembles furniture and artwork from the pre-exile home in Berlin (fig. 8.12). These clusters were set off against lightly painted walls as if to create deliberate reference points of familiar objects in the still-unfamiliar surroundings of the

Figure 8.11. Sigmund Freud's desk and chair, London. Used with permission of the Freud Museum London.

Figure 8.12. Corner in the living room with paintings and furniture brought over from Berlin, Marx house, London, 1935–36. Used with permission of Harry Weinberger.

new home—both in the sense of a *Zuhause*, the physical setting in a house, and a *Heimat* in London and England. Sigmund Freud was apparently aware of these subtle, but fundamental changes in the display of his art collection. He commented that the statues and antiques from all over the world were now more visible than they had been before. He continued writing that his collection was no longer a living one as he could no longer add new pieces to it.[47] Thus close to the end of his life the fate of the collection of antique statues was more on Freud's mind than its architectural display or even the setting of couch and chair, the symbols of psychoanalysis.

Towards a Life without Architecture

At the end of Second World War in Europe, Ernst L. Freud was fifty-three years old. His practice changed profoundly during the aftermath of the war. First, with regard to the number of commissions it never regained its pre-war size or even its size during the Berlin period. Second, it lost its almost-exclusive focus on domestic bourgeois architecture with other projects becoming more important. Freud continued to design, now and then, private homes, but they were either small, conversions, of anonymous character, or all three together. In 1948, he worked for the second time for Fritz and Ann Hess when he converted a garage into a mews home for the refugee couple whom he had already advised about the interior of their first London apartment in 1934. In the same year, Freud conceived a series of cottages for workers on an agricultural estate in Sussex; these were anonymous designs for unknown inhabitants and with a client who remains unidentified.

By 1945 Freud had lived in London for twelve years, just one year short of the time he had spent in Berlin. And similar to his position in the architectural scene of the Weimar Republic, Freud was again a society architect, even though on a smaller scale and at a later stage in his English career than in his German one, and with clients that were no longer almost exclusively drawn from an assimilated Jewish bourgeoisie. Rather, his post-war clientele came from the circles of exiled continental Europeans, Jewish and non-Jewish, and from the cultural elite of the British middle classes. In short, Freud's post-war architectural career illustrates the integration into the British society of those refugees that had managed to stay in the United Kingdom during the war and subsequently decided to remain in their new home country.[48]

Already by the 1940s Freud could count among his clients well-known members of the cultural bourgeois circles of London—for example, Julian (1887–1975) and Juliette Huxley (1895–1994). By approximately 1942 Freud worked for the couple on their new home at 31 Pond Street, London Camden, where he, among other things, designed shelves for nearly four thousand books.[49] Later clients like the Spenders and Ashcroft consolidated this image of a society architect as did some of Freud's non-domestic architectural projects. Three post-war projects in London exemplify the type of work Freud took on during the post-war period: a townhouse for an art collector, a neo-Elizabethan theatre for an actor, and a synagogue for a Jewish hospital.

The first project was for the art historian and art collector Count Seilern (1901–78), who was born in England to an American mother and an Austrian father, lived in various European countries, and returned for good to the United Kingdom in September 1939. After he had purchased his country home Hog Lane Farm at Ashley Green, Chesham, Buckinghamshire, he consulted with Freud about erecting a private gallery on his property for his extensive art collection. A second, later Freud project concerned the conversion of a property in Dulwich in the south of London into a private art gallery.[50] Finally, around 1947, Count Seilern took out a lease on 56 Princes Gate in London Kensington. Freud made changes to this building, though the exact scope of his work is not known, while the frame maker Paul Levi, himself a refugee from Nazi Germany, designed and created built-in furniture to display and store the Count's artwork.[51]

The second project was for the first neo-Elizabethan Mermaid Theatre that the actor Bernard Miles (1907–91) founded in 1951. The theatre took over a former school assembly hall in Acacia Road in the St. John's Wood area of London. Freud's intervention apparently concerned changes to the hall whereas the stage designers Michael Stringer and C. Walter Hodges dealt with the recreation of an Elizabethan stage.[52]

The third project was a small synagogue that Freud designed for the London Jewish Hospital in Stepney Green in 1958. This synagogue was the only religious building that Freud ever worked on. Even more, while throughout his life Freud was not overly religious, late in his life he designed this orthodox synagogue because 'it would have caused "difficulties for Orthodox Jews to attend any other service"', as Freud is quoted as saying in a contemporary publication.[53] Photographs show a restrained brick cube with a skylight for an interior hall with the *bimah* at its centre (fig. 8.13). The main front was emphasized by five slender, rectangular piers resting on a broad flight of a few, low steps. To the right and the left horizontal roofs on thin vertical supports connected the synagogue to the hospital while also providing covered walkways. Two doors gave access to the interior where the raised women's gallery was separated from the main space by a wrought iron 'token screen'[54] that integrated the motifs of the Star of David and the twin tablets of the Ten Commandments.

Figure 8.13. Interior of the British Synagogue, London Jewish Hospital, 1958, since demolished. Used with permission of the RIBA Library Photographs Collection.

These were prestigious even if smaller projects that illustrate well both the kind of clients Freud attracted later in his life and the degree of his professional acceptance among potential clients in London. They were, however, singular projects, as the dates of 1947, 1951, and 1958 show. They indicated not a late flourishing of a career but the gradual winding down of a long working life that had begun in imperial Vienna and Munich, reached its architectural high point in Weimar Berlin, was successfully transferred to London in the 1930s, and brought to a halt during the Second World War, after which it never again reached its earlier intensity. Ernst L. and Lucie Freud divided their years of his retirement between London and their cottage in Walberswick where Freud engaged increasingly in gardening (fig. 8.14). Together, they also began editing the writings of Sigmund Freud.

Figure 8.14. Ernst L. and Lucie Freud in front of their London home, 1968. Used with permission of Jane McAdam Freud.

Freud still accepted the odd commissions for conversions, new cottages, and holiday homes. One such late project was a design for a house near Falmouth, Cornwall, in the mid 1960s. The clients were Marcus and Rene Brumwell (died 2004), who had worked in advertising, were friends with many British modern artists and wished to accommodate their extensive collection of modern art. Symbolically, this project, whose plans have not been found, set an end point to Freud's career. Freud lost the commission when his clients consulted with their daughter, the architect Sue Rogers, and her husband, Richard Rogers. Both were co-founders of Team 4 which launched its career with Creak Vean (1966) in Feock, Cornwall, an outstanding piece of domestic architecture for Mrs. Rogers's parents.[55] Thus the baton was passed on to a younger generation of architects.

Notes

1. E. Weissweiler. 2006. *Die Freuds: Biographie einer Familie.* Cologne: Kiepenheuer & Witsch, 387.
2. The exact dates of Alexander Freud's stay in England are not known. At some point he moved on to Canada to join his son Harry Freud, where he passed away in 1943.
3. Letter from Alexander Freud to Ernst Freud, 30 December 1939 (folder Ernst Freud / Lucie Freud, 1938–53, box 1, Alexander and Sophie Freud papers, Manuscript Division, Library of Congress, Washington DC).
4. Notice from Alexander Freud and Ernst Freud, 13 October 1939 (folder Ernst Freud / Lucie Freud, 1938–53, box 1, Alexander and Sophie Freud papers, Manuscript Division, Library of Congress, WashinFagton DC).
5. A. Freud with D. Burlingham. 1973. *Infants without Families: Reports on the Hampstead Nurseries 1939–1945.* New York: International University Press, xxiii.
6. A. Freud, *Infants without Families*, 28–29.
7. Letter from Mathilde Hollitscher to Harry Freud, 22 October 1950 (folder Mathilde Hollitscher, box 7, Harry Freud papers, Manuscript Division, Library of Congress, Washington DC).
8. Letter from Lucie Freud to Harry and Heli Freud, 1 September 1948 (folder Ernst Freud / Lucie Freud, 1938–49, box 5, Harry Freud papers, Manuscript Division, Library of Congress, Washington DC).
9. Letter from Ernst Freud to Lucie Freud, 16 August 1933 (collection Esther Freud).
10. Letter from Ernst Freud to Lucie Freud, 28 June 1933 (collection Esther Freud).
11. Letter from Ernst Freud to Lucie Freud, 16 August 1933 (collection Esther Freud). The term 'old West' refers to the Tiergarten area to the west of the historic city centre.
12. Letter from Ernst Freud to Lucie Freud, 6 March 1934 (collection Esther Freud).
13. Letter from Sigmund Freud to Ernst Freud, 16 April 1935 (Sigmund Freud papers, Library of Congress, box 3, folder 5).
14. One of the first letters I have found that was directed to the new address was from Sigmund Freud to Ernst Freud, 21 November 1935 (Sigmund Freud papers, Library of Congress, box 3, folder 5).
15. A. H. 1928. 'Zu Hause', *Die Pyramide* 15 (August): 248–257; see chapter 1.
16. Information on material and colour taken from reverse of photograph 35132/7, RIBA, Library Photograph collection.
17. Photographs 35131/1-3, RIBA, Library Photograph collection.
18. P. Mebes. 1908. *Um 1800: Architektur und Handwerk im letzten Jahrhundert ihrer traditionellen Entwicklung*, 2 vols. Munich: F. Bruckmann.

19. I am grateful to Dr. Edina Meyer-Maril, Tel Aviv University, for her discussions with me of this point.
20. No photographs seem to exist of the interior of Matthäikirchstraße. However, some of the furniture pieces at 32 St John's Wood Terrace are identical to those at Regentenstraße 23, thus some furniture from the second Berlin apartment was fitted into the third Berlin apartment, and transferred to London.
21. N. L. Carrington. 1937. 'Ernst L. Freud. Interviewed at his new London House', *Decoration* 7 (November): 22–25; E. L. Freud and H. Bright. 1936. 'The Conquest of Space with the Aid of Electricity', *Good Housekeeping* October: 60–61, 104–105.
22. Apartment Gina Kaus, Vienna, c. 1930; see R. Hanisch. 1995. 'Die unsichtbare Raumkunst des Felix Augenfeld' in M. Boeckle (ed.). 1995. *Visionäre und Vertriebene: Österreichische Spuren in der modernen Architektur*. Berlin: Ernst & Sohn, 226–247 (231).
23. Ernst and Lucie Freud tried to sell the shelves in their last Berlin apartment to the next tenant (letter from Ernst Freud to Lucie Freud, 14 October 1933).
24. E. L. Freud and H. Bright, 'The Conquest of Space', 60–61, 104–105.
25. Letter from Marshall McLuhan to Elise, Herbert, and Maurice McLuhan, 27 February 1935 (M. Molinaro, C. McLuhan, and W. Toye [eds.]. 1987. *Letters of Marshall McLuhan*. Oxford: Oxford University Press, 62–63). Dr. Elizabeth Darling, Oxford, kindly brought this letter to my attention.
26. S. Claus. 2006. *Harry Rosenthal (1892–1966): Architekt und Designer in Deutschland, Palästina, Grossbritannien*. Zurich: gta, entry WK 26, 217.
27. Letter from Arnold Zweig to Sigmund Freud, 14 October 1937 (E. L. Freud [ed]. 1970. *The Letters of Sigmund Freud and Arnold Zweig*, trans. by Elaine and William Robson-Scott. New York: Harcourt, Brace & World, 148).
28. R. Negendanck. 2005. *Hiddensee: Die besondere Insel für Künstler*. Fischerhude: edition fischerhude kunstbuch.
29. P. Squenz [i.e. Josef Eberle (1901–86)]. 2005. 'Hiddensee 1924', in R. Seydel (ed) 2005. *Hiddensee: Geschichten von Land und Leuten*. Berlin: Ullstein, 238–242 (239, my translation).
30. A. Jürgensohn. 1924. *Hiddensee, das Capri von Pommern: Ein Reiseführer und Erinnerungsbuch*. Kloster auf Hiddensee: Karl Haertel, 159.
31. Letter from Florian Hülsen to author, 4 November 2008.
32. Letter from Ernst L. Freud, London, to Frau Dr. Harald Wolf, 27 June 1934 and 19 July 1934 (collection Florian Hülsen); Seydel, *Hiddensee*, 410.
33. Letter from Sigmund Freud to Ernst Freud, 17 January 1938 (E. L. Freud [ed.]. 1960. *Letters of Sigmund Freud*, trans. by T. and J. Stern. New York: Basic Books, letter 294).
34. It is not known if the house was named by the Freuds or if it had always been called Hidden House considering its 'hidden' location in the village green.
35. F. Krause. 2004. 'Hiddensee im Sommer 1907', in R. Seydel. 2004. *Hiddensee: Ein Lesebuch*. Berlin: Ullstein, 13–28 (13). Jürgensohn, *Hiddensee*, 163.
36. M. Faust. 2001. *Das Capri von Pommern: Geschichte der Insel Hiddensee von den Anfängen bis 1990*. Rostock: Ingo Koch Verlag, 177.
37. See chapter 1.
38. Krause, 'Hiddensee im Sommer 1907', in Seydel, *Hiddensee: Ein Lesebuch*, 28.
39. J. Cairney. 2004. *The Quest for Charles Rennie Mackintosh*. Edinburgh: Luath Press, 171–174.
40. Conversation with Stephen Freud, 9 July 2002.
41. Letter from Sigmund Freud to Max Eitingon, 6 June 1938 (E. L. Freud. 1960. *Letters of Sigmund Freud*, letter 299; the English phrase 'tower of strength' was used in the original).
42. Unless otherwise noted, all facts about 20 Maresfield Gardens are taken from Freud Museum (ed). 1998. *20 Maresfield Gardens: A Guide to the Freud Museum*. London: Serpent's Tail.

43. Letter from Sigmund Freud to Jeanne Lampl de Groot, 22 August 1938 (SF/K to N, box 17, Sigmund Freud Museum London), translated in Freud Museum, *20 Maresfield Gardens*, 7–8.
44. Letter from Sigmund Freud to Jeanne Lampl de Groot, 22 August 1938 (SF/K to N, box 17, Sigmund Freud Museum London), translated in Freud Museum, *20 Maresfield Gardens*, 8; I slightly amended the translation.
45. Letter from Sigmund Freud to Jeanne Lampl de Groot, 20 November 1938 (SF/K to N, box 17, Sigmund Freud Museum London), my translation.
46. The story of Freud's move into exile has often been told; I have relied here on P. Gay. 1998. *Freud: A Life for Our Time*. New York: W.W. Norton, 611–629.
47. Letter from Sigmund Freud to Jeanne Lampl de Groot, 8 October 1938 (SF/K to N, box 17, Sigmund Freud Museum London), my translation.
48. D. Snowman. 2002. *The Hitler Emigrés: The Cultural Impact on Britain of Refugees from Nazism*. London: Chatto & Windus.
49. J. Huxley. 1970. *Memories*. New York: Harper & Row, 263–64; J. R. Baker. 1978. *Julian Huxley: Scientist and World Citizen 1887–1975. A Biographical Memoir*. Paris: UNESCO, 48; J. Huxley. 1986. *Leaves of the Tulip Tree*. Topsfield, MA: Salem House, 184.
50. The building in question was possibly the neo-classical Georgian villa 'Belair', Gallery Road, Dulwich (email from Helen Braham, Courtauld Institute of Art, to author, 11 September 2005).
51. J. B. Shaw. 1978. 'Count Antoine Seilern (1901–1978)', *The Burlington Magazine* 120: 760–762. My thanks go to Paul Levi (1919–2008) and his wife in Reading, England, for many conversations about his and Freud's work for Count Seilern, and for a memorable visit to 56 Princes Gate which is today owned by Pepperdine University, Malibu, California. Additional information was provided in various emails from Helen Braham, Courtauld Institute of Art, London.
52. *Architects' Journal* 114 (11 October 1951): 427, 429; C. W. Hodges. 1968. *The Globe Restored: A Study of the Elizabethan Theatre*. London: Oxford University Press, 132, plate 51.
53. R. Wischnitzer. 1964. *The Architecture of the European Synagoge*. Philadelphia: Jewish Publication Society of America, 273.
54. Wischnitzer, *European Synagoge*, 273.
55. K. Powell (ed). 1999. *Richard Rogers Complete Works*, vol. 1. London: Phaidon, 14, 28–37, 307. Many thanks to Alan Powers, London, who alerted me to this project.

⌁ Chapter 9 ⌁

Architecture without Quality?
Some Concluding Remarks

As calm as his architecture was, Freud himself was equally as quiet when it came to writing about his architectural intentions and aesthetics. Clearly, he was not fond of describing and analyzing in words his projects and designs.[1] However, Freud's letter from October 1934 to the editor of *Design for To-Day* contains some important thoughts on modern architecture.[2] As cited in chapter 7, the letter begins with the usual observation by many exiled Continental European architects that England lacked modern architecture despite the fact, as Freud added, that there existed 'a great number of architects who are willing and prepared to express modern ideas in their work'.[3] This predicament could be overcome if modern clients would be 'inclined to accept and appreciate the principles of modern architecture, such as (a) Planning strictly in accordance with requirements; (b) Simplicity of forms and renunciation of the historical styles; (c) Use of the new materials and of their structural possibilities'.[4]

Considering the origin of modern architecture in Weimar Germany, Freud distinguished between a cause—'the complete lack of any real good tradition in German architecture, at least since the second part of the last century'—and an impulse that was rooted in the political changes of the revolution from 1918 when 'progressive parties took power'.[5] Thus the stage was set for an orderly evolution of modernist German architecture that passed through at least five overlapping phases. First, modern architects were appointed both as municipal architects and as teachers at educational, often state-subsidized institutions—for example, Hans Poelzig (1869–1936) at the Technische Hochschule in Berlin-Charlottenburg or Gropius at the Bauhaus in Weimar and, later, in Dessau. Second, municipal architects and planners like Ernst May (1886–1970) and Martin Wagner (1885-1957) designed modernist *Siedlungen* in, for example, Frankfurt-upon-Main and Berlin that made the new architecture more widely known. Freud called their work 'one of the greatest achievements of post-war Germany',[6] a statement that echoed the positive appreciation other contemporaries, like Plessner, had voiced. This popularity was furthered (phase three) by the modernist town halls, schools, hospitals, and office buildings for state-run social insurances, for example, that were commissioned by municipalities and 'municipally subsidized corporations'.[7] At the same time (phase four) modernist architecture gained a foothold among private businesses which demanded rational designs of functional factories, offices, and commercial buildings. Ultimately, in the fifth and final phase, this progression came to a happy ending when modern architecture was generally accepted for private homes: 'Almost universally the feeling of the public turned towards modern expression, and interest in architecture was aroused all through the German people.' The next sentence, however, sets a distinctly different tone: 'For many years nearly everything was built on modern lines and the erection of an old fashioned building was almost impossible.'[8]

Broadly, Freud was correct in identifying as one foundation of modernist architecture the nexus of state bureaucracy, subsidized building co-operatives, and modernist architects that existed in the Weimar Republic. What is debatable, however, is Freud's chronology that ignored both pre–Great War modern industrial buildings like, for example, the Fagus shoe last factory (1911–25) in Alfeld on the Leine, Germany, by Gropius and Adolf Meyer (1881–1929), as well as seminal domestic designs from well before the period of large-scale modernist social housing. Such designs would include, for example, residences by Mendelsohn in Berlin, like the Dr. Sternefeld house, and Mies van der Rohe's unrealized projects for two country houses made from concrete (1923) and brick (1924).

While the format of a short letter may have prevented a more detailed and more accurate historical account, the striking lack of the prophetic tone that characterized so many period manifestoes on modernist architecture was most likely Freud's choice. It is tempting to put down this restrain to the tactical considerations of an émigré who was keen to obtain work in his new home country. Yet the inconspicuous character of much of the pre-exile and post-exile work by Freud suggests that moderation was more likely an innate characteristic of his. Freud's own words reinforce this assumption. Architects were prepared to express modern ideas in their work, as if that was a matter of choice rather than of inner conviction as other contemporaries would have argued. Or, historic architecture was renounced instead of, for example, being swept away or overthrown; the former a decisively non-heroic act in comparison with the latter two that were advertised in period books on modernist architecture's emergence.[9] Similarly, factories were 'particularly suited to modern forms',[10] which suggests that the forms were not predetermined by the purpose of the building as, for example, Gropius would have proclaimed. Finally, the remark about the impossibility of erecting 'old fashioned' buildings expresses regret rather than relief over the passing of old-fashioned ways of building.

A letter to his wife, written much earlier on in his career than the 1934 document, sheds more light on Freud's last point. Staying in Oberstaufen in the Allgäu, Germany, in February 1920 in order to cure his lung ailment, Freud wrote: 'So much has always been written about architecture and music. The premise that "only a musical person can become a good architect" is quite often the conclusion. Of course that makes me a little sceptical. Certainly architecture is the art of making a mass bearable through a certain kind of rhythm. But the tasks of the modern day architect are mostly quite different; unfortunately I am sad that I must write to you in prose.'[11] Freud was most likely sceptical because he was not musically talented; and he was possibly sad because he wasn't poetically gifted either, forcing him to reply in prose to a poem his wife had composed for him in a preceding letter that is lost today. Architecturally, however, Freud's letter contested the opinion that, by definition, good architects worked poetically rather than prosaically, even if the circumstances of the time suggested or even demanded the latter.

In Freud's chronology of events, as laid out in 1934, domestic architecture was the last building task that fell under the spell of modernism. This did not indicate an undue delay, but offered the domestic architect a distinct advantage. Occupying the final place in the chain of events he could draw on the achievements of modernist architecture as developed earlier with regard to other building tasks without claiming for him, or even having to strive for, an avant-garde position. This made it, however, also more difficult to realize a more traditional building if only because the clients were fixated on modern architecture.

To read an œuvre like Freud's as a sequence in which time progresses in tandem with stylistic developments towards modernist architecture would impose a linear order that cannot easily explain, for example, why Freud harked back to such traditional architectural elements like a steep pitched roof when he began working on the Mosse country house in 1932, after he had climbed a few years earlier a pinnacle of modern domestic design with the cubic Frank country house. Rather, what might appear as a stylistic contradiction or even regression within a single architect's œuvre turns out to have been attempts to bridge, if not to unite, the poetic and the prosaic aspects of modern architecture: the various styles between which Freud moved with ease depending on his clients; the floor plans that confirmed rather than challenged bourgeois notions of domesticity; the interiors that occasionally combined symmetry and asymmetry in single rooms or adjacent ones; and the exteriors that now referenced early nineteenth-century architecture and then modern architecture.

Moreover, the stylistic heterogeneity suggests that Freud had adopted a basic Loosian approach to architecture that specified that buildings should visibly convey a sense of being appropriate to their purpose. Loos explained in his essay 'Architecture' from 1910 that, for example, a bank should appear solid and trustworthy, and domestic buildings comfortable and cosy without imposing themselves on their surroundings.[12] An equivalent diversity of architectural styles selected according to the purpose of buildings characterizes Freud's works. For example, the tobacco warehouse 'Problem' (1927–28) in Berlin, an industrial building, is a masterpiece of modernist architectural principles whose horizontally banded windows alternating with crisp bands of white stucco are balanced by the verticality of a stair tower of exposed brick (fig. 9.1). Against this skilful composition of bare volume, the equally masterfully arranged masses of the Frank country house convey a sense of professional solidity, educated taste, and relaxed, but not formless cosiness; entirely appropriate for the weekend retreat of a manager of one of Germany's largest banks.

Stylistic heterogeneity that references both traditional and modern architectural styles has occasionally been traced back to both bourgeois domesticity and, in the case of both Jewish architects and clients, to a distinct Jewish understanding of time. The latter condensed into a continuum 'past and future, present and eternity'.[13] This concept, it has been argued, was reflected, for example, in the 'light-hearted, frivolous mixture of styles'[14] of mid-nineteenth-century Berlin architecture for Jewish clients. In the decades flanking 1900, it could be found in the works of Alfred Messel, a converted Jew, and Hermann Muthesius, who counted among his clients various members of the Jewish bourgeoisie, whose domestic and commercial designs were at once 'modern and retrospective'.[15] Subsequently, singular pieces of art provided as 'accessories of history' a link with the past. Yet even in the 1920s some modern Jewish architects and clients aimed to root their modernist buildings in history. For example, in the 1921 remodelling by Mendelsohn and Neutra of the headquarters of the *Berliner Tageblatt*—owned by Rudolf Mosse into whose extended family Gerda Brasch, a sister of Lucie Freud, had married—a

Figure 9.1. Facade of the tobacco warehouse 'Problem', Berlin, 1927–28. Photograph from *Bauwelt*, 18 April 1929, used with permission of the Collection Centre Canadien d'Architecture / Canadian Centre for Architecture, Montréal.

striking addition rose upward at a street corner in order to extend sideward above the façades of the older structure.[16] To many architectural historians this streamlined, dynamic addition embodied the speed of the modern metropolis. To others, the expressive juxtaposition of the old and the new was a commentary on the Jewish understanding of the concept of space-time.[17] Without reaching the artistic heights and theoretical depth of Mendelsohn's architecture, Freud's œuvre does dovetail with such interpretations as is suggested, for example, by the use of the stylized tablets of law integrated into the design of the balustrade that held the handrail of the main stair in the Scherk house. Yet too little is known about the attitude of Freud and his clients, like the Scherk family, towards their Jewish heritage to consider conclusively from this angle both the stylistic heterogeneity of Freud's œuvre and the oscillations between the modern and the traditional within individual aspects of his domestic designs.

The issue of time in relation to eclectic architecture and interiors was also discussed when bourgeois domestic culture was analyzed. For example, in his autobiographic *Berlin Childhood around 1900*, Walter Benjamin (1892–1940) identified bourgeois apartments as places in which the progress of time had been overcome to the point that even death was banned.[18] Benjamin recalled the apartment of his maternal grandmother, who had lived in the now non-existent *Blumeshof* (Blume's court) that was located just across the Landwehrkanal, a little southwest of where the Freuds' Berlin homes were located.

Pondering the characteristics of bourgeois apartments as the central foci of the life of this class, Benjamin ascribed an active role to the furniture, commodities, and other objects that constituted the typical interior:

> What words can describe the almost immemorial feeling of bourgeois security that emanated from this apartment? ... For even if the products of the 1870s were much more solid than those of the Jugendstil that followed, their most salient trait was the humdrum way in which they abandoned things to the passage of time and in which they relied, so far as their future was concerned, solely on the durability of their materials and nowhere on rational calculations. Here reigned a type of furniture that, having capriciously incorporated styles of ornament from different centuries, was thoroughly imbued with itself and its own duration. ... In these rooms death was not provided for.[19]

Benjamin described of course an interior from the late nineteenth century when eclectic historicism flourished to the fullest. Others, like Siegfried Kracauer, contemplated manifestations of similar issues surrounding Weimar Republic bourgeois culture; Kracauer's writings help, by analogy, to appreciate the qualities of Freud's architecture.

Returning to the socio-economic changes that had effected the middles classes as described in *The Salaried Masses,* Kracauer portrayed in essays like 'The Biography as an Art Form of the new Bourgeois' (1930) and 'On Bestsellers and Their Audience' (1931)[20] a deeply insecure class that looked both ways, to the past where the roots and conditions for its rise lay, and to the future where it hoped to see the basis for its continuous role in the new Germany. By analogy, the often more-modern exteriors of domestic architecture designed by Freud may have reassured his clients and others that they, the bourgeoisie and middle classes, were still a socially and culturally driving force. The more conventional interiors at the same time refer back to notions of private domesticity, one of the roots of the social layer from which Freud drew his clients.

Kracauer argued that even though the bourgeoisie had become differentiated into 'a multiplicity of strata that extend from the high bourgeoisie down to the proletariat', it had remained socially influential. For example, it continued to shape the reading habits of the proletariat—'it reads up on what the bourgeoisie has already read'[21]—and assigned success to such individual authors who were not as artistically daring as Kafka but captured well 'the demands of a broad social stratum of consumers'.[22] Similarly, clients of Freud may not have all come from, strictly speaking, the bourgeoisie but they all accepted the bourgeois way of life as a goal for both their homes and lives.

While social changes may have led some contemporaries to expect the coming demise of the bourgeoisie, Kracauer instead asked if an 'unmasking of certain ideologies' indicated indeed a 'weakening of bourgeois consciousness'?[23] Ultimately, his answer was in the negative as the bourgeoisie stuck to their privileges and traditions if only in order to not '[be] drowned by the proletariat'.[24] The individual may have been on the retreat when faced with 'structural transformations' that, for example, made 'town and country planning transcend individual egotism'.[25] With this statement, Kracauer, a trained architect, referred to the contemporary debate about social-housing schemes versus single-family buildings as outlined in chapter 1. 'Yet', Kracauer continued, 'for the time being, these currents—which take into account both social reality and material imperatives—are far from determining the system in which they are developing.'[26] Comparable to Plessner, Kracauer accepted that the future of both the bourgeoisie and the individual was far from decided, even if he was much more critical of either than Plessner.

By analogy, a comparable affirmation of the bourgeois individual can be found in Freud's domestic architecture, for example, when looking at photographs of Freud-designed houses and interiors (many of Freud's design have only survived in the format of photographs or architectural drawings). Three larger groups of photographic images exist: first, exteriors of houses; second, sitting rooms and living rooms in private homes, often with an open fireplace; and, third, private offices with desks, shelves, and filing cabinets. That these types of rooms were among the most often photographed points towards a larger demand for them, especially as Freud used such images of his work for the acquisition of new commissions.

A typical Freudian sitting room was composed of comfort chairs perhaps arranged around a fireplace. For the latter, Freud preferred to use bricks, sometimes of a thin format that created a strong visual pattern when laid with joints of the same thickness. On other occasions, Freud placed comfort chairs opposite each other in front of bookshelves or combined them with sofas (fig. 9.2). Carefully placed objects like wall-mounted candle holders, vases with decorative flowers, ashtrays and smoking utensils, oriental rugs, thick floor cushions to sit on, antique carved Madonna figures (fig. 9.3), and, in at least one

Figure 9.2. Living room of the Goldschmidt house, Berlin. Used with permission of the RIBA Library Photographs Collection.

Figure 9.3. Unidentified living room with antique wood sculpture. Used with permission of the RIBA Library Photographs Collection.

case, a series of Holbein engravings (fig. 9.4), established in both a sense of bourgeois domesticity and historic continuity.

The comfort chairs are usually made from darker wood and covered in either leather, textiles sometimes printed with bold floral patterns, or soft cushions. Freud-designed chairs radiate an Austrian and southern German sense of comfort even when Freud worked with tubular steel. In the case of the office furniture for his friend Ginsberg, Freud balanced the nakedness of the steel with thickly padded cushions resulting in an Art

Figure 9.4. Unidentified living room with a series of Holbein prints. Used with permission of the RIBA Library Photographs Collection.

Déco look (fig. 9.5). Moreover, the metal furniture stood against walls surfaced with pale Japanese grass wallpaper that further softened the atmosphere. Typically, Freud mostly placed modernist tubular steel furniture into the more functional settings of business premises but rarely into private offices within domestic settings. When the latter happened, Freud used modernist metal furniture on terraces, as seen in the example of the Frank country house or in the Bermann-Fischer nursery; these are all examples of how

Figure 9.5. Bank office of Richard Ginsberg, Berlin, 1930. Used with permission of the Collection Centre Canadien d'Architecture / Canadian Centre for Architecture, Montréal.

Freud transferred into interior design a Loosian notion of a selectiveness of materials and forms depending on their tasks and purpose.

It is noticeable that in many photographs of private offices in houses and apartments the windows are often covered with sheers if not thicker curtains that shut out any light entirely (see chapter 5, fig. 5.5; fig. 9.6) Thus, the uncanny outside world was banned from the private realm, but only in order to be readmitted in the apparently less uncanny form of socially mediated work with which the inhabitant maintained a bond with society at large when conducting business at a Freud-designed desk (fig. 9.7). On the latter's surface, the neatly arranged selection of, for example, ink wells, fountain pens, telephones, and ash trays recalls the precarious alignment of antique statuettes and objects along the edges of Sigmund Freud's desk (fig. 9.8). These Rilkean household gods apparently helped guide the older Freud's manifold thoughts and interests through the labyrinth of the human soul and mind, while both the younger Freud and his clients aimed to control their places in modern society with the help of these office paraphernalia (see chapter 8, fig. 8.5). More objects, souvenirs, paintings, furniture, soft furnishings, and wallpaper were amassed within the sitting rooms and living rooms, in front of the fireplaces. These objects were from early childhood onwards carriers of meaning and memories, required in order to create a comfortable 'At Home' as the 1928 article in *Die Pyramide* had observed.

To return to the comparison between the Le Corbusian and the Freudian interiors with which this book began, the Corbusian modernist example, which had attempted

Figure 9.6. Unidentified office (possibly for Melanie Klein in London). Used with permission of the RIBA Library Photographs Collection.

Figure 9.7. Two writing desks in the library (front) and living room of the Matthew House, London, 1937–38. Used with permission of the Architectural Press Archive / RIBA Library Photographs Collection.

Figure 9.8. Sigmund Freud at his desk in Vienna, etching by Max Pollak, 1914. Used with permission of the Freud Museum London.

to overcome time in order to be timeless, nowadays looks dated and time-bound. It may speak eloquently of the architect's artistic skills, but as Walter Benjamin had pointed out, the hard and shiny surfaces of steel and glass would not accept the impressions and imprints of the inhabitants.[27]

In comparison, Freud's interiors and the houses relied on their inhabitants to bring them to life. Yet with many of them murdered, driven into exile and, by now, long passed away, images of Freud's architecture have fallen silent. However, in contrast to their modernist counterparts, Freud's architecture and designs do not, therefore, appear to be dated or time-bound. Instead, his work seems to lie outside of time entirely as it was created in the interaction between architect, clients, and artefacts. In this process Ernst L. Freud occupied a role comparable to the one his father Sigmund Freud had held in the psychoanalytical process, viz. crystallizing whatever associations came to the patient's mind. The case studies that the older Freud published convey what psychoanalysis could achieve and may have meant for the individual clients. Comparably, the remaining houses designed by Ernst L. Freud, the pieces of furniture that have survived, and the photographs and drawings of his œuvre offer glimpses into a bygone era of modern bourgeois culture of which otherwise memories would barely tell.

Notes

1. K. Klemmer. 1998. *Jüdische Baumeister in Deutschland: Architektur vor der Shoah*. Frankfurt: DVA, claims that it was characteristic for many Jewish architects to be equally well versed at both designing buildings and writing about architecture.
2. E. Freud. 1934. 'A foreign Architect Observes England', *Design for To-Day* 2 (October): 394–395.
3. E. Freud, 'A foreign Architect Observes England', 394.
4. E. Freud, 'A foreign Architect Observes England', 395.
5. E. Freud, 'A foreign Architect Observes England', 395.
6. E. Freud, 'A foreign Architect Observes England', 395.
7. E. Freud, 'A foreign Architect Observes England', 395.
8. E. Freud, 'A foreign Architect Observes England', 395.
9. W. C. Behrendt. 1927. *The Victory of the New Building Style* [1927], trans. Harry Francis Malgrave. Los Angeles, CA: The Getty; N. Pevsner. 1986. *Pioneers of Modern Design: From William Morris to Walter Gropius* [1936]. Harmondsworth: Penguin.
10. E. Freud, 'A foreign Architect Observes England', 395.
11. Letter from Ernst Freud, Kurhaus Aichele, Oberstaufen, Allgäu, to Lucie Freud, [Berlin], 29. February 1920 (Collection Esther Freud).
12. A. Loos. 1985. 'Architecture' [1910], in Y. Safran and W. Wang (eds.). *The Architecture of Adolf Loos*. London: Arts Council of Great Britain, 104–109 (108).
13. F. Bedoire. 2004. *The Jewish Contribution to Modern Architecture 1830–1930*. Jersey City, NJ: Ktav Publishing House, 212.
14. Bedoire, *The Jewish Contribution*, 213.
15. Bedoire, *The Jewish Contribution*, 260.
16. Bedoire, *The Jewish Contribution*, 265, 280–281.
17. B. Zevi. 1983. 'Hebraism and the Concept of Space-Time in Art', in A. Oppenheimer Dean (ed.). *Bruno Zevi on Modern Architecture*. New York: Rizzoli, 155–166 (164). See also Bedoire, *The Jewish Contribution*, 280, 211–212.
18. Here I broadly follow Bedoire's line of argument in *The Jewish Contribution*, 211–212.
19. W. Benjamin. 2002. *Berlin Childhood around 1900* [1938], in H. Eiland and M. W. Jennings (eds.). *Walter Benjamin. Selected Writings Volume 3 1935–1938*, trans. by E. Jephcott et. al. Cambridge, MA: Belknap Press, 344–413 (369).
20. S. Kracauer. 1995. *The Mass Ornament: Weimar Essays*, trans. and ed. by T. Y. Levin. Cambridge, MA: Harvard University Press, 101–105, 89–98.
21. Kracauer, *Mass Ornament*, 92.
22. Kracauer, *Mass Ornament*, 91–92.
23. Kracauer, *Mass Ornament*, 93, 94.
24. Kracauer, *Mass Ornament*, 94.
25. Kracauer, *Mass Ornament*, 93.
26. Kracauer, *Mass Ornament*, 93.
27. W. Benjamin. 2001. 'Experience and Poverty' [1933], in M. W. Jennings (ed.). *Walter Benjamin Selected Writings, vol. 2 1927–1934*, trans. by R. Livingstone et. al. Cambridge, MA: Belknap Press, 731–736 (734).

❦ Selected List of Works ❦

The list is organized into groups and subgroups:

    1.0 Domestic architecture
        1.1 Private houses (newly designed)
        1.2 Private houses (refurbished, converted, or extended)
        1.3 Multi-apartment buildings and houses designed for anonymous users
    2.0 Domestic interiors (for houses, apartments, and individual rooms)
    3.0 Domestic furniture (individual pieces and sets)
    4.0 Professional, business, and commercial premises, interiors, and furniture
        4.1 Psychoanalytic spaces and furniture
        4.2 Shops, offices, kitchens, and other business premises
    5.0 Miscellaneous designs

Within each group projects are listed chronologically and within the same year alphabetically, first, by location (with unknown location last), and, second, by the names of either client or project. Dates are taken from either drawings or publications. If several dates are given, all are noted but the project is listed under the earliest.

Furniture designs are not individually identified, only the overall number is noted in parentheses.

Information that could not be confirmed from archival evidence has been placed in square parentheses.

References to literature and other sources are listed chronologically, with frequently cited reference works abbreviated. Selected entries have been annotated.

With very few exceptions, only projects that could be dated and for which either the client name or the location could be established have been included. The Ernst L. Freud collection at the Royal Institute of British Architects in London contains hundreds of drawings that have not been identified.

Abbreviations of Frequently Used Sources

BAB, [year]: Umlauf, K. (ed). 1983. *Adressbuch für Berlin und seine Vororte 1919–1932*. Munich: Saur.
Benton, 1995: Benton, C. 1995. *A Different World. Émigré Architects in Britain 1928–1953*. London: Heinz Gallery, 1995.
BioHB: Röder, W., et al. (eds.). 1980–83. *Handbuch der deutschsprachigen Emigration nach 1933*. Munich: Saur.

Brecht, 1985: Brecht, K., et al. (eds.). 1985. *"Hier geht das Leben auf eine merkwürdige Weise weiter ... " Zur Geschichte der Psychoanalyse in Deutschland.* s.l.: Michael Keller.

Danto, 2005: Danto, E. A. 2005. *Freud's Free Clinics. Psychoanalysis & Social Justice, 1918–1938.* New York: Columbia University Press.

Gould, 1977: Gould, J. 1977. *Modern Houses in Britain, 1919–1939.* London: Society of Architectural Historians of Great Britain.

Haberlandt, [volume, year]: *Haberlandts Bautennachweis für Berlin und Umgebung* 1 (1891)–49 (1940).

Hajos, 1928: Hajos, E. M., and L. Zahn. 1928. *Berliner Architektur der Nachkriegszeit.* Berlin: Albertus.

JAB, 1931: *Jüdische Adressbuch für Gross-Berlin. Ausgabe 1931.* Berlin: Arani, 1994.

Klemmer, 1998: Klemmer, K. 1998. *Jüdische Baumeister in Deutschland. Architektur vor der Shoah.* Stuttgart: DVA.

Ladwig-Winters, 1998: Ladwig-Winters, S. 1998. *Anwalt ohne Recht. Das Schicksal Jüdischer Rechtsanwälte in Berlin nach 1933.* Berlin: be.bra Verlag.

Ladwig-Winters, 2007: Ladwig-Winters, S. 2007. *Anwalt ohne Recht. Das Schicksal jüdischer Rechtsanwälte in Berlin nach 1933.* Berlin: be.bra Verlag.

LMA: London Metropolitan Archive.

LoC: Library of Congress, Anna Freud papers, Harry Freud papers, Sigmund Freud papers.

Mossner, [year], [volume]: Mossner, C. (ed.). 1928–30. *Adreßbuch der Direktoren und Aufsichtsräte.* Berlin: Finanz-Verlag. 1927–28: vol. II, sorted alphabetically by company names; 1929 and 1930: vol. I, sorted alphabetically by names of individuals.

RIBA d: Royal Institute of British Architects, London, Drawings & Archives collections.

RIBA p: Royal Institute of British Architects, London, Photographs collection.

Strauss, 1983: Strauss, H., et al. 1987. *Emigration. Deutsche Wissenschaftler nach 1933 Entlassung und Vertreibung. List of Displaced German Scholars 1936. Supplementary List of Dipslaced German Scholars 1937. The Emergency Committee in Aid of Displaced Foreign Scholars, Report 1941.* Berlin: Technische Universität.

Thomson, 1999: Thomson, C. 1999. 'Contextualising the Continental: The Work of German Émigré Architects in Britain 1933–1945', PhD Dissertation. Warwick: University of Warwick.

Welter, 1992: Welter, V. 1992. 'Landhaus Frank (c. 1928–1930) in Geltow bei Berlin Architekt: Ernst L. Freud (1892–1970)', architectural historical report for Atelier Christoph Fischer Dipl.-Ing. Architekt. Berlin.

Wenzel, 1929: Wenzel, G. (ed.). 1929. *Deutscher Wirtschaftsführer. Lebensgänge deutscher Wirtschaftspersönlichkeiten. Ein Nachschlagebuch über 13000 Wirtschaftspersönlichkeiten unserer Zeit.* Hamburg: Hanseatische Verlagsanstalt.

Worbs, 1997: Worbs, D. 1997. 'Ernst Ludwig Freud in Berlin', *Bauwelt* 88 (42): 2398–2403.

1.0 Domestic architecture

1.1 Private houses (newly designed)

1921

—Maretzki house
Berlin, Dahlem, Zietenstraße 2, today Reichensteinerweg 25
Design for a detached house including furniture
Clients: Dr. jur. Ernst Maretzki (born c. 1890) and Eva Maretzki (née Liebrecht, born c. 1898)
sources and literature:
BAB 1920, 1921, 1922.
RIBA d, p.

Hajos, 1928.
Welter, 1992.
Klemmer, 1998.
Ladwig-Winters, 1998.
Email correspondence with Thomas Maretzki, 2004–6.

1922

—**G. Levy and Adolf Hofer houses**
Berlin, Dahlem, Im Dol 44–44a
Two semi-detached houses, together with architect Schäfer, western house destroyed
sources and literature:
RIBA p.
Hajos, 1928.
Welter, 1992.
Worbs, 1997.
Klemmer, 1998.
Thomson, 1999.

1922

—**Schimek house (fig. 5.1)**
Berlin, Charlottenburg, Halmstraße 10a–11
Detached house for two families, demolished 1973
Clients: Joseph Schimek (1859–1934) and Amalia Schimek (1864–1930) for two of their daughters and their husbands: Ilka (1894–1968) and Paul Schimek (1883–1965, née Isaac), and Margit Charlotte Schimek (1899–1947) and Herbert M. Picard (1893–1952)
sources and literature:
RIBA p.
Landesarchiv Berlin, building file Halmstraße 10/11a, Charlottenburg, Berlin, Rep 207, Acc 2372.
Hajos, 1928.
Claims Tribunal Conference, http://www.crt-ii.org/_awards/_apdfs/Schimek_Ilka.pdf (accessed 24 March 2004).
Email correspondence and telephone conversations with Deborah Browning Schimek, Paul Schimek, Henry Picard, and Karen Prow, February 2008.

1925–26

—**Lampl house (figs. 5.2, 5.4, 5.5, 5.6)**
Berlin, Grunewald, Schuhmacherplatz 2, today Waldmeisterstraße 2
Detached house including furniture designs (40)
Clients: Hans Lampl (1889–1958) and Jeanne [Adriana] Lampl-De Groot (1895–1987)
sources and literature:
RIBA d, p.
Haberlandt, 34 (1925), 1 October 1925, no. 432-34 (1926), 1 February 1926, no. 436.
Hajos, 1928.
H. G. 1928. 'Vom Neuen Bauen', *Die Pyramide* 14 (7): 205–213, image before 205.
A. H. 1928. 'Zu Hause', *Die Pyramide* 14 (8): 248–257 (255).
H. Hoffmann. 1929. *Neue Villen*. Stuttgart: Julius Hoffmann, 100–101.
M. Speyer. 1937."'And So To Bed" The Suggestion has echoed throughout the centuries, but what a different bed awaits us from those of our forebears knew', *Good Housekeeping*, August, 64–65, 125.

E. Mühlleitner. 1992. *Biographisches Lexikon der Psychoanalyse.* Tübingen: Edition Diskord, 199–200, 202–203.
Welter, 1992.
Worbs, 1997.
Klemmer, 1998.
Email and letter correspondence with Edith Berkovits-Lampl, September 2004–July 2007.

1926–27
—Weizmann house
Jerusalem
Design for detached house as part of campus for Hebrew University, never built
Clients: Chaim (1874–1952) and Vera (1881–1966) Weizmann
sources and literature:
Letter from Frank Mears to Chaim Weizmann, 12 October 1926 (L12/39, Central Zionist Archives, Jerusalem).
Letter from Sigmund Freud to Ernst L. Freud, 12 October 1926 (LoC, Sigmund Freud papers, box 3, folder 3).
Letter from Ernst Freud to Chaim Weizmann, 20 April 1927 (file 1134, The Weizmann Archives, Rehovot).

1928–30
—Frank country house (figs. 5.7–5.16, 5.18)
Geltow near Berlin, Am Franzensberg
Design for a country house including interior design, most furniture, and an adjacent gardener or chauffeur house, together with Alexander Kurz (born 1887)
October, and November 1929, March, June, and August 1930 (dates furniture designs)
Clients: Dr. phil. h.c. Theodor Frank (1871–1953) and Margot Frank (1889–1942)
Apparently, Mrs. Franks met Freud at a party, perhaps a music evening at their townhouse, where the architect saw the plans for the country house. He convinced Mrs. Frank that 'she was about to permit the creation of a monstrosity of the worst kind'. The Franks accepted alternative plans by Freud and thus his most prestigious project got underway.
sources and literature:
RIBA d, p.
Hajos, 1928.
Mossner, 1929, vol. I, 452–453.
Wenzel, 1929, column 639.
Anita. 1930. 'Landhaus am See', *Die Dame,* August, issue 23, 10–13.
JAB, 1931, 101.
G. A. Platz. 1933. *Wohnräume der Gegenwart.* Berlin: Propyläen, 74–75, 237, 252, 352.
'Country House on a Lake near Berlin designed by Ernst L. Freud'. 1934. *Architects' Journal* 79 (21 June): 892–893.
'Modern Brick—and Flowers'. 1934. *The Ideal Home,* April, 223–226.
M. Speyer. 1934. 'Dining Rooms 1834–1934', *Design for To-Day* 2 (September): 350–353.
C. G. Holme (ed.). 1934. [no title], *Decorative Art: The Studio Year Book.* London: The Studio, [no volume number], 85.
H. A. L. Degener (ed.). 1935. *Degeners Wer ist's?* Berlin: Herrmann Degener, 431.
'Contemporary Brick Building'. 1936. *Architectural Review* 79 (May): 217–228.
L. Thurn and Taxis. 1991. 'Rätsel um das Haus am Schwielowsee. Eine Villa der Moderne im Wechsel der Zeit', *Die Tageszeitung,* 13 November.

Welter, 1992.
G. Zohlen. 1994. 'Das Haus am See', *Die Zeit* (1 April): 80.
L. Gall et al. (eds.). 1995. *The Deutsche Bank 1870–1995*. London: Weidenfeld & Nicolson, 294–299.
Worbs, 1997.
Klemmer, 1998.
S. von Campe. 2002. 'Ernst Ludwig Freud, die Villa Frank in Geltow und das Neue Bauen', MA dissertation. Germany: Freie Universität Berlin.

1930–31

—**Ludwig Scherk house (figs. 5.21, 7.2)**
Berlin, Lankwitz, Mozartstraße 10 / Kaulbachstraße 25
Design for a detached house, together with Alexander Kurz (born 1887), including furniture designs (12)
October and November 1930
sources and literature:
RIBA d, p.
JAB 1931.
C. Lichtenstein (ed.). 1985. *Otto R. Salvisberg. "Die andere Moderne"*. Zurich: gta, 52–53.
'Two Modern Houses'. 1934. *Home & Gardens*, March, 504–506.
P. Bucciarelli. 1991. *Fritz Höger maestro anseatico 1877–1949*. Venice: Arsenale, 115–116.
Welter, 1992.
Worbs, 1997.
Klemmer, 1998.
Letters from Herta Scherk, 3 May 2004, 28 February 2008.

c. 1932–33

—**Carl and Gerda Mosse house (fig. 5.22)**
Krampnitz, near Potsdam/Berlin
Design of a country house, together with Alexander Kurz, including furniture designs (31) and a chauffeur house
sources and literature:
RIBA d, p.
Conversations with Carola Zentner, July 2002 to July 2005.

1935–36

—**Dr. Adolf Marx and Heide Marx house (figs. 7.3, 7.4, 8.12)**
London, Hampstead N2, 14 Neville Drive
Design for a detached house, sold after 1962, today altered
Dr. Adolf Marx was a banker with Singer & Friedländer Bank in Berlin who left Germany together with his wife in either 1932 or 1933. Their daughter Annie Marx married the art historian Dr. Wolfgang Herrmann; the couple were client-friends of Ernst and Lucie Freud [see entries in 1.2 and 3.0]
sources and literature:
RIBA p.
LMA p.
JAB, 1931, 271.

W. Herrmann. 1992. 'Journey from Berlin: Oral History Transcript', Los Angeles: UCLA, Special Collections, Oral History collection, 236–237.
Thomson, 1999.
Letter from Frank Herrmann, 14 August 2002.
Conversation with Harry Weinberger, 18 October 2002.

1937–39

—**Cottington-Taylor house 'The Weald' (fig. 7.13)**
Pebble Hill, Betchworth, Surrey
Design of a detached house
Clients: Dorothy Daisy Mash (died 1944, widowed Cottington-Taylor, née Gale), and Albert Edward Louis Mash
sources and literature:
D.D. Cottington Taylor and Ernest L. Freud. 1937. 'To buy or to build? Mrs. Taylor's long years of experience at Good Housekeeping Institute are being turned to good account now that she is building a house for herself', *Good Housekeeping*, June, 76–77, 146–148.
'The Weald, Betchworth near Reigate'. 1948. Sales particulars. England: Surrey History Centre, Woking, 2173/3/84.
Gould, 1977.
Benton, 1995.

1949

—**'Cottage at Walberswick'**
Walberswick, Suffolk
Design for a new cottage
Client: [Dr. Willi Hoffer]
sources and literature:
RIBA d.

mid 1960s

—**Cottage at Walberswick**
Walberswick, Suffolk
Design for a new cottage
sources and literature:
RIBA d.

1.2 Private houses (refurbished, converted, or extended)

1921

—**Eitingon house**
Berlin, Tiergarten, Rauchstraße 4
Refurbishment of a two-storey apartment
Clients: Max Eitingon (1881–1943) and Mirra Eitingon (1877–1943)
sources and literature:
Letter from Anna Freud to Sigmund Freud, 12 November 1920 (LoC, Sigmund Freud papers, box 12, folder 15).
Letter from Minna Eitingon to Ernst Freud, 23 January 1921 (Lux Papers, box A–K, Freud Museum).

M. Schröter (ed). 2004. *Sigmund Freud Max Eitingon, Briefwechsel 1906–1939*, 2 vols. Tübingen: Edition Diskord.
Mossner, 1930, vol. I, 384.

—**Dr. jur. Heinz Henneberg House**
Berlin, Dahlem, Podbielskiallee 68
Refurbishment of a villa
sources and literature:
Letter from Ernst Freud to Richard Neutra, 18 September 1921 (California State Polytechnic University, Pomona, College of Environmental Design, Archives-Special Collection, Richard Neutra collection, box 36).

1924 or later
—**Ernst and Lucie Freud cottage (fig. 8.7)**
Hiddensee, Vitte, Dorfstraße 15 (later Norderende 17)
Refurbishment of a cottage from 1850
sources and literature:
A. Jürgensohn. 1924. *Hiddensee, das Capri von Pommern. Ein Reiseführer und Erinnerungsbuch.* Kloster auf Hiddensee, Karl Haertel, 159.
R. Seydel (ed.). 2005. *Hiddensee. Geschichten von Land und Leuten.* Berlin: Ullstein, 410.
Email correspondence with Jana Leistner, Heimatmuseum Hiddensee, August–October 2008.
Correspondence with Florian Hülsen, October–November 2008.

1925–26
—**Mrs. Leopold Lindemann house**
Berlin, Dahlem, Podbielskiallee 65
Refurbishment of a villa
sources and literature:
Haberlandt, 34 (1925), 1 November, no. 434-35 (1926), 1 March 1926, no. 437.
Letter from Ernst Freud, Berlin, to Lucie Freud, United Kingdom, 16 October 1933 (Collection Esther Freud).

1927
—**Otto Levy house**
Berlin, Nikolassee, An der Rehwiese 4
Refurbishment of a villa, demolished
sources and literature:
Haberlandt, 36 (1927), 1 May 1927, no. 451-1, July 1927, no. 453.
JAB, 1931, 238.

1927
—**Dr. Arno Wittgensteiner house**
Potsdam, Neubabelsberg, Luisenstraße 19–21 [8], today Virchowstraße
Conversion and partially rebuilding of the former country house Schade von Westrum
Wittgensteiner was a lawyer who served on the boards the Lindemann & Co. A.-G., Berlin, the Kaufhaus Grand A.-G., Spandau, and the Rudolf Karstadt AG, Hamburg.
sources and literature:
RIBA p.
Haberlandt, 36 (1927), 1 August 1927, no. 454-1, September 1927, no. 455.

Hajos, 1928.
Mossner, 1927–28, vol. II, 753–754.
Mossner, 1929, vol. I, 2043.
Mossner, 1930, vol. I, 2087.
Welter, 1992.
Worbs, 1997.

1928–29

—**Buchthal house** (figs. 5.19, 5.20)
Berlin, Charlottenburg, Halmstraße 13–14/Lindenallee 22
Refurbishment of a detached house including a second storey, and furniture designs
Clients: Eugen Buchthal (1878–1954) and Thea Buchthal (1886–1968, née Wolff)
sources and literature:
RIBA d, p.
Haberlandt, 37 (1928), 21 August 1928, no. 466b-1, October 1928, no. 468.
Hajos, 1928.
Brüder Luckhardt und Alfons Anker. Berliner Architekten der Moderne. 1990. Berlin: Akademie der Künste, 194.
Welter, 1992.
Worbs, 1997.
Klemmer, 1998
BioHB.

1929–30

—**Bermann-Fischer house** (fig. 4.9)
Berlin, Grunewald, Gneiststraße 7, building demolished
Refurbishment of a detached house, including interior designs and a nursery extension with furniture
June and August 1930
Clients: Gottfried Bermann (1897–1995) and Brigitte Bermann-Fischer (1905–91)
sources and literature:
RIBA d, p.
JAB, 1931, 30.
Anonymous. 1933. [no title], *Design for To-Day* 1 (October): 237.
I. Grubrich-Simitis. 1993. *Back to Freud's Texts. Making Silent Documents Speak*, trans. Philip Slotkin. New Haven, CT: Yale University Press, 50.

1931 or earlier

—**Freud and Tiffany Burlingham country cottage**
Hochrotherd, in the Semmering, near Vienna
Design, with Anna Freud, for the refurbishment of a cottage, execution by Karl Hofmann, partner of Felix Augenfeld & Karl Hoffmann architects
Clients: Anna Freud (1895–1982) and Dorothy Burlingham (1891–1979)
sources and literature:
Young-Bruehl, E. 1988. *Anna Freud.* New York: Summit, 191.
M. J. Burlingham. 1989. *The Last Tiffany. A Biography of Dorothy Tiffany Burlingham.* New York: Atheneum, 216.
R. Harnisch. 1995. 'Die unsichtbare Raumkunst des Felix Augenfeld', in Matthias Boeckle (ed.). *Visionäre & Vertriebene.* Berlin: Ernst & Sohn, 238.

after 1933

—Second Dr. Wolfgang and Annie Herrmann house
London, Hampstead, 89 Kingsley Way
Refurbishment of a house including interior designs
sources and literature:
RIBA p.
Strauss, 1983.
Thomson, 1999.
W. Herrmann. 1992. 'Journey from Berlin: Oral History Transcript', Los Angeles: UCLA, Special Collections, Oral History collection, 236–237.
Letter from Frank Herrmann, 14 August 2002.
Conversation with Harry Weinberger, 18 October 2002.

1936

—Gill music room at Pine House (figs. 7.6, 7.7)
Churt, Hindhead, Surrey
Extension of an early twentieth-century country house with a music room
Clients: Ms Nellie Muriel Gill (1881–1970), called Ms K. Gill, and Ruby Davison
sources and literature:
RIBA p.
N. Carrington. 1936. 'Music Room at Pine House, Churt, Surrey', *Country Life*, 26 September, xxxvi, xxxviii.
R. Edwards. 1936. 'Modern Furniture The Artist as Designer', *Country Life*, 10 October, xxxxi.
Thomson, 1999.
J. Ubbens et al. (eds.). 2000. *Karin von Leyden (1906–1977) Ernst von Leyden (1892–1969)*. Haarlem: Ars et Animation.
Conversation with Stephen Freud, 9 July 2002.
Correspondence and conversation with J. Penticost, August 2002.

c. 1936

—'Maysland' farmhouse
Conversion of an Elizabethan farmhouse
Great Easton, Essex
Client: 'Pink' W. C. Crittall
When Gerda Mosse, the sister of Lucie Freud, and her three children fled Germany in 1936, W. C. Crittall, who was a friend of Ernst L. Freud, offered them a farm house to live in near the Crittall metal window factory. The Mosses stayed there until c. 1946.
sources and literature:
Conversation with Carola Zentner, 12 July 2002.
Email Carola Zentner, 7 September 2005.

1937

—Ernst and Lucie Freud cottage 'Hidden House' (fig. 8.8)
Walberswick, Suffolk
Refurbishment and extension of an existing cottage
sources and literature:
E. and Lucie Freud (eds.). 1980. *Sigmund Freud Briefe 1873–1939*, 3rd improved ed. Frankfurt: S. Fischer, letter 17 January 1938.
R. Seydel (ed.). 2005. *Hiddensee. Geschichten von Land und Leuten*. Berlin: Ullstein, 410–411.

182 Selected List of Works

1937–38

—M. M. Gill house (figs. 7.8, 8.6)
London, South Kensington, 8 Alexander Place
Refurbishment of a terraced house, including interior designs
sources and literature:
RIBA d.
M. Whirter. 1939. 'New Rooms for Old', *The Ideal Home*, March, 164–165.
Email Ray Leigh, Gordon Russell Museum, Broadway, Worcs, England, 12 November 2006.

—Dr. David and Mrs. A. A. Matthew house (figs. 7.9, 9.7)
London, Hampstead, Hampstead Way 43
Refurbishment of a detached house, originally built by Barry Parker and Raymond Unwin
sources and literature:
RIBA p.
LMA, d.
'Replanning of a House in Hampstead'. 1939. *Architectural Review* 86 (November): supplement 221–222.
D. Coke (ed.). 1995. *Hans Feibusch. The Heat of Vision.* London: Lund Humphries.
A. Powers. 1997. 'Historical Context', in Paul Foster (ed.). *Feibusch Murals Chichester and Beyond. An Exploration of Approach.* Chichester: Chichester Institute of Higher Education, 20–25.
Letter from M. Marmot, 11 September 2002.

1938

—Sigmund and Martha Freud house (figs. 8.10, 8.11)
London, Hampstead, 20 Maresfield Gardens
Refurbishment, including a consulting room, and extension with winter garden and loggia of a detached house from the 1920s
sources and literature:
RIBA p.
LMA d.
Worbs, 1997.
Freud Museum London (ed). 1998. *20 Maresfield Gardens—Guide to the Freud Museum.* London: Serpent's Tail.

1938–40

—Rickman cottage 'Cocks Cottages' [Cock's Lodge]
Sandon, near Baldock, Hertfordshire
Merger of two semi-detached cottages into a single cottage
Clients: Dr. John (1891–1951) and Lydia Lewis Rickman (1885–1971)
sources and literature:
Lucy Rickman Baruch, p.
Letters and email correspondence with Lucy Rickman Baruch, April 2004–November 2005.

1942–43

—Julian and Juliette Huxley house
London, 31 Pond Street
Refurbishment of a terraced house, including interior designs and shelving for four thousand books
sources and literature
J. Huxley. 1970. *Memories.* New York: Harper & Row, 263–264.

J. R. Baker. 1978. *Julian Huxley. Scientist and World Citizen 1887–1975*. Paris: UNESCO, 48.
J. Huxley. 1986. *Leaves of the Tulip Tree. Autobiography*. Topsfield, MA: Salem House, 184.
National Monument Records, English Heritage, Images of England #477784, http://www.imagesofengland.org.uk (accessed 13 February 2009).

1945

—**Dame Peggy Ashcroft house**
London, Frognal Lane, No. 40 Manor Lodge
Repair and refurbishment of a detached house
sources and literature:
Email from Lady Natasha Spender, London, 20 September 2004.

—**Stephen and Lady Natasha Spender house**
London, 15 Loudoun Road
Repair and refurbishment of a detached house
sources and literature:
Email from Lady Natasha Spender, London, 20 September 2004.

1946–47

—**Mrs. O. F. Thompson house**
London, Hampstead, Ossulton Way 98
Rebuilding and alteration of a war-damaged detached house
sources and literature:
LMA d.

—**Anna Freud cottage 'Far End'**
Walberswick, Suffolk
Refurbishment of a cottage
Anna Freud purchased 'Far End' at an auction in 1946. Apparently, Ernst Freud also worked on a cottage for Dorothy Burlingham.
sources and literature:
E. Young-Bruehl. 1988. *Anna Freud*. New York: Summit Books, 287.
Conversation with Carola Zentner, 12 July 2002.

1948

—**Fritz and Ann Hess mews house**
London, NW3, 1 Daleham Mews
Conversion of a garage into a mews dwelling
November 1948
Apparently, Freud also worked on a cottage for the couple in Walberswick.
sources and literature:
RIBA d.
Conversations with Carola Zentner, 12 July 2002, and Stephen Freud, 9 July 2002.

—**Count Seilern house**
London, South Kensington, 56 Princes Gate, Exhibition Road
Refurbishment of a terraced town house
Client: Antoine Edward Count Seilern (1901–78)
sources and literature:
Conversation with Stephen Freud, London, 9 July 2002.

Email from Helen Braham, Curator of Sculpture and Applied Arts Courtauld Gallery, 17 October 2002.
Letters and conversation with Paul Levi, 2002–5.

1950s

—**Wolfgang Mosse house**
London, Hampstead NW8, 28 Clifton Hill
Addition of a new staircase at the garden side of a terraced house
sources and literature:
Letter from Lucie Freud to Harry and Leli Freud, 1 September 1948 (LoC, Harry Freud papers, box 5, folder Ernst L. Freud and Lux Freud 1938–49).
Conversation with J. Mosse, London, 23 July 2002.

—**Gill Cottage 'Longshore house'**
Walberswick, Suffolk
Refurbishment of a cottage
Client: Ms Nellie Muriel Gill (1881–1970), called Ms K. Gill
sources and literature:
RIBA p.
Conversation with Stephen Freud, 9 July 2002.

1956

—**Stephen and Ann Freud house**
London, Chiswick, 74 Park Road
Extension of a house with a small bay window
sources and literature:
Conversation with Stephen and Ann Freud, London, 9 July 2002.

1963

—**Marcus and Rene Bromwell house**
Creek Vean, Feock, Cornwall, England
Design for refurbishment and extension of an existing building, never built
sources and literature:
Email from Sue Rogers, London, 2 August 2004.
B. Appleyard. 1986. *Richard Rogers. A Biography.* London: Faber and Faber, 111.
K. Powell. 1999. *Richard Rogers. Complete Works.* London: Phaidon, vol. 1, 29–35, 307.

—**Third Dr. Wolfgang and Annie Herrmann house**
London, Hampstead, 11 Pilgrim's Lane
Refurbishment of a detached house, including interior designs
Some of the furniture that Freud had designed for the Herrmanns on earlier occasions was moved into the new house as can be seen on a photograph of the couple by their son, the photographer Frank Herrmann.
sources and literature:
RIBA p.
Strauss, 1983.
F. Herrmann. 1988. *Portrait Photography.* Sparkford near Yeovil: Oxford Illustrated Press, 147.
W. Herrmann. 1992. 'Journey from Berlin: Oral History Transcript'. Los Angeles: UCLA, Special Collections, Oral History collection, 236–237.

Thomson, 1999.
Letter from Frank Herrmann, 14 August 2002.
Conversation with Harry Weinberger, 18 October 2002.

1965

—**Cottage next to the Hidden House**
Walberswick, Suffolk
Refurbishment of a cottage next to the Hidden House
sources and literature:
Letter from Ernst L. Freud to Harry Freud, 10 May 1965 (LoC, Harry Freud papers, box 5, folder Ernst L. Freud and Lucie Freud 1950–66 and undated).

1.3 Multi-apartment buildings and houses designed for anonymous users

1937–38

—**Frognal Close town houses (fig. 7.10)**
London, Hampstead, 1–6 Frognal Close
Design of a group of six town houses
Client: [Ralph Davies]
sources and literature:
RIBA p.
Exhibited in 1934 at 'International Architecture 1924–1934' at RIBA new HQs Portland Place [RIBA photos: Ba157].
N. Stephen. 1938. 'Hampstead—two centuries of House Architecture', *Building* 13 (July): 268–273.
'Group of Houses in Hampstead: designed by Ernst L. Freud'. 1938. *Architects' Journal* 88 (1 September): 373–375, 377.
'A Group of Houses in Hampstead'. 1938. *Architectural Review* 84 (August): 54–56.
1938. *The National Builder* 18 (4): 121.
C. H. Reilly. 1939. 'The Year's Work at Home'. *Architects' Journal* 89 (January): 133–146.
P. Abercrombie (ed.). 1939. *The Book of the Modern House. A Panoramic Survey of Contemporary Domestic Design.* London: Hodder & Stoughton, 100, plate 79.
Gould, 1977.
Benton, 1995.

—**Belvedere Court apartment building (fig. 7.12)**
London, Hampstead Garden, Lyttelton Road
Design of fifty-six apartments in three connected blocks
sources and literature:
RIBA p.
LMA
'"Belvedere Court," Lyttleton Road, Hampstead Garden Suburb'. 1939. *The Builder* 156 (10 February): 239–240.
Benton, 1995.

1939 or earlier

—**Belsize Park Gardens apartment buildings**
London, Hampstead, 25 Belsize Park Gardens, and 1 Belsize Park Gardens
Conversion of two townhouses into apartments

25 Belsize Park Gardens was owned by Gerda Mosse (née Brasch) while 1 Belsize Park Gardens was owned by her, Ernst Freud, and a Mrs. Böhm. During World War 2, 25 Belsize Park Gardens housed staff from the Hampstead War Nurseries.
sources and literature:
Conversation with Carola Zentner, 12 July 2002.
A. Freud and D. Burlingham. 1973. *Infants without Families. Reports on the Hampstead Nurseries 1939–1945.* New York: International University Press, 28–29.

1939

—4 Maresfield Gardens apartment building
London, Hampstead, NW3
Design for a conversion of a townhouse into apartments, never built, building sold in 1945
sources and literature:
Notice on file jointly written by Alexander Freud and Ernst L. Freud, 13 October 1939 (LoC, Alexander and Sophie Freud papers, box 1, folder Ernst L. Freud and Lucie Freud, 1938–53).
Letters from Ernst L. Freud to Harry Freud, 17 December 1940, 31 May 1941, 15 June 1942, 11 June 1943, 12 June 1945 (LoC, Harry Freud papers, box 5, folder Ernst Freud and Lucie Freud 1938–49).
Letter from Ernst L. Freud to Alexander Freud, 22 November 1942 (LoC, Alexander and Sophie Freud papers, box 1, folder Ernst L. Freud and Lucie Freud 1938–53).

1945

—Hampstead apartment buildings
London, Hampstead
Designs for conversions of single-family houses into apartment buildings
sources and literature:
Letter from Ernst L. Freud to Harry Freud, 2 September 1945 (LoC, Harry Freud papers, box 5, folder Ernst L. Freud and Lucie Freud 1938–49).

1946

—Littlehampton apartment building
Littlehampton
Design for a conversion of a townhouse into five small apartments
Exhibited in at 'New Homes from Old', exhibition organized by Housing Centre and held at tea Centre, London [1946].
sources and literature:
'Conversion of Houses—Seaside Flats Little Hampton'. 1946. *The National House Builder and Building Digest* 6 (November): 28–29.

1948

—Cottages for agricultural workers
Sussex
Designs for two semi-detached cottages, one detached cottage, and the alteration of an existing cottage
November and December 1948
sources and literature:
RIBA d, p.

1950

—Hampstead apartment house
London, Hampstead NW3
12 October 1950
Conversion of an existing townhouse into one or two self-contained apartments
Drawing initialled G.C.B.
sources and literature:
RIBA d.

1951

—Golden Lane Housing Estate
London
Entry for a social-housing competition, never built
Freud worked on this scheme together with the architect Arthur Erickson (1924–2009) who recalled that Freud's office was located in the garage. Each afternoon, tea was taken inside the Freud home where the Freuds led an active social life.
sources and literature:
Newsletter, *The Circle*, 18 March 1952 (RIBA Archive C/1/1).
Corporation of London Records Office, list of participants in competition.
E Iglauer. 1981. *Seven Stones. A Portrait of Arthur Erickson, Architect.* Madeira Park, BC: Harbour Publishing, 54.
Email from Arthur Erickson, 24 March 2005.

1952 or later

—43 Elsworthy Road apartments
London, 43 Elsworthy Road
Design for a block of six apartments to replace a war-damaged building
sources and literature:
RIBA p.
Letter from Lucie Freud to Harry Freud, 10 November 1952 (LoC, Harry Freud papers, box 5, folder Ernst L. Freud and Lucie Freud 1950–66 and undated).
'Flats on a Bomb Site'. 1955. *Architecture and Building* 30 (January): 30–32.
Benton, 1995.

1965

—'Proposed erection of three cottages on a half acre site at Walberswick near Southwold Suffolk'
Walberswick, Suffolk
Design for three cottages
29 March 1965
sources and literature:
RIBA d.

2.0 Domestic interiors (for houses, apartments, and individual rooms)

1921

—Karl Abraham study
Berlin, Grunewald, Bismarckallee 14

Refurbishment of a study
sources and literature:
E. Falzeder (ed.). 2002. *The Complete Correspondence of Sigmund Freud and Karl Abraham 1907–1925*. London: Karnac, letter 401A.

1921 or later
—Seidmann-Freud apartment
[Berlin, Charlottenburg, Schillerstraße 12/13]
Interior and furniture designs (24)
Client: Tom (Martha-Gertrud) Seidmann-Freud (1892–1930)
Painter and poet Tom Seidmann-Freud was the daughter of one of Sigmund Freud's sisters. She wrote and illustrated children's books. In 1921, she married Jankew Seidmann, an orthodox Jew who published Judaistic literature. Seidmann committed suicide in October 1929 when his publishing house went bankrupt. His wife followed him three months later.
sources and literature:
RIBA d.
B. Murken. 1984. *Tom Seidmann Freud—Leben und Werk*. Frankfurt: Institut für Jugendbuchforschung.

1923
—Apartment for an anonymous client
Leipzig
sources and literature:
Letter from Ernst Freud to Lucie Freud, 20 March 1923 (collection Esther Freud).

1924–25
—Second Ernst and Lucie Freud apartment (figs. 1.3, 8.1, 8.2, 8.3)
Berlin, Tiergarten, Regentenstraße 23
Interior and furniture designs
Before 1925 Ernst and Lucie Freud lived at Regentenstraße 11. For 1923, Ernst Freud also had an address in Steglitzer Straße 69. From c. 1924–32 they occupied an apartment at Regentenstraße 23, which they gave up for a new one at Matthäikirchstraße 4 in c. October 1931. There they lived until they emigrated in late 1933.
sources and literature:
RIBA d, p.
BAB 1920–1933.
H. G. 1928. 'Vom Neuen Bauen', *Die Pyramide* 14 (7): 205–213, image before 205.
A. H. 1928. 'Zu Hause', *Die Pyramide* 14 (August): 248–257.
Letter from Ernst Freud to Lucie Freud, 5 October 1933 (collection Esther Freud).

1927
—First Dr. Wolfgang and Annie Herrmann house
Berlin, Dahlem, [Im Gehege 15]
Interior and furniture designs (26)
Clients: Dr. Wolfgang Herrmann and Annie Herrmann, née Marx
Art historian Dr. Wolfgang Herrmann and his wife Annie, née Marx, moved into a new house in Berlin, Dahlem, in 1927. On that occasion they commissioned designs by Freud. After 1933, Freud worked in London for both Wolfgang and Annie Herrmann and the parents of the latter, Adolf and Heide Marx (see entry in 1.1).

sources and literature:
RIBA d.
JAB, 1931, 155.
W. Herrmann. 1992. 'Journey from Berlin: Oral History Transcript'. Los Angeles: UCLA, Special Collections, Oral History collection, 236–237.
Letter from F. Herrmann, 17 July 2002.

1930

—**Dr. (B.[enno]) Cohn dwelling**
unknown location [Berlin, Charlottenburg], Eichkamp, Preussenallee
Interior and furniture designs (47)
November and December 1930
sources and literature:
RIBA d.
Lux papers, box L–Z, Freud Museum, London.
Ladwig-Winters, 1998, 112, 113.
Ladwig-Winters, 2007, 136.

—**Krojanker apartment**
[Berlin, Schöneberg, Innsbrucker Straße 18]
Interior and furniture designs
February 1930
Client: Dr. jur. Gustav Krojanker (1891–1945)
Freud was a friend of Gustav Krojanker since they both studied in Munich where they met through their memberships in Jewish fraternities; Krojanker in the *Jordania* and Freud in *Hasmonaea*. Krojanker was the son of Hermann Krojanker (1885–1935) who owned 'Conrad Tack & Cie', one of the largest European shoe factories located in Burg near Magdeburg. Krojanker held a PhD in economics and worked with his brother in the family business. His Zionist interested led him to move to Berlin in 1929. In 1930, he became the director of both the Jüdische Verlag and the Weltverlag, both dedicated to the Zionist cause. In 1932, Krojanker emigrated to Palestine.
sources and literature:
RIBA d.
BAB 1931.
Email correspondence with Leorah Kroyanker, November 2005–July 2008.

—**Michael apartment**
[Berlin, Tiergarten, Brückenallee 4]
Interior and furniture designs (44)
January 1930
Clients: Dr. Fritz Michael and Hanna Michael (née Schwab)
Fritz Michael was a research chemist who came from a wealthy Berlin Jewish family. He married in 1928 or 1929 when Freud was commissioned to design the furniture for the apartment of the couple. Their exile took them to The Netherlands, the United Kingdom, and Mexico before they settled in Israel in 1947.
sources and literature:
RIBA d.
JAB, 1931, 282.
Email correspondence with Ben Schwab, May 2004–March 2008.

—**Stefan Neumann dwelling**
unknown location

Furniture designs (48)
August, September, and November 1930
Some drawings stamped 'Alexander Kurz Regentenstraße 23'
sources and literature:
RIBA d.

—**Generaldirektor Pulvermann dwelling**
unknown location [Berlin]
Furniture designs (18)
December 1930
sources and literature:
RIBA d.

—**Dr. Salomon apartment**
[Berlin, Charlottenburg, Wielandstr. 15]
Interior and furniture designs (32)
April 1930
sources and literature:
RIBA d.

—**Adolf Soberheim dwelling**
unknown location
Furniture designs (21)
August and September 1930
Some drawings stamped 'Alexander Kurz'
sources and literature:
RIBA d.

1931

—**Goldmann dwelling**
unknown location
Furniture designs (17)
April 1931
sources and literature:
RIBA d.

1931

—**Schönheimer dwelling**
unknown location
Furniture designs (39)
February 1931
Some drawings stamped 'Frau Erna Cohn im Atelier der Architekten Dipl. Ing. Ernst L. Freud und Dipl. Ing. Alexander Kurz, Regentenstraße 23'
sources and literature:
RIBA d.

1932

—**Third Ernst and Lucie Freud apartment**
Berlin, Tiergarten, Matthäikirchstraße 4
Interior and furniture designs for the architect's own apartment

sources and literature:
BAB, 1933.

1933

—**Hamburger house (fig. 4.11)**
London, St John's Wood, St John's Wood Park 45
Interior design for an existing house, including fitting of furniture brought from Germany
Client: Richard Hamburger (1884–1940)
sources and literature:
RIBA d.
JAB, 1931, 146.
M. Speyer. 1935. 'Decoration—the Doctor's Dilemma', *Design for To-day* 3 (June): 228–230.
BioHB.
Strauss, 1983.
M. Hamburger. 1973. *String of Beginning. Intermittent Memoirs 1924–1954.* Manchester: Carcanet.
T. Lennert, 'Die Entwicklung der Berliner Pädiatrie', in W. Fischer et al. (eds). 2000. *Exodus der Wissenschaften aus Berlin.* Berlin, New York: Walter de Gruyter, 529–551.
E. Seidler. 2000. *Kinderärzte 1933–1945, entrechtet—geflohen—ermordet.* Bonn: Bouvier, 148–149.
Letters from Michael Hamburger, 31 July 2002, 10 August 2002, 8 October 2002.

1934

—**Fritz and Ann Hess apartment**
London, Highgate, Millfield Lane, 16 West Hill Court
Advice on the interior design of a small apartment, including selection of wallpapers and curtains, and the purchase of furniture
sources and literature:
Letters from Ernst Freud to Lucie Freud 27 March 1934 and 28 March 1934 (collection Esther Freud).

1935

—**Mona Beardsley apartment**
London, Crawford Street
Design for interior and furniture of an apartment, including chairs, a long sofa, an s-shaped table and teak-veneer cabinets
sources and literature:
Letter from Tony Birks-Hay, 26 September 2007.

—**Ernst and Lucie Freud house (figs. 8.3, 8.4, 8.5, 8.14)**
London, Hampstead NW3, 32 St John's Wood Terrace
Conversion of a terraced house, interior design, including fitting of furniture from their last apartment in Berlin
sources and literature:
RIBA, p.
N. Carrington. 1935. 'Ernst L. Freud interviewed at his new London House', *Decoration*, no. 7 new series, November: 22–25.
E. L. Freud and Harold Bright. 1936. 'The Conquest of Space with the Aid of Electricity', *Good Housekeeping*, October, 60–61, 104–105.

192 *Selected List of Works*

Letter from Ernst L. Freud to Harry Freud, 17 December 1940 (LoC, Harry Freud papers, box 5, folder Ernst L. Freud and Lucie Freud 1938–49).
Letter from Ernst Freud to Harry Freud, 15 June 1942 (LoC, Alexander and Sophie Freud papers, box 1, folder Ernst L. Freud and Lucie Freud 1938–53).
Letter from Lucie Freud to Harry Freud, [18 December 1951] (LoC, Harry Freud papers, box 7, folder Mathilde Hollitscher 1950–59).
Benton, 1995.

1939
—**Rie apartment**
London, 18 Albion Mews, Hyde Park; the interior is today in the Kaiserliches Hofmobiliendepot, Vienna
Fitting of existing built-in and moveable furniture into a mews building
Client: Lucie Rie (née Gomperz, 1902–95)
When living in her native Vienna, Lucie Rie had in 1928 an apartment designed by architect Ernst A. Plischke (1903–92). When she emigrated in 1938, Plischke sent the furniture together with working drawings to London, where Freud fitted them into a building in Albion Mews in early 1939.
sources and literature:
Ernst Anton Plischke. Vienna: Akademie der Künste, 1983.
T. Birks. 1987. *Lucie Rie.* London: Alphabooks.
E. A. Plischke. 1989. *Ein Leben mit Architektur.* Vienna: Löcker
E. B. Ottilinger. 1999. 'Die Wohnung Lucie Rie. Das "Opus 1" von Ernst A. Plischke im "Kaiserlichen Hofmobiliendepot"', *Parnass* 4: 82–88.
E. B. Ottilinger. 2001.'Home again', *Crafts* May/June: 34–37.

1950s
—**Interior of a study for unknown client**
London, Alexandra Place
Design for a study and furniture
sources and literature:
RIBA p.

3.0 Domestic furniture designs (individual pieces and sets)

1920
—**Atelier Alexander Baerwald (1877–1930)**
Berlin, Dahlem, Takustraβe 3
Design for a table
15 February 1920
sources and literature:
RIBA d.

1921
—**anonymous clients [Eitingon]**
[Berlin, Tiergarten, Rauchstraβe 4]
Furniture designs (8)
20 April 1920

sources and literature:
RIBA d.

1925
—Baron Uexkuell
Berlin
Furniture design (1)
sources and literature:
Inventory Regentenstraße 11 (Lux Papers, box L–Z, Freud Museum, London).

1928–30
—Dr. Oskar Tokayer
Berlin, Friedrich-Wilhelm-Straße 23
Furniture designs (3)
sources and literature:
RIBA d.

1929
—Schmidt
unknown location
Furniture designs (8)
August 1929
sources and literature:
RIBA d.

1929 or earlier
—Rudolf Gleimius (1890–1977)
Berlin, Gatow, Kladower Damm 43
Design for a radio cabinet
Gleimius was a businessman and banker who was a board member and director of various businesses and banks in Berlin and Germany. He was married to Ilse Goldmann since 1926. They lived on a large estate at Kladower Damm overlooking the river Havel. Freud designed for them a cupboard that accommodated a radio. In 1929, the Gleimius couple visited the US. After their return they planned for a new building on their property in an 'American bungalow style'. Apparently, Gleimius produced the design that Freud was asked to realize. Already earlier, Freud had designed the bedroom furniture for the main house at the waterfront of the property.
sources and literature
Mossner, 1929, vol. I, 535.
Wenzel, 1929, column 733.
Letters from Klaus-Egon Bossart, 4 October and 8 December 2005.

1930
—Dr. [Arno] Wittgensteiner
Neubabelsberg, Luisenstraße 3
Furniture designs (3)
February 1930
sources and literature:
RIBA d.

—Anonymous client
unknown location, Taunusstraβe 10
Furniture designs (3)
November 1930
sources and literature:
RIBA d.

—Aron Werke
unknown location [Berlin]
Design for a music cupboard and a loudspeaker encasement
May and September 1930
sources and literature:
RIBA d.
'Aron Elektricitätszähler-Fabrik G.m.b.H. Heliowatt Werke Elektrizitätsgesellschaft m.b.H. Wilmersdorfer Straße 39', in H. Engel et al. (eds). 1986 *Geschichtslandschaft Berlin. Orte und Ereignisse. Charlottenburg. Teil 1. Historische Stadt.* Berlin: Nicolai, vol. 1, 178–199.

—Dr. Braunthal
unknown location [Berlin]
Furniture designs (3)
January 1930
sources and literature:
RIBA d.

—Dr. Bürgner
unknown location [Berlin]
furniture designs (13)
December 1930
sources and literature:
RIBA d.

—Dr. Halpern
unknown location
Furniture designs (10)
April 1930
sources and literature:
RIBA d.

—Constanze [called Tania] Marie Matilde Kurella (1904́–1995)
[Berlin, Tiergarten, Potsdamer Straße 21]
Design for a bedstead
November 1930
sources and literature:
RIBA d.
BAB 1930, 1931.
N. Jenkins. 1994. 'James Stern 1904–1993', *Auden Society Newsletter* 12 (April).

—Dr. Landshoff
[Berlin]
Furniture designs (2)
February 1930
sources and literature:
RIBA d.

—**Dr. Pietrkowsky**
unknown location [Berlin]
Furniture designs (3)
March 1930
sources and literature:
RIBA d.

—**Dr. Schoenbeck**
unknown location
Furniture designs (8)
May 1930
sources and literature:
RIBA d.

—**Dr. [Karl] Selowski (1889–after 1949)**
unknown location [Berlin]
Furniture design
October 1930
sources and literature:
RIBA d.
Ladwig-Winters, 1998, 207.

1930 or earlier

—**Dr. Goldschmidt country house (fig. 9.2)**
Berlin, Dahlem
Furniture designs (7)
sources and literature:
RIBA d, p.

—**Alwin Schönbach**
Berlin, Charlottenburg, Kaiserdamm 67, 4th floor
Furniture designs (3)
Schönbach (born 27 March 1891) was director of Fa. Saß & Martini bank in Kanonierstraße 39 in Berlin.
sources and literature:
RIBA d.
Mossner, 1929, vol. I, 1650.
Wenzel, 1929, column 2022.
BAB 1931.
JAB 1931, 368.

1931

—**anonymous client**
Berlin, Schöneberg, Lietzenburgerstraße 1
Furniture designs (5)
15 November 1931
sources and literature:
RIBA d.

—**Margot Joachimsthal (1901–1995)**
unknown location [Berlin]

Furniture designs (6)
One of the drawings stamped 'Erna Cohn'
February 1931
Margot Joachimsthal was born in Berlin, lived briefly in Hamburg, and moved to Switzerland shortly before the war. She met her husband George Giusti (1908–90) in Switzerland and the couple and their son went to New York in 1938. They took some of the furniture with them as recalled by their son Robert Giusti.
sources and literature:
RIBA d.
Email and telephone conversation with Robert Giusti, March 2004.

—Walter Neumark
unknown location
Furniture designs (10)
January 1931
sources and literature:
RIBA d.

—Gen. Dir. Pulvermann
Design for a tubular steel comfort chair
16 April 1931
sources and literature:
RIBA d.

c. 1931

—Trudi [Gertrud] Ornstein
unknown location [Berlin, Schönberg, Speyerer Straße 18]
Design for a child's bed
sources and literature:
RIBA d.
BAB, 1931.

between 1933 and 1937

—Dr. jur. Edward Heims (1884–1964) and Hildegard Heims (1906–1987)
London, address not know
Furniture design (11), among them a dining table and eight dining chairs, which were built by Gordon Russell furniture company
Dr. jur. Edward Heims, whose name was Heymann until 1917, was a Berlin-born lawyer and banker who lived in Berlin with his second wife Hildegard Heims (née Hartmann). From 1914–19, Edward Heims worked in the German foreign ministry, and from 1919–23 he was on the staff of Walter Simons, Germany's foreign minister from 1920–21. Heims was also the general manager for the International Mortgage and Investment Corporation (IMIC) with offices in Berlin and Baltimore, MD (in the US), and served on the boards of directors for various other companies, among them Banque Commerciale Société Anonym in Luxemburg. Hildegard Heims held a masters degree in economics. In 1929 they lived at Potsdamer Straße 121 in Berlin. In 1933, the couple went into exile to London where they commissioned the furniture from Freud. In 1937, the family left for Los Angeles, California.
sources and literature:
Mossner 1929, vol. I, 680.
Mossner 1930, vol. I, 697.

Email correspondence and telephone conversations with Dr. Evelyn Parker, September–October 2006.
Email Ray Leigh, Gordon Russell Museum, Broadway, Worcs, England, 12 November 2006.
Ladwig-Winters, 2007, 170.

1936

—**light fittings and occasional table**
Design for ceiling fittings and a metal tube table with glass top
sources and literature:
'Ceiling Fittings'. 1936. *Decoration*, no. 18, new series, October: 50.
'Occasional Table in Chromium and Rough-Cast Glass'. 1936. *Decoration*, no. 20, new series, December, 47.

4.0 Professional, business, and commercial premises

4.1 Psychoanalytic Spaces and furniture

1920

—**Karl Abraham waiting room**
Berlin, Grunewald, Bismarckallee 14
Redecoration of a waiting room
sources and literature:
E. Falzeder (ed). 2002. *The Complete Correspondence of Sigmund Freud and Karl Abraham 1907–1925*. London: Karnac, letter 374A.

—**Poliklinik für Psychoanalytische Behandlung nervöser Krankheiten**
Berlin, Tiergarten, Potsdamer Straße 29 (today number 74)
Interior designs for five treatment rooms and furniture designs
opened 15 February 1920
sources and literature:
Report of Poliklinik, March 1920–June 1922 (Freud Museum, London).
Danto, 2005, 53.

1927

—**Psychoanalytische Klinik Sanatorium Schloβ Tegel (Figs. 6.6, 6.7, 6.8, 6.9, 6.12)**
Berlin, Tegel
Refurbishment of existing sanatorium building, including interior design and furniture design (49), clinic opened in April 1927 and closed in November 1931, building demolished
sources and literature:
RIBA d.
Sanatorium Schloβ Tegel Psychoanalytische Klinik Berlin Tegel. 1927. S.l.: no publisher.
Letter from Ernst Simmel to Sigmund Freud (LoC, Sigmund Freud papers, box 42, folder 3).
Brecht, 1985.
Danto, 2005, 185–186.

—**Radó consulting room and dwelling**
Berlin, Schmargendorf, Ilmenauerstraβe 2A
Interior and furniture design (11) for consulting room and other spaces in a private dwelling
Client: Dr. Sandor Radó (1890–1972), psychoanalyst

Radó moved to the US in September 1931. 'We had our apartment in Berlin; I brought out some furniture. This desk in my office now is part of my original furniture designed by Freud's son Ernst. This was my original analytic chair, covered with leather I did not like so it was recovered; and I am still using my original analytic couch in my office.' 'Peter [SR's son] also discarded Radó's office furniture which was designed by Ernst Freud. Radó had brought the pieces from Berlin and was very proud of his analytic couch and chairs. After Radó's death and Peter's marriage, Peter and his wife thought the furniture seemed shabby and it was discarded, much to Peter's largest regret.' (Roazen and Swerdloff, 1995)

sources and literature:
RIBA d.
P. Roazen and B. Swerdloff (eds.). 1995. *Heresy: Sandor Rado and the Psychoanalytic Movement.* Northvale, NJ: Jason Aronson, 109, 110, 181.

1928

—**Berliner Psychoanalytische Institut (Poliklinik and Lehranstalt) of the Deutsche Psychoanalytische Gesellschaft (DPG) (figs. 6.3, 6.4, 6.5)**
Berlin, Tiergarten, Wichmannstraße 10
Interior designs for the relocated Poliklinik, opened on 30 September 1928.
sources and literature:
Deutsche Psychoanalytische Gesellschaft (ed.). 1930. *Zehn Jahre Berliner Psychoanalytisches Institut (Poliklinik und Lehranstalt).* Vienna: Psychoanalytischer Verlag.
Brecht, 1985.
Danto, 2005, 201–202.

1928–29

—**Spitz consulting room and villa**
Berlin, Grunewald, Taubertstraße 5
Interior and furniture design for consulting room and other spaces in a private villa
Client: Dr. René (Arpad) Spitz (1887–1974)
The Spitz family moved to Berlin from Vienna in c. 1928 or 1929. Freud worked on an interior design for a villa for the family that included a sound proof psychoanalytic consulting room, a glass-enclosed garden room, and a large couch, placed in the centre of the living room, that could be divided by bolsters into four sections each seating two to three people. This couch went with the family into exile to New York. Before they reached the US, the family fled to Paris where Paul Bry worked as their interior designer. Later in the 1950s, Spitz relocated to Denver, Colorado, where he employed Victor Hornbein (1913–95) as his architect.
sources and literature:
BAB, 1931.
JAB, 1931, 394.
Email correspondence with Eva Maria Spitz-Blum, 2 February, 25 March, and 30 May 2004.

1933

—**Klein consulting room and house (fig. 6.15)**
London, St John's Wood NW8, 42 Clifton Hill
Refurbishment and interior design for an existing house including a consulting room
Client: Melanie Klein (1882–1960)
sources and literature:
M. Speyer. 1935. 'Decoration—the Doctor's Dilemma', *Design for To-day* 3 (June): 228–230.
P. Grosskurth.1986. *Melanie Klein: Her World and Her Work.* New York: Knopf, 200.

Letter from G. Munro Ferguson, 20 August 2002.
Letter from Dr. S. Smith, September 2002.
Email from W. Chubb, 3 September 2002.
Conversation with Dr. D. Meltzer, 4 October 2002.
Email correspondence and telephone conversation with D. Brimblecombe, September–October 2007.

1934

—Maas and Misch Sanatorium

London, Hampstead, located opposite an existing hospital
Project for the remodelling and furnishing of an existing building as a psychoanalytic sanatorium, never built
Clients: Hilde Maas and Dr. med. Käthe Misch (i.e. Kate Friedlaender [1903–49])
sources and literature:
Letters from Ernst Freud to Lucie Freud, 12 July 1933, 13, 14, and 22 March 1934, 9 and 11 April 1934 (collection Esther Freud).
Letter from H. Kennedy, 26 August 2002.
T. Müller. 2000. *Von Charlottenburg to Central Park West. Henry Lowenfeld und die Psychoanalyse in Berlin, Prag und New York.* Frankfurt: Déjà Vue, 303.
Danto, 2005, 260.

1934 or earlier

—Friedlaender consulting room

London, 32 St Anne's Terrace, St John's Wood, later at 2, Harley House, Harley Street, London NW1
Client: Dr. med. Kate Friedlaender (1903–49, née Frankl, divorced Misch)
sources and literature:
JAB, 1931, 285.
Email correspondence with Gerda Flöckinger CBE, November 2006 to January 2007.
Letter from H. Kennedy, 26 August 2002.
Psychoanalytikerinnen in Europa. Biografisches Lexikon (http://www.psychoanalytikerinnen.de/, ad vocem, accessed 15th January 2007).

1935–36

—Jones consulting room and cottage

Sussex, Midhurst, Elsted, The Plat
Extension of a Jacobean cottage (1625) with a two-storey wing including a consulting room on the ground floor
sources and literature:
West Sussex Record Office, Chichester, d.
R. A. Paskauskas (ed.). 1993. *The Complete Correspondence of Sigmund Freud and Ernest Jones 1908–1939.* Cambridge, MA: Harvard University Press, letter 637 (27 June 1935), letter 644 (27 February 1936).
E. Jones. 1959. *Free Associations. Memories of a Psycho-Analyst.* London: Hogarth, 15–16, 252.
R. Davies. 1994. *Yr Eneth Ddisglair Annwyl: Morfydd Owen (1891–1918). Ei Bywyd mewn Llunian.* Llandysul, Dyfed: Gomer.

—Psychoanalytische Vereinigung Wien

Vienna, Berggasse 7

Interior design of an apartment used as office, including a conference room
sources and literature:
Letter from Anna Freud to Ernst Freud, 30 December 1935 (Freud Museum London).
M. Molnar (ed.). 1992. *The Diary of Sigmund Freud 1929–1939*. London: Hogarth, 5 June 1936.
Letter from Anna Freud to Lou Andreas-Salomé, 28 December 1935 (LAS/AF letter 408).
Sigmund-Freud Museum Vienna, photograph of conference room.

1938

—**Sigmund and Martha Freud house**
London, Hampstead, 20 Maresfield Gardens
Installation of furniture from the Vienna consulting room and study in a new consulting room in the London home (see entry in 1.2)

1941

—**Babies' Rest Centre for Hampstead War Nurseries**
London, Hampstead, 5 Netherhall Gardens
Refurbishment of an existing house as a nursery for babies
The Hampstead War Nurseries began with a Children's Rest Centre at 13 Wedderburn Road in Hampstead in January 1941 where Freud apparently installed a safe room as protection against bombing raids. In March 1941, talks began about a second location for the Hampstead War Nurseries. The Babies' Rest Centre opened in summer 1941 at the same time as New Barn in Chelmsford, Essex, was established as a third, out-of-London location of the War Nurseries.
sources and literature:
Letter from Ernst L. Freud to Harry Freud, 8 February 1941 (LoC, Harry Freud papers, box 5, folder Ernst L. Freud and Lucie Freud 1938–49).
Letter from Robert Hollitscher to Alexander Freud, 22 March 1941 (LoC, Alexander and Sophie Freud papers, box 6, folder Mathilde and Robert Hollitscher 1939–64).
Letter from Mathilde Hollitscher to Alexander Freud, 26 April 1941 (LoC, Alexander and Sophie Freud papers, box 6, folder Mathilde and Robert Hollitscher 1938–64).
Letter from Ernst L. Freud to Dorothy Burlingham, 6 May 1946 (LoC, Anna Freud papers, box 28, folder 13 Ernst L. Freud and Lucie Freud 1946–52 correspondence).
A. Freud and D. Burlingham. 1973. *Infants without Families. Reports on the Hampstead Nurseries 1939–1945*. New York: International University Press.

1951

—**First House for The Hampstead Child Therapy Course and Clinic**
London, Hampstead, 12 Maresfield Gardens
Planning of a kitchen and canteen in a detached house, both at a later stage converted into a nursery school
sources and literature:
Letters from Ernst L. Freud to Anna Freud, 13 December 1956, 14 January 1958 (LoC, Anna Freud papers, box 28, folder 14, Ernst L. Freud and Lucie Freud 1953–61 correspondence).
Letter from H. Kennedy, 17 August 2002.

1955–56

—**Second House for The Hampstead Child Therapy Course and Clinic**
London, Hampstead, 21 Maresfield Gardens
Conversion of a detached house including the merger of all ground floor living rooms into a large meeting room that spanned the width of the house

sources and literature:
Jenks, Percival, Pidgeon & Co., London: 'Balance Sheet and Account 1955', 22 February 1956, for Hampstead Child-Therapy Course and Clinic (LoC, Anna Freud papers, box 132, folder 4).
Letter from Ernst L. Freud to Anna Freud, 14 January 1958 (LoC, Anna Freud papers, box 28, folder 14, Ernst L. Freud and Lucie Freud 1953–61 correspondence).
Letter from H. Kennedy, 17 August 2002.

1967–1968
—Third House for The Hampstead Child Therapy Course and Clinic
London, Hampstead, 14 Maresfield Gardens
Renovation and alteration of the detached building adjacent to 12 Maresfield Gardens
sources and literature:
Fuller, Jenks, Beecroft & Co., 'Balance Sheet and Account 1967', 15 March 1968, for Hampstead Child-Therapy Course and Clinic (LoC, Anna Freud papers, box 133, folder 1).
Letter from H. Kennedy, 17 August 2002.
E. Young-Bruehl. 1988. *Anna Freud*. New York: Summit, 379.

4.2 Shops, offices, kitchens, and other business premises

1924–25
—[Eduard] Lingel shoe shop
Berlin, [Mitte, Werderstraße 7]
Shop front with display window
sources and literature:
RIBA p.
Mossner, 1927–1928, vol. II, 26.

1927–28
—Tobacco warehouse 'Problem' (Fig. 9.1)
Berlin, Prenzlauer Berg, Greifswalderstraße 212–213
Warehouse for cigarette company 'Problem', owned by Szlama Rochmann, in collaboration with Heinz Jacobsohn, architect
sources and literature:
RIBA p.
Haberlandt, 37 (1928), 1 January 1928, no. 459-1, July 1928, no. 465.
Hajos, 1928.
Anonymous. 1929. 'Tabakspeicher für die Zigarettenfabrik "Problem"', *Bauwelt* 20 (16): 1–3.
Sp. 1929. 'Tabakspeicher der Zigarettenfabrik Problem in Berlin', *Der Industriebau* 20 (July): 231–233.
V. Welter. 1992. '*Tabakspeicher der Zigarettenfabrik "Problem"*'. Germany: Berlin.
Worbs, 1997.
Thomson, 1999.

1928–29
—Werkstätten für Ofen und Kaminbau
Berlin, Tiergarten, Genthiner Straße 15
Tiled shop front and entrance
Some tiles inscribed with 'Inh. K. Lindner, Arch. E. Freud Dipl. Ing.', bottom tile signed [Parzigens], shop no longer exists, building demolished

sources and literature:
RIBA p.
BAB 1928, 1929.
JAB 1931, 250.

1929

—Ruths GmbH Offices
Berlin, Tiergarten, Bellevuestraße 11
Office interiors and furniture designs
June and August 1929
When Sigmund Freud stayed in Berlin in 1928 to receive cancer treatment, Johannes Ruths, a Swedish businessman and entrepreneur who had developed a water tank that kept water at boiling temperature, was one of Freud's patients.
sources and literature:
RIBA d.
Letter from Sigmund Freud to Ernst L. Freud, 16 December 1928 (LoC, Sigmund Freud papers, box 3, folder 4).
BAB 1929.
C. Tögel. 2006. *Freud und Berlin*. Berlin: Aufbau-Verlag, 101–104.

—Restaurant Kolonie Zschornewitz
Zschornewitz
Design for restaurant tables
19 November 1929
sources and literature:
RIBA d.

1930

—Richard Ginsberg director's office (fig. 9.5)
[Berlin, Mitte, Charlottenstraße 42]
Interior and furniture designs (29)
March and October 1930
sources and literature:
RIBA d, p.
Wenzel, 1929, column 729.
Mossner 1929, vol. I, 530.
BAB 1930.
JAB 1931, 117.
B. Butt. 1934. 'Study Where Work is Easy. Psychology Plays Part in Its Decoration', *The Daily Telegraph* (9 April): 8.
B. Butt. 1934. 'Banishing Noise from the Home. Modern Sound-Proof Materials and their Possibilities', *New Health* (March): 18–19.
M. Speyer. 1935. 'The Continental Office', *Architectural Design and Construction* 5 (8): 338–339.
F. Karsch. 2005. *Joachim Karsch: Werkverzeichnis der Plastiken*. Weimar: VDG, entries 1930–2, 1930–4, and 1932–3.

—Mitteldeutsche Bodencredit-Anstalt
Berlin, Mitte, Charlottenstraße 42
Interior and furniture designs (13) for bank offices
October 1930

sources and literature:
RIBA d.
Mossner, 1927–28, vol. II, 838–839.
Wenzel, 1929, column 729.
BAB, 1931.

1938

—Fashion shop for 'Robell' (Stiassny Ltd.)
London, W1, 48 Baker Street
Client: Mathilde Hollitscher, née Freud
Design (exterior and interior) for a fashion shop
sources and literature:
'A Daughter of Freud is a dress-designer now in London—and the architect son of the famous Professor has designed her modern Salon'. 1939. *Jewish Chronicle* 98 (15 Tebeth 5699/6 January): 8.
Thomson, 1999.

1940

—Good Housekeeping Institute
London, 30 Grosvenor Gardens
Design of testing and research kitchens, and a laundry
sources and literature:
RIBA p.
P. L. Garbutt. 1940. 'Once again The Institute leads the Way', *Good Housekeeping* (April): 36–37, 100.
P. L. Garbutt. 1940. 'The New Institute opens its Doors', *Good Housekeeping* (September): 29–32.
E. L. Freud. 1940. 'A Domestic Laboratory The Good Housekeeping Institute', *The National Builder* 20 (October): 49–51.
Benton, 1995.
Thomson, 1999.

1940 or later

—Wartime Meals Centre for the Good Housekeeping School of Canteen Cookery, Good Housekeeping Institute
London, 30 Grosvenor Gardens Mews North
Alterations of the façade of a building
sources and literature:
RIBA p.
Benton, 1995.
Thomson, 1999.

1941

—School of Cookery, Good Housekeeping Institute
London, 30 Grosvenor Gardens
Design of junior and senior kitchen for a cookery school
sources and literature:
P. L. Garbutt. 1942.'The new Good Housekeeping School of Cookery approved by the Ministry of Food', *Good Housekeeping* (January): 28–29.

1943

—Offices for Good Housekeeping Institute
London, 30 Grosvenor Gardens
Reorganization of office spaces in basement and ground floor
sources and literature:
LMA d.

1945–49

—Kitchen for Corpus Christi College Cambridge
Design of a kitchen in the fourteenth-century Old Hall
sources and literature:
RIBA p.
'Kitchen for Corpus Christi College, Cambridge'. 1949. *Architects' Journal* 109 (6 January): 11–12.
Archives of Corpus Christi College, Parker Library, Cambridge.

1950s

—Shop Walpole Brothers (London Ltd)
London, 87–91 New Bond Street
Design for a shop for a manufacturer of bed linen and bathroom towels
sources and literature:
RIBA p.
Thomson, 1999.

1954–55

—Restaurant and Bar 'La Boîte'
London, Bayswater, Hereford Road
Design for a restaurant and bar operated by Clement Freud (1924–2009)
The weaver Peter Collingwood was commissioned to produce seventy-five feet of rush matting from imported plaited Dutch rushes and sisal that was dyed bright red.
sources and literature:
C. Freud. 1995. *Freud Ego*. London: BBC, 130–131.
Email correspondence with Matthew Parrington, V&A Museum Senior Research Fellow (Applied Arts), August 2007–February 2008, and Peter Collingwood, September 2007–August 2008.

5.0 Miscellaneous Designs

1915

—Memorial for fallen comrades from k. u. k. Feldkanonenregiment Nr. 8
Medeazza, Doberdoplateau, above Monfalcone at the Isonzo river
Design for a memorial
sources and literature:
E. Falzeder et al. (eds). 2000. *The Correspondence of Sigmund Freud and Sándor Ferenczi*. 3 vols. Cambridge, MA: Harvard University Press, vol. 2, letter 573, 31 October 1915.
E. Pfeiffer (ed.). 1972. *Sigmund Freud and Lou Andreas-Salomé Letters*. London: Hogarth Press, letters 9 November 1915, 18 November 1915.

1939

—**Tombstone for Sigmund Freud (Fig. 4.4)**
London, Golders Green Crematorium, East Columbarium
Design for a tombstone; a slender, triangular column, made from Derbyshire Birdseye marble and mounted with an Etruscan vase (period 250 BC) from Sigmund Freud's collection of antiques
sources and literature:
'Professor Sigmund Freud Memorial at Golders Green'. 1940. *Pharaos. Official Journal of the Cremation Society and the Federation of British Cremation Authorities* 6 (no. 2, May): 9.
Benton, 1995.
Worbs, 1997.

1948

—**unknown project, anonymous client**
London
Ernst Freud was fined a penalty of £750 for contravening the conditions of a building license. Work was not to exceed £750, but the actual cost was £3,800. Freud had already been fined £50 for a similar offence in August 1947.
sources and literature:
Evening Standard, 22 October 1948.

1951

—**The Mermaid Theatre for Lord Bernard Miles (1907–91)**
London, St John's Wood, Acacia Road
Conversion of a school assembly hall into a theatre in collaboration with theatre designers Michael Stringer and C. Walter Hodges
sources and literature:
Anonymous. 1951. 'Mermaid Theatre', *Architects' Journal* 114 (11 October): 427, 429.
C. W. Hodges. 1968. *The Globe restored. A Study of the Elizabethan Theatre*. London: Oxford University Press, 132, plate 51.

1955

—**unknown project in Nigeria**
Nigeria
Early in January 1956 Freud gave a lecture on a work project for which he had recently twice visited Nigeria.
sources and literature:
The Circle newsletter (RIBA Archive C/1/3).

1958

—**British synagogue at London Jewish Hospital (fig. 8.13)**
London, Stepney Green E1
Design for a synagogue as part of London Jewish Hospital, demolished in the early 1980s
sources and literature:
RIBA p.
R. Wischnitzer. 5724 [1964]. *The Architecture of the European Synagogue*. Philadelphia, PA: Jewish Publication Society of America, 273–274.
Benton, 1995.

꙳ Selected Bibliography ꙳

Archival Collections consulted

Archiv zu Schloß Tegel, Berlin
Cal Poly Pomona, College of Environmental Design, Archives-Special Collection
Central Zionist Archives, Jerusalem
Centre Canadien d'Architecture / Canadian Centre for Architecture, Montréal
Deutsche Bank AG, Historisches Institut, Frankfurt
Freud Museum London
Getty Research Institute, Research Library, Special Collections
Kriegsarchiv Wien, Austria
Landesarchiv Berlin
Library of Congress, Manuscript Division, Washington DC (LoC)
Ludwig-Maximilians-Universität München, Archiv (ALMU)
RIBA, Library Drawings Collection and Photographs Collection, London
Surrey History Centre, Woking
Technische Universität München, Historisches Archiv (HATUM)
Technische Universität Wien, Archiv (TUWA)
University of California at Los Angeles, Charles E. Young Research Library, Department of Special Collections
Yad Weizmann, The Weizmann Archives, Rehovot

Publications written and edited by Ernst L. Freud (ordered chronologically)

Freud, E. L. 1934. 'A Foreign Architects observes England', *Design for To-Day* 2 (October): 394–395.
Carrington, N. 1935. 'Ernst L. Freud interviewed at his new London House', *Decoration* 7 new series (November): 22–25.
Freud, E. L., and H. Bright. 1936. 'The Conquest of Space with the Aid of Electricity', *Good Housekeeping* (October): 60–61, 104–105.
Cottington Taylor, D. D., and E. L. Freud. 1937. 'To buy or to build? Mrs. Taylor's long years of experience at Good Housekeeping Institute are being turned to good account now that she is building a house for herself', *Good Housekeeping* (June): 76–77, 146–148.
Freud, E. L. 1940. 'A Domestic Laboratory The Good Housekeeping Institute', *The National Builder* 20 (October): 49–51.
Freud, E. L. 1945. 'Conversion. Some Notes by Ernst L. Freud', *Architects' Journal* 101 (15 February): 351–356.

Reifenberg, H. J., and E. L. Freud. 1955. 'German Architecture Today. A Preview of the R.I.B.A. Exhibition', *Architecture and Building* 30 (February): 44–47.
Freud, E. L. (ed.). 1960. *Letters of Sigmund Freud*, trans. by Tania and James Stern. New York: Basic Books.
Freud, E. L., and H. Meng (eds.). 1963. *Sigmund Freud/Oskar Pfister: Briefe 1909–1939*. Frankfurt: S. Fischer.
Abraham, H. C., and E. L. Freud (eds.). 1965. *Sigmund Freud Karl Abraham Briefe 1907–1926*. Frankfurt: S. Fischer.
Freud, E. L., and L. Freud (eds.). 1968. *Sigmund Freud Briefe 1873–1939*, 2nd enlarged edition. Frankfurt: S. Fischer.
Freud, E. L. (ed.). 1968. *Sigmund Freud und Arnold Zweig Briefwechsel*. Frankfurt: S. Fischer.
Freud, E. L., and L. Freud (eds.). 1980. *Briefe 1873–1939*, 3rd edition. Frankfurt: S. Fischer.
Freud, E.L., L. Freud, and I. Grubrich-Simitis (eds.). 1989. *Sigmund Freud: Sein Leben in Bildern und Texten*. Frankfurt: Insel Verlag.

Publications on and referring to Ernst L. Freud's architecture and life

Abercrombie, P. (ed.). 1939. *The Book of the Modern House: A Panoramic Survey of Contemporary Domestic Design*. London: Hodder & Stoughton, 100, plate 79.
Anita. 1930. 'Landhaus am See', *Die Dame* (August): issue 23, 10–13.
Anonymous. 1927. *Sanatorium Schloß Tegel Psychoanalytische Klinik Berlin Tegel*, s.l.: no publisher.
Anonymous. 1929. 'Tabakspeicher für die Zigarettenfabrik "Problem"', *Bauwelt*, 20 (16), 1–3.
Anonymous. 1933. [no title], *Design for To-Day*, 1 (October), 237.
Anonymous. 1934. 'Country House on a Lake near Berlin designed by Ernst L. Freud', *Architects' Journal*, 79 (21 June), 892–893.
Anonymous. 1934. 'Two Modern Houses', *Home & Gardens*, March, 504–506.
Anonymous. 1934. 'Modern Brick—and Flowers', *The Ideal Home*, April, 223–226.
Anonymous. 1936. 'Contemporary Brick Building', *Architectural Review*, 79 (May), 217–228.
Anonymous. 1936. 'Ceiling Fittings', *Decoration*, no. 18, new series, October, 50.
Anonymous. 1936. 'Occasional Table in Chromium and Rough-Cast Glass', *Decoration*, no. 20, new series, December, 47.
Anonymous. 1938. 'Group of Houses in Hampstead: Designed by Ernst L. Freud', *Architects' Journal*, 88 (1 September), 373–375, 377.
Anonymous. 1938. 'A Group of Houses in Hampstead', *Architectural Review*, 84 (August), 54–56.
Anonymous. 1938. [No title], *The National Builder* 18 (4): 121.
Anonymous. 1939. 'A Daughter of Freud is a Dress-Designer now in London—and the Architect Son the famous Professor has Designed her Modern Salon', *Jewish Chronicle* 98 (15 Tebeth 5699/6 January 1939): 8.
Anonymous. 1939. '"Belvedere Court", Lyttleton Road, Hampstead Garden Suburb', *The Builder* 156 (10 February): 239–240.
Anonymous. 1939. 'Replanning of a House in Hampstead', *Architectural Review* 86 (November): supplement 221–222.
Anonymous. 1940. 'Professor Sigmund Freud Memorial at Golders Green', *Pharaos: Official Journal of the Cremation Society and the Federation of British Cremation Authorities* 6 (no. 2 / May): 9.
Anonymous. 1946. 'Conversion of Houses—Seaside Flats Little Hampton', *The National House Builder and Building Digest* 6 (November): 28–29.

Anonymous. 1949. 'Kitchen for Corpus Christi College, Cambridge', *Architects' Journal* 109 (6 January): 11–12.
Anonymous. 1951. 'Mermaid Theatre', *Architects' Journal* 114 (11 October): 427, 429.
Anonymous. 1955. 'Flats on a Bomb Site', *Architecture and Building* 30 (January): 30–32.
Augenfeld, F. 1981, 'Erinnerungen an Adolf Loos', *Bauwelt* 72 (42): 1907.
Benton, C. 1995. *A Different World: Émigré Architects in Britain 1928–1958*. London: Heinz Gallery.
Butt, B. 1934. 'Study Where Work is Easy. Psychology Plays Part in Its Decoration', *The Daily Telegraph* (9 April): 8.
Butt, B. 1934. 'Banishing Noise from the Home: Modern Sound-Proof Materials and their Possibilities', *New Health* (March): 18–19.
Carrington, N. 1936. 'Music Room at Pine House, Churt, Surrey', *Country Life* (26 September): xxxvi, xxxviii.
Deutsche Psychoanalytische Gesellschaft (ed.). 1930. *Zehn Jahre Berliner Psychoanalytisches Institut (Poliklinik und Lehranstalt)*. Vienna: Psychoanalytischer Verlag.
Edwards, R. 1936. 'Modern Furniture The Artist as Designer', *Country Life* (10 October): xxxxi.
Eitingon, M. 1923. *Bericht über die Berliner Psychoanalytische Poliklinik (März 1920–Juni 1922)*. Leipzig: Internationaler Psychoanalytischer Verlag.
Freud Museum London (ed.). 1998. *20 Maresfield Gardens: Guide to the Freud Museum*. London: Serpent's Tail.
G., H. 1928. 'Vom Neuen Bauen', *Die Pyramide* 14 (July): 205–213, image before 205.
Garbutt, P. L. 1940. 'Once again The Institute leads the Way', *Good Housekeeping* (April): 36–37, 100.
Garbutt, P. L. 1940. 'The New Institute opens its Doors', *Good Housekeeping* (September): 29–32.
Garbutt, P. L. 1942. 'The new Good Housekeeping School of Cookery approved by the Ministry of Food', *Good Housekeeping* (January): 28–29.
Gorion, E. bin et al. (eds.). 1992. *Philo-Lexikon: Handbuch des jüdischen Wissens* [1936]. Frankfurt: Jüdischer Verlag im Suhrkamp Verlag, 38–39.
Gould, J. 1977. *Modern Houses in Britain, 1919–1939*. London: Society of Architectural Historians of Great Britain.
H., A. 1928. 'Zu Hause', *Die Pyramide* 14 (August): 248–257.
Hajos, E. M., and L. Zahn. 1928. *Berliner Architektur der Nachkriegszeit*. Berlin: Albertus.
Hodges, C. W. 1968. *The Globe Restored: A Study of the Elizabethan Theatre*. London: Oxford University Press, 132, plate 51.
Hoffmann, H. 1929. *Neue Villen*. Stuttgart: Julius Hoffmann, 100–101.
Holme, C. G. (ed.). 1934. *Decorative Art: The Studio Year Book*. London: The Studio, 85.
Ingenweyen, B. 2004. 'Villa Frank und Park in Geltow bei Potsdam erbaut von Ernst Ludwig [sic] Freud 1928–1930', in L. Scharnholz. 2004. *Die unbekannte Moderne von Luckenwalde nach Löbau*. Berlin: Philo & Philo Fine Arts, 14–19.
Oberndorf, C. P. 1926. 'The Berlin Psychoanalytic Policlinic', *The Psychoanalytic Review* XIII: 318–322.
Platz, G. A. 1933. *Wohnräume der Gegenwart*. Berlin: Propyläen.
Reilly. C. H. 1939. 'The Year's Work at Home', *Architects' Journal* 89 (January): 133–146.
Schröter, M. (ed.). 2010. *Sigmund Freud: Unterdess halten wir zusammen. Briefe an die Kinder*. Berlin: Aufbau.
Schultz, U., and L. M. Hermanns. 1987. 'Das Sanatorium Schloß Tegel Ernst Simmels—Zur Geschichte und Konzeption der ersten Psychoanalytischen Klinik', *Psychotherapie, Psychosomatik, Medizinische Psychologie* 37 (2 February): 58–67.
Sp. 1929. 'Tabakspeicher der Zigarettenfabrik Problem in Berlin', *Der Industriebau* 20 (July): 231–233.

Speyer, M. 1934. 'Dining Rooms 1834–1934', *Design for To-Day* 2 (September): 350–353.
Speyer, M. 1935. 'The Continental Office', *Architectural Design and Construction* 5 (8): 338–339.
Speyer, M. 1935. 'Decoration—the Doctor's Dilemma', *Design for To-Day* 3 (June): 228–230.
Speyer, M. 1937. '"And So To Bed" The Suggestion has echoed throughout the centuries, but what a different bed awaits us from those of our forebears knew', *Good Housekeeping* (August): 64–65, 125.
Stephen, N. 1938. 'Hampstead—two centuries of House Architecture', *Building* 13 (July): 268–273.
Thurn und Taxis, L. 1991. 'Rätsel um das Haus am Schwielowsee. Eine Villa der Moderne im Wechsel der Zeit', *Die Tageszeitung* (13 November).
Thomson, C. 1999. 'Contextualising the Continental: The Work of German Émigré Architects in Britain 1933–1945', PhD dissertation. Warwick, England: University of Warwick.
Welter, V. 1992. 'Landhaus Frank (c. 1928–1930) in Geltow bei Berlin Architekt: Ernst L. Freud (1892–1970)', architectural historical report for Atelier Christoph Fischer Dipl.-Ing. Architekt. Germany: Berlin.
Welter, V. 1992. 'Tabakspeicher der Zigarettenfabrik "Problem"', architectural historical report for Atelier Christoph Fischer Dipl.-Ing. Architekt. Germany: Berlin.
Welter, V. M. 2005. 'Ernst L Freud—Domestic Architect', in S. Behr and M. Malet (eds.). 2004. *Arts in Exile in Britain 1933–1945: Politics, and Cultural Identity* [The Yearbook of the Research Center for German and Austrian Exile Studies, vol. 6]. Amsterdam and New York: Rodopi, 201–237.
Wilmers, M.-K. 2009. *The Eitingons: A Twentieth-Century Story*. London: Faber and Faber.
Whirter, M. 1939. 'New Rooms for Old', *The Ideal Home* (March): 164–165.
Wischnitzer, R. 5724 [1964]. *The Architecture of the European Synagogue*. Philadelphia, PA: Jewish Publication Society of America, 273–274.
Worbs, D. 1997. 'Ernst Ludwig Freud in Berlin', *Bauwelt* 88 (42): 2398–2403.
Zohlen, G. 1994, 'Das Haus am See', *Die Zeit* (1 April): 80.

Index

Abraham, Karl, 1, 54, 96, 187–8, 197
Adler, Leo, 10
Amadeus Quartet, 125
Andreas-Salomé, Lou, 35, 38–9
Architecture
    bourgeois, 2–5, 10–13, 16, 18–19, 41–46, 50, 60–61, 69–71, 97–98, 120, 125, 141–43, 146, 154, 163–67
    domestic, 1–4, 7, 10–13, 16, 18–20, 33, 41–46, 59, 62, 69–73, 76, 78–91, 125, 132–35, 143, 146, 154–55, 158, 162–68
    Expressionist, 50, 88–89, 123
    Jewish, 3, 34, 56, 163–64
    modernist, 2–3, 9–12, 15–19, 33, 50, 60, 73, 87, 100, 104, 118, 120, 125, 130, 132, 142–43, 145–46, 150–51, 161–63, 168–69, 171
    traditional, 2, 7, 9–10, 12, 17, 19–20, 31, 33, 42–43, 50, 86, 89, 120, 126, 143, 163–64
Aron Werke, Berlin, 194
Ashcroft, Peggy, 134, 155, 183
Augenfeld, Felix, 25, 31, 42–3, 101–2, 143, 153, 180
Austria
    Grinzing, 150
    Hochrotherd, near Semmering, 25, 31, 180
    Vienna, 4–5, 24–32, 34, 39, 41–44, 46, 52–54, 56, 60, 67, 69, 73, 76, 98–103, 111, 113, 119, 139, 143, 150–51, 153, 157, 171, 192, 198, 199–200
        Berggasse 19, 26–31, 98–101, 104, 116, 139, 150
Austria-Hungary. *See* Austria

Baerwald, Alexander, 34, 56–58, 67n46, 68n56, 192
Beardsley, Mona, 191
Benjamin, Walter, 1–2, 98, 164–65, 171

Berliner Architektur der Nachkriegszeit, 16–17, 73, 82
Bermann-Fischer, Gottfried and Brigitte, 62, 120, 168, 180
Bernays, Martha. *See* Freud, Martha, (née Bernays)
Bernays, Minna, 24, 29–30, 151, 178
Bloch, Martin, 123
Böhm, Franz, 133, 138, 140, 150, 186
Bonaparte, Marie, 151
Brasch, 54, 60, 72
    Gerda. *See* Mosse, Gerda, (née Brasch)
    Josef and Elise, 51, 72
    Käte, 51, 68n66
    Lucie. *See* Freud, Lucie, (née Brasch)
Braunthal, Dr., 194
Britten, Benjamin, 125
Brumwell, Marcus and Rene, 158, 184
Bry, Paul, 198
Buber, Martin, 57
Buchthal
    Eugen and Thea, 62, 88–89, 180
    Hugo, 88, 180
Bürgner, Dr., 194
Burlingham, Dorothy, 139, 180

Chaikin, Benjamin, 60
Charreau, Pierre, 2
Checkley, George, 120–21
Chermayeff, Serge, 120
Cohn, Benno, 189
Cohn, Erna, 54, 190, 196
Cohn, Harry, 119
Corpus Christi College, Cambridge, 133, 204
Cottington-Taylor, Dorothy Daisy, (née Gale), 130, 133, 178. *See also* Good Housekeeping Institute
Count Seilern, Antoine Edward, 155, 160, 183
Crittall, Walter Francis, 123, 137n38, 181

Davies, Ralph, 185
Deutsche Werkbund, 3, 18, 32
Dexel, Grete and Walter, 10–11
Dorn, Marion, 126–27

Eder, David, 58–59, 119
Eitingon
    Chaim, 56
    Max and Mirra, 1, 54, 56, 59, 72–73, 96, 150, 178, 192
Engelman, Edmund, 28–30, 99, 102
Engelmann, Paul, 42
England
    Ashley Green, near Chesham, Buckinghamshire, 155
    Betchworth, Surrey, 130, 132, 178
    Cambridge, 120–21, 133–34, 204
    Elsted, near Midhurst, Sussex, 123, 199
    Feock, Cornwall, 158, 184
    Great Easton, Essex, 123, 181
    Littlehampton, 134, 186
    London
        Bayswater, 204
        Dulwich, 119, 155, 160n50
        Golden Lane Housing Estate, 134, 187
        Hampstead, 115, 122–23, 127, 133–34, 139–40, 150, 177, 181–87, 191, 199–201
        Hampstead Child Therapy Course and Clinic, 114, 140, 186, 200, 201
        Hampstead Garden Suburb, 127, 185
        Hampstead War Nurseries, 139–40, 186, 200
        Kensington Palace, King's Gallery, 126
        Maida Vale, 123
        South Kensington, 126, 145–46, 150, 182–83
        St. John's Wood, 112, 122–3, 133–34, 140, 143, 145–46, 155, 159n20, 191, 198–99, 205
        Westminster, 133, 140
    Sandon, near Baldock, Hertfordshire, 123, 182
    Sussex, 7, 123, 139, 154, 186, 199
    Walberswick, Suffolk, 147, 149–50, 157, 178, 181, 183–85, 187
Erickson, Arthur, 134, 187

Feibusch, Hans, 127, 129, 182
Fichtl, Paula, 29, 151

Finetti, Giuseppe De, 42
Fischer, Samuel, 62
Fischer, Theodor, 32–33
France
    Garches, 7–8
    Paris, 2, 113, 150–51, 198
Frank, Josef, 3
Frank, Theodor and Margot, 10, 60, 78, 87–88, 94n33, 94n37, 119, 176
Freud
    Alexander, 139, 186
    Anna, 24, 28–9, 39, 46, 51, 69, 92, 101, 108, 110114, 139, 150–1, 153, 180, 183. *See also* London, Hampstead Child Therapy Course and Clinic, and War Nurseries
    Clemens (Clement) Raphael, 9, 54–5, 65, 133, 135–37
        and 'La Boîte', restaurant and bar, 204
    Ernst L.
        and *Bauschule* of Adolf Loos, 41–43, 61
        family homes in Berlin, 9, 54, 66n22, 66n24, 92, 96, 141–43, 159n20, 188, 190
        Jewish student corporation *Hasmonaea*, 56, 189
        lung ailment, 53, 162
        and McLuhan, Marshall, 145
        and Mendelsohn, Erich, 62, 120, 129
        military service, 33–34, 36n32, 36n35, 49, 72, 133, 204
        and Neutra, Richard, 25, 28, 31, 42, 60, 66n22, 67n46, 72, 129
        relationship with clients, 72–73, 118, 161
        comparison with Rietveld, Gerrit, 142
        studies in Munich, 4, 20, 25, 31–34, 36n30, 36n35, 38–39, 42, 49–51, 56, 60, 66n22, 119, 145, 157, 189
        comparison with Taut, Max, 148
        wedding with Lucie Brasch, 34, 50–54
        and Zionism, 26, 56–57, 59–60, 119, 145
    Harry, 92
    Jean Martin, 24
    Lucian Michael, 9, 54–55, 140
    Lucie, (née Brasch), 34, 39, 47, 50–52, 54–55, 57, 60, 65n6, 91–92, 118,

133–34, 139–40, 145, 147–8, 157, 163, 177, 179, 181, 188, 190–91
Martha, (née Bernays), 24, 26, 29–31, 58, 139, 150, 182, 200
Mathilde. *See* Hollitscher, Robert and Mathilde (née Freud)
Sigmund, 1, 4, 24, 26–31, 34–5, 38–39, 46, 51–53, 55–56, 58, 73, 97, 99–104, 108, 110, 113, 139, 147, 150–51, 153–54, 157, 169, 171, 182, 188, 200, 202, 205
Sophie. *See* Halberstadt, Sophie, (née Freud)
Stephan (Stephen) Gabriel, 9, 54–55, 138n61, 139, 184
Friedlaender, Kate (Käthe) (née Frankl, divorced Misch), 113–14, 199

Gay, Peter, 13
Geddes, Sir Patrick, 57–60, 68n52, 149
Geiger, Theodor, 14
Germany
    Berlin
        Alt Moabit, 62
        Charlottenburg, 51, 62, 161, 175, 180, 188–90, 195
        Dahlem, 1, 69–70, 72–73, 123, 125, 174–75, 179, 188, 192, 195
        Grunewald, 1, 62, 69, 175, 180, 187, 197–98
        Lankwitz, 69, 177
        Nikolassee, 69, 179
        Schmargendorf, 1, 197
        Tegel, 1, 98, 105–112, 197
        Tiergarten, 1, 9, 54, 69, 72, 79, 140, 158, 178, 188–90, 192, 194, 197–98, 201–2
        Westend, 62, 69–70, 73, 78, 88
        Zehlendorf, 73, 75, 129, 131
    Hamburg, 4, 51, 53, 64, 68n66, 196
    Hiddensee, 51, 111, 118, 147–49, 179
    Krampnitz, near Potsdam, 91–92, 177
    Leipzig, 147, 188
    Munich, 32, 38, 119
    Potsdam, Neubabelsberg, 179, 193
    Zschornewitz, 202
Gerson, Hermann, 54
Gill, Nellie Muriel, 125–26, 146–47, 150, 181, 182, 184
Gindler, Elsa, 65
Ginsberg
    Käthe, 57, 67n45
    Marianne, 57, 67n45
    Oliver, 57, 67n45
    Richard, 57, 136n23, 167, 169, 202. *See also* Mitteldeutsche Bodencredit-Anstalt, Berlin
Gleimius, Rudolf and Ilse, (née Goldmann), 67n45, 193
Goldmann, 44, 190
Goldmann, Ilse. *See* Gleimius, Rudolf and Ilse
Goldschmidt, Dr., 166, 195
Good Housekeeping Institute, London, 130, 133, 203–4. *See also* Cottington-Taylor, Dorothy Daisy, (née Gale)
Groot, Jeanne de. *See* Lampl, Hans and Jeanne (née de Groot)
Gropius, Walter, 33, 49, 161–62
Gutkind, Erwin, 73

Halberstadt, Sophie, (née Freud), 24, 52–53
Halpern, Dr., 194
Hamburger, Richard, 63–4, 68n66, 115, 120, 123, 136n34, 191
Hawksmoor, Nicholas, 126
Hebrew University, Jerusalem, 57–58, 176
Heckel, Erich, 123
Heims, Dr. jur. Edward and Hildegard (née Hartmann), 196
Henderson, Ian, 126
Henneberg, Heinz, 69, 72, 179
Henningsen, Poul, 104
Herrmann, Wolfgang and Annie (née Marx), 123, 177, 181, 184, 188
Herzl, Theodor, 26, 56
Hess, Fritz and Ann, 122, 154, 183, 191
Höger, Fritz, 89
Hofer, Adolf, 54, 70, 93n11, 175
Hoffer, Willi, 150, 178
Hofmann, Karl, 25, 180
Hollitscher, Robert and Mathilde (née Freud), 24, 96, 139–40, 203
    and 'Robell' fashion shop, London, 140, 203
Hopkins, Pryns, 102
Hornbein, Victor, 198
Hüttenbach, Alfred, 82
Huxley, Julian and Juliette, 155, 182

Israel
    Haifa, 56, 67n48
    Jerusalem, 57, 119, 176
    Rehovot, 57–8

Jacobsohn, Heinz and Katharina, 54, 66n28, 201
Jeanneret, Pierre. *See* Le Corbusier
Joachimsthal, Margot, 195–6
Jones, Ernest, 102, 119, 122–23, 147, 150–51, 199
Jüdische Student, Der, 52, 66n22

Karsch, Joachim, 57, 67n45, 145
Kerschbaumer, Anton, 123
Klein, Alexander, 16–17, 19, 86
Klein
    Melanie, 97, 112–14, 119, 122, 170, 198
    Melitta, 119, 136n16
Kornberg, Fritz, 67n48
Kracauer, Siegfried, 3–4, 13–4, 16, 165–66
Krojanker, Gustav, 56–57, 145, 189,
Kurella, Constanze Marie Matilde, 65, 194
Kurz, Alexander, 54, 133, 137n52, 176–77, 190

Lampl, Hans and Jeanne (née de Groot), 1, 73–78, 175
Landauer, Fritz, 34, 119
Landshoff, Dr., 194
Le Corbusier, 7–9, 169
Levi, Paul, 155, 160n51
Levy, G., 54, 70, 93n11, 175
Levy, Otto, 179
Leyden, Ernst von, 125, 181
Liebrecht, Eva. *See* Maretzki, Ernst and Eva (neé Liebrecht)
Lindberg, Paula. *See* Salomon, Paula, (née Lindberg)
Lindner, K., 201
Lingel, Eduard, 201
Loos, Adolf, 4, 26, 34–35, 38, 41–46, 48n39, 61, 76, 85, 146, 163, 169
Luckhardt, Hans and Wassili, 73, 88
Lutyens
    Edwin Landseer, Sir, 119
    Robert, 119

Maas, Hilde, 114–15, 122, 199
Mackintosh, Charles Rennie, 149
Maretzki, Ernst and Eva (neé Liebrecht), 70, 72, 93n15, 174
Marks, Simon, 119
Marx
    Adolf and Heide, 123–25, 147, 153–54, 177, 188

    Annie. *See* Herrmann, Wolfgang and Annie (née Marx)
Matthew, David and A. A., 127, 129, 170, 182
Mears, Frank, Sir, 57–60
Mebes, Paul, 142
Meltzer, Donald, 112, 117n47
Mendelsohn, Erich and Louise, 3, 33, 49, 57–8, 62, 72–3, 75–76, 78, 86, 90, 91, 93n15, 119–20, 129, 131, 162–64
Messel, Adolf, 3, 163
Michael, Fritz und Hannah (née Schwab), 61, 189
Mies van der Rohe, Ludwig, 17–19, 22n64, 49, 73, 78, 86–87, 162
Miles, Lord Bernard, 155, 205
Misch
    Käthe. *See* Friedlaender, Kate (Käthe) (née Frankl, divorced Misch)
    Walter, 113
Mitteldeutsche Bodencredit-Anstalt, Berlin, 57, 202
Moore, Riette Sturge, 127
Mosse, 93n15, 118, 139
    Carl, 51, 91
    Gerda, (née Brasch), 51, 91–92, 137n38, 139–40, 163, 177, 181, 186
    Rudolf, 51, 91–92, 139, 163, 177
    Wolfgang, 184
Müller, Otto, 123
Müller-Wulckow, Walter, 10
Muthesius, Hermann, 3, 12–13, 62, 163

National Socialism, 5, 49, 62, 88, 91–92, 118
Neumann, Stefan, 62, 72, 189
Neumark, Walter, 196
Neutra, Richard J., 25, 28, 31, 42–43, 48n39, 60, 66n22, 67n46, 72–73, 75–76, 91, 93n15, 94n20, 129, 131, 163
Nicholson, Christopher, 108–10

Ornstein, Gertrud ('Trudi), 196

Palyi, Melchior, 119
Parker, Barry, 127, 182
Pears, Peter, 125
Pechstein, Max, 123
Pepinski, Eryk, 88
Philo-Lexikon: Handbuch des jüdischen Wissens, 2
Pietrkowsky, Dr., 195
Pinner, Dr., and Neumann, 66n22, 93n12

Platz, Gustav Adolf, 10–13, 20n20, 120
Plessner, Helmuth, 3–4, 10, 14–15, 18–20, 22n53, 39–40, 100, 161, 166
Plischke, Ernst A., 192
Pocock, J. C., 7–8
Poliklinik für psychoanalytische Behandlung nervöser Krankheiten, Berlin, 1, 96, 98, 103–5, 108, 110, 197
Pritchard, Rosemary (Molly), 108–10, 117n41
Problem cigarette company, Berlin, 54, 201
psychoanalytic consulting rooms, 1–2, 5, 27–28, 35, 46, 76, 97–104, 108–110, 112–13, 116n20, 116n25, 117n41, 122–23, 151–53, 182, 197–200
psychoanalytic couch and chair, 1–2, 96–104, 106, 108, 110–13, 116n20, 117n47, 151–54, 198
Pulvermann, Generaldirektor, 190, 196
Pyramide, Die, 7, 10, 19, 46, 54, 57, 141, 148, 169

Radó, Sandor, 1, 197–8
Rickman, John, 108, 123, 182
Rie, Lucie, 192
Rilke, Rainer Maria, 4, 34–35, 38–41, 45–46, 46n4, 46n5, 46n6, 47n9, 96, 101, 169
Rochmann, Szlama, 201
Rogers, Sue, (née Brumwell), 158
Rosenfeld, Eva, 111–12
Rosenthal, Harry, 147–48
Rothwell, Evelyn, 125
Ruths GmbH, Berlin, 202

Salvisberg, Otto Rudolf, 33, 49, 89, 125
Salomon
    Albert and Paula, (née Lindberg), 62, 190
    Charlotte, 62, 68n62
Samuel, Edwin Herbert, 119
Sanatorium Schloß Tegel, Berlin, 1, 98, 105–12, 117n36, 197
Schimek family, 71, 88, 93n7, 175
Schindler, Rudolf, 42
Schleicher, Gustav, 42
Schmideberg, Walter, 119, 136n16
Schmidt, 193
Schmutzer, Ferdinand, 103
Schoenbeck, Dr., 195
Schönheimer, 66n26, 190
Schwab, A. *See* Sigrist, Albert
Schwab, Hannah. *See* Michael, Fritz und Hannah (née Schwab)

Scotland, 133
    Edinburgh, 136n34
Seidmann-Freud, Tom (Martha-Gertrud), 188
Selowski, Dr. Karl, 117n38, 195
Sigrist, Albert (i.e. A. Schwab), 3, 11
Simmel, Ernst, 1, 96, 105–10, 117n36, 197
Soberheim, Adolf, 190
Sommerfeld, Adolf, 75, 129, 131, 137
Spender, Stephen and Lady Natasha, 133–34, 137n54, 155, 183
Spitz, René Arpad, 1, 198
Stern, Harold, 98
Stern, James, 65
Student corporations, Jewish
    Hasmonaea, 56, 189
    Jordania, 36n30, 56, 189

Taut, Bruno, 49
Team 4, 158
Thompson, Mrs. O. F., 183
Tönnies, Ferdinand, 3, 14
Tokayer, Oskar, 193
Tugendhat, Grete, 17

Uexkuell, Baron, 193
Unwin, Raymond, 127, 182

Vyvyan, Jennifer, 125

Wagner, Otto, 25–26, 31, 34, 42, 103
Wagner-Freinsheim, Helmut von, 42
Walpole Brothers (London Ltd), 204
Weimar Republic, 1, 4, 7, 10, 13–4, 17, 49–50, 69, 82, 92, 147, 155, 157, 161–62, 165
Weinberger, Harry, 124, 154
Weizmann, Chaim and Vera, 57–60, 67n48, 68n52, 68n56, 69, 119, 149, 176
Werkstätten für Ofen und Kaminbau, Berlin, 201
Wijdeveld, Hendrik Theodorus, 120
Wittgenstein, Ludwig, 42
Wittgensteiner, Arno, 179, 193
Wren, Christopher, 126

Yerbury, Francis Rowland, 119

Zionist Organisations
    Blau-Weiss, 56
    Kadimah, 56
Zweig, Arnold, 147, 150–51

www.ingramcontent.com/pod-product-compliance
Lightning Source LLC
Chambersburg PA
CBHW051157290426
44109CB00022B/2489